The Global Climate Regime and Transitional Justice

T0298585

Geopolitical changes combined with the increasing urgency of ambitious climate action have reopened debates about justice and international climate policy. Mechanisms and insights from transitional justice have been used in over thirty countries across a range of conflicts at the interface of historical responsibility and imperatives for collective futures. However, lessons from transitional justice theory and practice have not been systematically explored in the climate context. The comparison gives rise to new ideas and strategies that help address climate change dilemmas.

This book examines the potential of transitional justice insights to inform global climate governance. It lays out core structural similarities between current global climate governance tensions and transitional justice contexts. It explores how transitional justice approaches and mechanisms could be productively applied in the climate change context. These include responsibility mechanisms such as amnesties, legal accountability measures, and truth commissions, as well as reparations and institutional reform. The book then steps beyond reformist transitional justice practice to consider more transformative approaches, and uses this to explore a wider set of possibilities for the climate context.

Each chapter presents one or more concrete proposals arrived at by using ideas from transitional justice and applying them to the justice tensions central to the global climate context. By combining these two fields the book provides a new framework through which to understand the challenges of addressing harms and strengthening collective climate action. This book will be of great interest to scholars and practitioners of climate change and transitional justice.

Sonja Klinsky is Assistant Professor in the School of Sustainability at Arizona State University, USA.

Jasmina Brankovic is Senior Researcher at the Centre for the Study of Violence and Reconciliation, South Africa.

Routledge Advances in Climate Change Research

For more information about this series, please visit: www.routledge.com/Routledge-Advances-in-Climate-Change-Research/book-series/RACCR

The Global Climate Regime and Transitional Justice

Sonja Klinsky and Jasmina Brankovic

LONDON AND NEW YORK

First published 2018 by Routledge

2 Park Square, Milton Park, Abingdon, Oxfordshire OX14 4RN
52 Vanderbilt Avenue, New York, NY 10017

Routledge is an imprint of the Taylor & Francis Group, an informa business

First issued in paperback 2019

British Library Cataloguing-in-Publication Data
A catalogue record for this book is available from the British Library

Library of Congress Cataloging-in-Publication Data
A catalog record for this book has been requested

ISBN: 978-0-415-78602-7 (hbk)
ISBN: 978-0-367-43022-1 (pbk)

Typeset in Goudy
by Apex CoVantage, LLC

Contents

Illustrations

Figure

Tables

Acknowledgments

Our names are on this book, but full credit for all of its useful and creative parts belongs to a much wider community. At its heart this book emerges from an attempt to integrate fields that have rarely interacted, which is inevitably exciting and accident prone. We ourselves come to this issue from entirely different perspectives. Sonja Klinsky is a climate change scholar who has focused largely on issues of justice and equity within climate policy decision making at multiple scales. Jasmina Brankovic is a transitional justice practitioner and scholar who has critiqued narrow and technical understandings of the field and focused on attempts to address historical injustices and structural inequalities through transitional justice mechanisms.

As such, this book could only emerge due to some strategic and courageous risk taking by a number of people and organizations. Specifically, we are indebted to the crucial contributions of the Climate Strategies research network secretariat and the KR Foundation. Sonja had been thinking of a project like this for some time, but had not pursued it until Henry Derwent encouraged her to collaborate with the Climate Strategies research network to explore it in earnest. Subsequently the KR Foundation generously agreed to take a chance and fund the exploratory work, and particularly a series of workshops, out of which this book emerged.

Throughout this process the Climate Strategies secretariat – in particular Henry Derwent, Andrzej Błachowicz, Eleonora Arcese, and Alex Carr – was invaluable. In addition to the primary project funding from the KR Foundation, The Hague Institute for Global Justice, the Konrad Adenauer Foundation, and the Center for Development Research at the University of Bonn generously provided financial and in-kind support for the workshops. We also received the support of two undergraduate assistants, Gavriella Berk and Parker Shea, facilitated by the Center for the Study of Religion and Conflict Fellows Program at Arizona State University. Meanwhile, the incisive, constructively critical, and genuinely interested contributions we received from all of the workshop participants and interlocutors were absolutely essential in allowing us to think through the possibilities and contradictions of the integration we were exploring.

During this whole process we both received support, friendship, insightful critiques, and good ideas from a vast number of people – far too many to list individually – across multiple countries. Particular personal notes of thanks go to Robert Viergutz, Aaron Klinsky, Fatima Ahmad Owens, the entirety of Bondstone, and Sadie the dog for unwavering friendship; Nora Timmerman for the writing retreats; Hallie Eakin, Michael Schoon, and Katja Brundiers for unparalleled collegial encouragement; and the School of Sustainability at Arizona State University for its support. More thanks go to Hugo van der Merwe and colleagues at the Centre for the Study of Violence and Reconciliation for making space for this book project; the Brankovics and Anna Selmeczi for their curiosity and support; and one Brankovic Moger for the inspiration.

This book was written across vast distances and disciplinary divides. Logistically speaking, Sonja was in Tempe, Arizona, and Jasmina was in Cape Town, South Africa. It may sound whimsical but it is simply true, none of this would have been possible without Skype, WhatsApp, email, and digital file sharing. Nor would it have been possible without explicit intentions from both authors to reach across and over the boundaries in which we reside. Questions about justice are compelling, fluid, and intense at the best of times. The conceptual complications of working in this area are amplified when attempting to integrate ideas from traditions that are both evolving as we speak. We thank the reader in advance for taking what we have offered in the spirit in which it was intended.

Finally, we wrote this as a contribution, we hope, to the collective work of trying to build a more just world. Our final thanks go to all of the people who steadily persist in this effort, despite the profound challenges they face in doing so.

Introduction

A transitional justice approach to the climate change context

Emotions were running high at the end of the 2015 United Nations Climate Change Conference in Paris. After years of difficult negotiations the world had a universal climate agreement that set a target of keeping global temperatures to below 2°C change from preindustrial levels, possibly 1.5°C. The concluding tweet sent by the executive secretary of the United Nations Framework Convention on Climate Change (UNFCCC) at the time, Christiana Figueres, was short, sweet, and inclusive: "We must. We can. We did!" (Figueres 2015).

Articulations of the need for solidarity and collective action in the face of climate change ran throughout the lead-up to and during the Paris negotiations. President Barack Obama's statement at the beginning of the Paris talks illustrated the depth of the call for universal engagement, concern for the future, and the powers of a common vision when he argued that, "[H]ere, in Paris, we can show the world what is possible when we come together, united in common effort and by a common purpose" (Obama 2015).

And yet, despite the overwhelming applause, tears, and embraces that erupted as Conference of the Parties (COP) President Laurent Fabius gaveled the meeting closed, there were undercurrents of tension even amid the celebration. These were most clearly articulated by Nicaragua, which, despite taking significant climate action at home, objected to the agreement on the basis that "the concept of universal responsibility and voluntary commitments doesn't work. Universal responsibility is a spin. It's a spin on historical responsibility and common, but differentiated, responsibilities" (Oquist 2015).

Debates about justice have always been part of climate change negotiations. How could they not be? The central dynamics driving climate justice debates are relatively straightforward, although the details can become philosophically complex. Historically there have been uneven contributions to global emissions, which are also associated with uneven benefits from fossil energy exploitation. As a result of changes in industrialization over time, however, without emission reductions even from those who have not traditionally been high emitters, it may not be possible to avoid deepening climate impacts. Simultaneously, the experience of climate impacts has been and is expected to continue to be deeply uneven across states, communities, and individuals, posing potentially existential threats to some people and populations, whereas others may be comparably protected, in part because of resources generated through past emissions. And all of this tumult is integrated with a variety of local and global processes that have resulted in profoundly uneven levels of human well-being. Although climate change is by no means the only factor with the potential to increase inequality, we may wish to try to design policies that diminish, rather than deepen, existing inequalities.

Concerns about justice in the climate context come from both moral and political angles. For some people justice is a core moral value that ought to be pursued for its own sake, regardless of other outcomes this might provide. For others, justice is largely an issue of political expediency. From the latter perspective justice is important only to the extent that states with different interests see a global deal as 'fair enough' to enable them to present it to their domestic publics. Either way, concerns about justice in the climate context are not going away any time soon.

It is against this backdrop that the negotiators of the Paris Agreement attempted to reach a collective pathway that would facilitate rapid reductions of greenhouse gas (GHG) emissions and establish a basis for protecting those who are most vulnerable to climate impacts. Despite the energy and momentum generated by the Paris Agreement, however, justice-related challenges may be set to intensify due to mounting pressures to rapidly reduce GHG emissions and deal with steadily increasing climate impacts. In its Fifth Assessment report the Intergovernmental Panel on Climate Change (IPCC) suggests that atmospheric stabilization consistent with a roughly 2°C increase would require emission reductions of 70 to 107 percent of 2010 levels (Edenhofer et al. 2014). Meanwhile, climate impacts are becoming more fully understood, and it is apparent that they are set to become more serious over time: any additional emissions now will contribute to the intensification of impacts.

This book emerges out of a conviction, a concern, and a question. We are convinced that we need the kind of collective momentum and solidarity the Paris Agreement attempted to establish. It is difficult to imagine how the social and economic as well as institutional and technical changes needed to ensure that *all* people have the means to flourish could be achieved without these deep commitments to one another across time and space. However, we are also concerned that in the face of pressures for rapid mitigation and responses to increased climate impacts, failing to adequately address historically rooted claims about justice could hinder the ability of the global community to meet its objective of avoiding 'dangerous anthropogenic climate change,' either by eroding trust and collective action for emission reductions or by failing to provide sufficient support to those in greatest need of protection from climate impacts. We suggest that a global agreement capable of achieving sustained, deep mitigation targets and sufficient responses to climate impacts will have to integrate backward-looking claims of historical responsibility with forward-oriented promotion of inclusive low-carbon development pathways.

Herein lies our question. Climate change is not the only time people have been faced with historically rooted collective action challenges involving justice disputes. Could other experiences suggest new strategies for building solidarity and addressing the justice tensions at the heart of global climate change negotiations?

What would an approach to global climate policy capable of meeting backward- and forward-oriented climate needs look like?

'Transitional justice' represents one set of tools that has been adapted to many diverse contexts at the interface of historical responsibility and imperatives for new collective futures. For over thirty years, communities, scholars, practitioners, and policy makers have experimented with a range of strategies for enabling conflict-ridden societies to develop greater long-term peace and solidarity. Transitional justice emerged during the 1980s and 1990s, as many countries in Latin America and Eastern Europe underwent regime change and faced the challenge of rebuilding their societies after periods of dictatorship and violence. It has since become a globally accepted field and go-to solution for contexts attempting to address past harms. The goal of transitional justice processes is to recognize and at least partially remedy injustices while also building a sense of unity or solidarity. Such processes have evolved to include a range of mechanisms, most particularly accountability measures such as amnesties, prosecutions, and truth commissions; reparations for those harmed; and institutional reforms that aspire to prevent future harms.

Lessons from transitional justice have not been examined for the climate context, although they provide useful concepts and practices for reconciling past-oriented concerns about historical responsibility with future-oriented desires for broader and deeper collective action. It is precisely this gap that the book attempts to fill.

Analogous thinking

At first, transitional justice processes may seem like an unusual inspiration for climate change policy making. However, the two fields share a number of contextual and structural similarities that allow us to think about the ways societies have attempted to deal with profound losses, harms, and injustices in the face of pressures to develop or maintain collective identities even across these fissures. Analogous thinking is a common strategy for problem solving because it can facilitate creativity and lead to new insights (Bonnardel 2000). Instead of seeing the climate context as an opportunity for a direct application of transitional justice, we are using transitional justice as a lens that allows us to see climate conflicts in a new way and identify options for moving forward that might otherwise be left unexplored.

Contextually, transitional justice and efforts to address climate change are rooted in evolving discussions about the nature and extent of international norms of justice and the institutional arrangements that are most useful for upholding these norms. These evolved from discussions regarding states' obligations toward each other in the wake of World War I and II, as well as the rise of human rights norms after the Cold War and the attendant focus on states' obligations to individuals. In the case of transitional justice, the resulting developments in international human rights law, international humanitarian law, and international criminal law initially informed and later were also shaped by the field. These developments in international treaty and customary law influenced the kinds of institutional arrangements used by transitional justice actors at the international level, as well as ways in which they were either domesticated or rejected at the national and community levels in countries facing legacies of past harms, primarily in the global South but also increasingly in the global North.

The climate context is similarly marked by continual contestation and the evolution of international norms about the scope of obligations we have to one another and about how best to design institutions capable of facilitating the fulfillment of those obligations. The shifting discourse on adaptation – purposeful efforts to manage climate impacts – is one example. The early years of climate negotiations were dominated by mitigation efforts focused on the reduction of GHG emissions. Despite acknowledgment of the potentially existential threats climate change posed for some communities, the chief obligations of states parties to the UNFCCC were seen to revolve around their capacity to contribute to mitigation. Although mitigation commitments remain central to any discussion of justice and climate change, the focus has now broadened to recognize a wider scope of obligations. The Paris Agreement includes a global goal for adaptation, and the Green Climate Fund aspires to have a portfolio equally weighted across mitigation and adaptation. Meanwhile long-standing discussions of loss and damage have resulted in the development of the Warsaw International Mechanism for Loss and Damage and in greater attention to the potential for climate impacts to have profound implications for human well-being, even with mitigation and adaptation efforts. Climate justice is now not only a question of how to allocate efforts for mitigation, but also more broadly what obligations the global community has in the face of serious and uneven climate impacts.

In both transitional justice and climate efforts we see an evolution of what justice might entail and of the types of claims recognized as valid moral arguments. For example, within the transitional justice arena it is now accepted that new regimes will provide some form of reparation to states and individuals affected by gross human rights violations committed by the previous regime, even in cases where they had nothing to do with those violations. The increasing calls for reparations due to slavery and systemic racism in both the United States (Coates 2014; Valls 2007) and the Caribbean (Caribbean Reparations Commission n.d.; Beckles 2013), in addition to the long-standing claims of indigenous populations worldwide, demonstrate how actions once perceived as just come to be recognized as profoundly wrong. Whether one agrees with Martin Luther King Jr.'s assertion that "the moral arc of the universe is long but it bends towards justice" (King Jr. 1965) or not, the background of re-examination and re-engagement with morality and the boundaries of responsibility and harm is relevant to both the transitional justice and climate change communities. We cannot forget that our very instincts about what is morally abhorrent change constantly, facilitating recognition that practices we see as 'normal' may in fact be deeply problematic and in need of repair.

In no case have concepts about obligations or moral duties evolved 'naturally' or without guidance. In fact, the potential for norm entrepreneurs, such as activists, affected communities, and policy makers, to actively shape the ways we come to understand our obligations is a core theme heightened by the juxtaposition of the climate change and transitional justice contexts. Recognizing norm entrepreneurship changes the way we can talk about justice and institution building in these contexts. The institutions we have now are not fixed and never will be. Instead, we are this moment in the middle of the work of shaping how we can, or ought to, address the tensions of an increasingly globally connected world. With this book we therefore not only observe these changes, but also seek to contribute to them. As will be seen in the chapters on accountability, reparations, and institutional reform, we have consciously used examples of norm entrepreneurship in both fields to suggest new approaches to the climate conundrum.

On top of these broad resonances, there are also a number of structural similarities between the climate and transitional justice contexts. For instance, in both, compromise positions may not be desired by any of the various actors involved, but may be essential due to forced interdependence and the mounting costs of continued stalemates. However, these situations are also rooted in local, national, regional, and international political contexts characterized by power imbalances and deal making. Efforts to recognize and deal with justice claims in these contexts cannot stay at the level of ideals, but need to be placed in the concrete and specific debates central to actors' claims. Transitional justice and climate are thus both highly politicized fields. Importantly, deeply held differences about the appropriate role of past events in shaping future obligations or actions lie at the heart of both fields. How much should past actions dictate the future positions or roles of actors? How much of the past needs to be dealt with to enable a better future?

Similarly, because of the diffuse, highly complex, and multifaceted nature of the harms experienced and the pathways by which they emerge, efforts to use legal means to address them, through both international and national legal systems, face fundamental challenges in terms of capacity and structural mismatches. This does not mean that legal means are irrelevant for the climate context, but that we are unlikely to be able to rely on them as a sole strategy for either mobilizing mitigation or addressing climate impacts. Finally, in both contexts, we are forced to deal with profound and diverse losses, some of which may fit neatly into models of compensation but others of which may require a broader conversation about acts of repair. How ought – or can – a governance system deal with the realities of individuals and communities facing climate-related loss?

Outlining new approaches

This book provides a first attempt at systematically examining transitional justice concepts and tools for their utility in the climate context. The ideas we present were developed and honed through a series of workshops and multistakeholder events. From late 2015 until the end of 2016, a team led by Sonja Klinsky and the secretariat of Climate Strategies, an international research network centered on climate policy dilemmas, held four international workshops explicitly designed to scope out and develop early ideas about how transitional justice mechanisms could be used in this context. Each workshop sought to bring the insights from the previous one into the next. It was through this iterative workshop process that Jasmina Brankovic became involved in the project and joined the team.

The workshops were attended by international climate negotiators, advisors, activists, and scholars, as well as transitional justice scholars and practitioners. By the time of our fourth and final participatory event, a round-table dinner hosted in parallel with COP22 in Marrakech, we had directly involved over ninety individuals with a wide range of expertise in the discussion, in addition to others we reached through less participatory means such as side events during the UNFCCC negotiations in December 2015, May 2016, and November 2016. Our ideas in this book unabashedly grew out of the engagement the project made possible.

In the chapters that follow we examine how transitional justice has implemented institutional responses such as accountability mechanisms, reparations, and institutional reform, leveraging these experiences to imagine what new ideas they suggest for the climate context. Just as we would have to do in any other conflict situation, we have designed our suggestions around the specificities of the climate context. We have taken well-tested transitional justice approaches and integrated them with institutions and norms already in existence in the climate context. We are attempting to stretch existing strategies for managing climate justice tensions in the climate space, but in ways that remain true to the political, social, economic, and ecological limitations from which these debates emerge.

In Chapter 1 we start our exploration of transitional justice approaches in the climate context by revisiting the core justice challenges that have emerged and that will continue to be central to the global climate regime's attempt to meet the objectives of the Convention and the Paris Agreement. This includes debates about uneven historical emissions, unevenly distributed climate harms, and the way that both of these issues intersect with pre-existing and profound inequalities globally. We introduce transitional justice, its mechanisms and history, and some major debates in the field that hold lessons for the climate context. We then explicitly explore the conceptual basis for applying transitional justice insights in the climate context. What are the structural similarities between these two arenas, and where are the limitations of this exercise in analogous thinking?

However, it is important to first understand what has already been tried before we can meaningfully suggest a new pathway forward. Accordingly, in Chapter 2 we review how four key strategies have been used to deal with climate justice tensions: 1) fair burden sharing; 2) green growth; 3) legal liability; and 4) grassroots climate justice mobilization. As we discuss in the chapter, each of these brings important conceptual and material resources to the table, but alone none of them is fully capable of addressing the urgency and complexity of the justice tensions in the climate context. We see these strategies as providing the foundation for our work, although any of them independently is unlikely to be sufficient.

After establishing the urgency and complexity of the climate justice conundrum and pointing out the promise but limitations of current ways of resolving it, we start our systematic exploration of the potential for transitional justice to contribute to the international climate regime. Chapters 3, 4, and 5 each discuss a common transitional justice measure and imagine how it could be applied in the climate context.

In Chapter 3 we examine responsibility mechanisms. Some form of accountability is essential in any transitional justice process, and we outline various approaches to amnesty, individual (and collective) legal accountability, and truth commissions in the field. Establishing responsibility has been a very difficult area in climate negotiations, at least partially due to fear that acceptance of responsibility might lead to punitive demands to account for potentially profound (and expensive) climate impacts. In light of these political sensitivities, we focus on three pathways for better including responsibility within the climate context: 1) an acknowledgment process to manage the political temptations and long-term repercussions of de facto amnesty; 2) a process like a truth commission that would have truth-seeking and truth-telling components and generate recommendations for financial and nonfinancial contributions from state and nonstate actors toward both reparations for harm and forward-oriented action; and 3) continuing efforts to apply legal accountability norms to individuals and collective actors (such as states and corporations).

These measures could operate individually, but they could also feed into each other. For instance, stronger pursuit of legal accountability could generate substantial pressure on recalcitrant actors to acknowledge responsibility via nonretributive pathways. As seen in many transitional justice contexts, mechanisms like truth commissions or nonpunitive forms of acknowledgment can offer powerful actors who feel under threat from accountability measures a more palatable avenue for productive engagement. These proposed measures could also feed into other categories of mechanism entirely, including reparations. For example, a truth commission that includes state and nonstate actors could be instrumental in generating additional resources for reparations or informing how acts of repair could be designed to resonate with the self-identified needs of affected communities.

Chapter 4 steps away from questions of responsibility to address the issue of reparations. Transitional justice has established the norm of providing reparations to those most affected by harms, defining reparations broadly to include compensation, restitution, rehabilitation, satisfaction, and efforts to promote nonrecurrence. Reparations occur between states and between states and individuals, and they may be individual or collective, material or symbolic. The issue of reparations has been extremely contentious in the climate context – almost toxically so – but individuals and communities are already being harmed by climate change, and will continue to be. There are already climate impacts, which will be increasingly serious, and they are unevenly experienced and linked to the generation of GHG emissions.

We suggest that, as in many transitional justice contexts, separating the issues of responsibility and repair has political benefits. Separating these issues allows us to take a nonpunitive approach to reparations aimed explicitly at ameliorating climate-related harms, leaving responsibility to be managed through the mechanisms described earlier. Specifically, we propose a pathway in which a Reparations Commission housed within the UNFCCC could facilitate the creation of a much broader set of resources and forms of repair than currently included in the climate context. One of the most important contributions from transitional justice practice has been the articulation of multiple ways to address harm, including noncompensatory forms of repair. The Reparations Commission would also work to connect community-based claims of harm to appropriate reparations. Because climate harms will evolve depending on global mitigation efforts, we propose a dynamic reparations process tied to these achievements.

Institutional reforms are another central mechanism in transitional justice processes, and we explore these in Chapter 5. Reforms of existing institutions and the establishment of new institutions signals a commitment to building a new future, with the aspirational goal of creating an environment in which harms are less accepted and more difficult to inflict. In the climate context, this focus on avoiding further harms highlights the importance of facilitating deep, future-oriented climate action that resonates with both mitigation and adaptation challenges. By recognizing that the Paris Agreement is itself a form of institutional reform purposefully designed to lay the groundwork for an improved future, we can focus on what particular aspects would be needed to enable it to develop the depth of legitimacy and momentum it needs to achieve its goals.

By limiting our analysis specifically to reforms that would be uniquely identified by using a transitional justice lens, we propose the following: 1) improving finance and resourcing mechanisms by widening the range of potential contributors (and forms of contribution) and by increasing the transparency of contributions to all means of implementation; 2) creating a mechanism for due process aimed particularly at market mechanisms; 3) initiating loss and damage scoping studies accompanied by support for permanent in-country expert panels; and 4) more thoroughly engaging commitments for education and capacity building. Notably this would include commitments to develop capabilities for enhancing domestic legal accountability for climate action. All of these are designed to leave long future-oriented shadows in terms of facilitating much more robust mitigation and adaptation action.

There are many potential pathways by which accountability measures, reparations, and institutional reforms could interact in the climate space, strengthening the likelihood that each of them would be able to substantively contribute to the goals identified. We return to this question at the end of the book.

In writing this volume, we have grappled with the ramifications of relying on liberal thought to shape international norms and institution building in both the climate and transitional justice contexts. Transitional justice emerges from a liberal democratic tradition and human rights discourse that foregrounds political (and economic) liberalization and individual agency over addressing social and economic conditions and structural inequalities. Similarly, as the Paris Agreement is built around the voluntary contributions of sovereign states, it, too, takes a liberal approach to notions of global society. What kind of a global society are we trying to build? What kinds of justice ought all people be able to enjoy, regardless of where they were born? As expressed by civil society activists in both contexts, when are incremental efforts at change inadequate or forms of cooptation in themselves, and when are they truly the only politically viable option? How do we decide where on the continuum of reform to transformation we ought to place our focus?

We address the limitations of liberal approaches in Chapter 6, in which we revisit calls for transformation that go well beyond the immediate bounds of the UNFCCC or states themselves. We suggest that there have been two dominant narratives of transformation in the climate justice context – one emerging from grassroots mobilization and the other emerging from efforts to drive rapid mitigation through green growth and technological developments. By reflecting on these narratives we were able to identify three strategies that emerge out of the creative tension between them: 1) supporting inclusive low-carbon development pathways that go beyond technicist emission pathways to include political realities, cultural perspectives, and lived experiences; 2) developing and using justice-oriented tools for policy analysis; and 3) envisioning an expanded approach to capacity building. Each of these strategies could be pursued independently, but also could be partially integrated into the responsibility, reparations, and institutional reform measures described earlier. Each strategy also purposefully attempts to engage with more emergent and widespread forms of mobilization.

In our concluding chapter, we return to the central motivation of the book: to identify ways of building the solidarity and collective action needed to adequately address climate change in a global context of profound inequality. We reflect on the notion of solidarity and identify how the suite of transitional justice–inspired proposals we make could be integrated to support efforts toward this goal.

In a context of imperfect justice

During the writing of this book we frequently faced the question, posed by others and ourselves, whether we were valorizing transitional justice experiences. These experiences have not – by any means – been universally beneficial. Although many cases do demonstrate relatively productive steps toward greater peace, other cases also raise concerns about the extent to which elites can co-opt transitional justice or coerce those most affected by harms to 'forgive and forget' in the name of some collective goal which may, or may not, benefit them. This book is not an advertisement for transitional justice writ large, nor does it present anything near an exhaustive account of concepts and practices in the field, but we have attempted to build on insights about what has and has not been productive in terms of people's abilities to lead dignified lives in transitional contexts. For instance, many of our thoughts about the potential use of amnesty in the climate context, which we conclude is likely to be very hard to avoid due to political pressure, focus on understanding how amnesties have led to weaknesses in transitional regimes that have relied on them without also engaging in other transitional justice mechanisms. The analogy of transitional justice is useful not because it proposes simple solutions, but because it offers new ideas and practices that go 'outside the box' for those attempting to navigate the complexity of the climate justice knot.

In our approach, justice is aspirational. We recognize full 'justice' may never be realized but that moving toward a more just and mutually beneficial co-existence is better than not trying to move in this direction at all. This is particularly the case if resolving some aspects of the worst injustices is essential not only to remedying these particular wrongs but also to supporting systemic change that may avoid further harms.

For us, 'working toward justice' includes some reckoning with harms already inflicted, and that will inevitably emerge through climate impacts, in ways that meet the demands and needs of those most affected. It also moves us toward a state in which harms are lessened, or avoided entirely, in the future. For us as authors, our conceptualization of justice goes beyond strict legal interpretations of justice and extends to encompass claims of human needs, human rights, and basic human dignity. In resonance with Amartya Sen (2000) and Martha Nussbaum (2003), the notion of justice we work with posits true human freedom at its core and necessarily speaks to economic and social material experiences in addition to the narrower suite of civil and political human rights commonly included in liberal justice discourses. It is important to remember, however, that to be effective and responsive to the specificities of each context, mechanisms that address harms should be tailored to the conception of justice held by those most affected by those harms.

In this book we have attempted to be both idealistic and pragmatic in seeking innovative ways to address climate harms. We have attempted to look beyond the scope of immediate conventions and notions of political feasibility to suggest new pathways. And yet we have also attempted to avoid idealism that fails to root itself in the political, institutional, and material difficulties we are facing in the climate context. We think it is exactly the commonality of these challenges in the climate and transitional justice contexts that gives credence to this work. We are not proposing or promising a panacea. We are not insisting on visions of perfect justice that fail to recognize the complexities of each context. Instead we wrote this book in full recognition of the creativity, courage, trust, and determination it takes to attempt to build a more just future.

References

Beckles, Hilary McD. 2013. *Britain's Black Debt: Reparations for Slavery and Native Genocide*. Kingston: University of West Indies Press.

Bonnardel, Nathalie. 2000. "Towards Understanding and Supporting Creativity in Design: Analogies in a Constrained Cognitive Environment." *Knowledge-Based Systems* 13(7–8): 505–13.

Caribbean Reparations Commission. n.d. http://caricomreparations.org.

Coates, Ta-Nehisi. 2014. "The Case for Reparations." *Atlantic*. http://www.theatlantic. com/magazine/archive/2014/06/the-case-for-reparations/361631.

Edenhofer, Ottmar, Ramon Pichs-Madruga, Youba Sokona, Ellie Farahani, Susanne Kadner, Kristin Seyboth, and Anna Adler. 2014. "Summary for Policy Makers: Climate Change 2014: Mitigation of Climate Change." *Contribution of Working Group III to the Fifth Assessment Report of the Intergovernmental Panel in Climate Change*. Cambridge: Cambridge University Press.

Figueres, Christina. 2015. "We Must. We Can. We Did! #COP21 #ParisAgreement." *Tweet*. https://twitter.com/cfigueres/status/675750563431215105?lang=en.

King Jr., Martin Luther. 1965. "Sermon at Temple Israel of Hollywood." http://www.americanrhetoric.com/speeches/mlktempleisraelhollywood.htm.

Nussbaum, Martha. 2003. "Capabilities as Fundamental Entitlements: Sen and Social Justice." *Feminist Economics* 9(2–3): 33–59.

Obama, Barack. 2015. "Remarks by President Obama at the First Session of COP 21." *United Nations Framework Convention on Climate Change*. http://unfccc.int/files/meetings/paris_nov_2015/application/pdf/cop21cmp11_leaders_event_usa.pdf.

Oquist, Paul. 2015. "We Do Not Want to Be an Accomplice: Nicaragua Rejects Global Consensus on Voluntary Emission Cuts." *Democracy Now*. www.democracynow.org/2015/12/4/we_do_not_want_to_be.

Sen, Amartya. 2000. *Development as Freedom*. New York: Anchor Books.

Valls, Andrew. 2007. "Reconsidering the Case for Black Reparations." In *Reparations: Interdisciplinary Inquiries*, edited by John Miller and Rahul Kumar, 114–29. Oxford: Oxford University Press.

1   From climate harms
to climate action

In 2013 the World Sikh Organization of Canada released a video entitled, "It Matters: The Legacy of Residential Schools." The video acknowledges that as Canadians, Sikhs had 'turned their faces' from the reality of residential schools, which forced over 150,000 aboriginal children to attend schools designed to assimilate them into white settler society. Thousands of children died, even more were abused, and First Nations continue to grapple with the social, economic, and psychological effects of several 'lost generations' and torn cultural continuity. The script of the video reads:

> We turned our faces away as thousands of students died in residential schools. We turned our faces away for decades. Today we refuse to turn our faces away. Today we see and we acknowledge what has happened. Today it matters . . . It matters as a Sikh because we are a faith that was founded in social justice . . . It matters as a Canadian because it's part of our history and we need to understand our entire history.
>
> (WSO 2013)

What is particularly interesting is that the Sikh community was not directly responsible for the residential schools in Canada and composes only 1.4 percent of the Canadian population. Unlike the Anglican and Catholic Churches (which have since offered formal apologies), the Sikh community never ran residential schools. Moreover, Sikhs themselves faced, and to some extent continue to face, systematic discrimination in Canadian society.

This statement of acknowledgment is part of a larger process, in which the Canadian Truth and Reconciliation Commission (TRC) toured the country to collect public statements both from victims of residential schools and from the full range of Canadian society. Like many others, this statement acknowledges indirect responsibility for the atrocities experienced in Canadian history, based in part on the broader benefits stemming from claiming Canadian identity. It affirms the centrality of the Sikh community to Canada, and accordingly accepts some of the moral weight of this history, despite the lack of immediate, direct responsibility and a deeply complicated relationship with the government of Canada and settler communities.

At first glance, this story of Sikh engagement with the Canadian TRC seems at odds with a chapter focused on the intersections of climate change and justice. And yet the statement of acknowledgment speaks to many of the challenges we see in the climate justice space. The relationships between those who experienced harms and those who caused them are complicated, and direct causality may play a role but is not, alone, sufficient for thinking about responsibility. Some obligations may be perceived not through direct causality but through a form of shared identity in which members recognize that they have accrued some benefits merely by being part of the collective. The Sikh statement is a contribution toward creating a new set of relationships broadly based on reconciling tensions within a divided society, but it is not the product of a legal obligation.

The questions raised by the Canadian TRC thus resonate with the ones we must face in the climate justice context. What does justice look like? Where are the boundaries and overlaps between moral and legal accounts of harm and obligations? When and how will we choose to look forward, and when does this require looking backward? How will we deal with ambiguous causal pathways of harm? What does it take to build solidarity?

In this chapter we focus on the underlying suite of tensions about justice and climate change that have emerged in scholarly and political contexts and situate the Paris Agreement within these debates. In recognition of the dual pressures to deal with deeply rooted historical responsibility claims and to find a pathway for collective action at a scale never yet seen in the climate context, this chapter introduces transitional justice as a potential framework for thinking through the dynamics of these challenges. It outlines the mechanisms of transitional justice and the historical factors that gave rise to them, as well as some debates in the field that may hold lessons for the climate context, before exploring the structural similarities between the transitional justice and climate contexts that make the comparison relevant.

Climate change and justice

Two underlying lines of argument – moral and political – appear repeatedly in explanations of why we might be interested in the intersections of justice and climate change. For some, climate change is fundamentally an issue of moral concern. As Don Brown has argued, "because climate policy will likely determine which people, plants, and animals will live and die, human-induced climate change must be understood to raise the most momentous ethical questions" (Brown 2003: 229). From this perspective climate change is an issue of justice because it challenges basic well-being, in some cases even existence, and because these threats emerge from our relationships with each other and the biophysical processes at play.

This line of moral reasoning is at the heart of Pope Francis' encyclical in which he reflects on the uneven distribution of harms from climate change and challenges us to acknowledge that "our lack of response to these tragedies involving our brothers and sisters points to the loss of that sense of responsibility for our fellow men and women upon which all civil society is founded" (Pope Francis 2015: para. 25). To echo the Sikh statement, climate justice matters because we are all citizens of one geographically contained community (i.e., Earth) and what happens to one member in this community affects the story and identity of all of us. What kind of a society do we wish to be?

Such moral claims have been the center of the vast and growing philosophical literature on climate change and of climate justice advocacy.[1] The literature has attempted to systematically identify the exact forms of moral claim within the climate context, while climate justice advocacy has spread rapidly as a frame for understanding climate change. This literature and practice have contributed theoretically clarity (and sometimes more complicated questions) to the specific debates within the climate justice context.

Others, however, have come to the climate justice table not necessarily out of moral concern as much as out of acknowledgment of the power justice claims have politically. Those concerned about climate change justice from a political perspective point to the necessity of having a 'fair enough' agreement to which all states parties to the UNFCCC can agree (Müller 2001). International law is dependent on the willingness of states to create and ratify agreements and then to implement them. Even if an ideal climate agreement was judged to be perfectly just by a set of profoundly wise philosophers, without political buy-in from sovereign states there is no guarantee that this agreement would be signed or used to guide climate policy.

The problem is, of course, that states do not all agree on what justice entails, in part because their core national interests are different and may be in direct competition. For instance, there was enormous pushback when experts from Brazil, India, China, and South Africa released a joint set of reports, all of which featured historical responsibility for GHG emissions as a core element of future-oriented obligations (BASIC Experts 2011). This historically based claim lay in direct opposition to some parties' positions. At the same Conference of the Parties (COP17) during which the experts released this document, the United States special envoy on climate change, Todd Stern, was purportedly heard declaring, "If equity's in, we're out," during the final negotiations of the Durban Platform for Enhanced Action.[2] This American position was not new. Almost fifteen years previously, the United States Senate unanimously adopted the Byrd-Hagel Resolution, which called upon the United States not to agree to any international climate agreement until all countries, including the large developing countries[3] (such as India and China), also accepted hard emission limits (Byrd and Hagel 1997). Many would say that this is not objectively just. However, in a situation of realpolitik discourses of justice are profoundly powerful in shaping national – and thus international – policy processes.

Claims about justice are central to the international climate negotiation space because of the sovereignty of states and the potential for climate actions to shape national interests; but they have also been crucial in domestic policy contexts. Calls for climate justice can be used to promote certain forms of climate action, as is seen by growing global mobilization of local actors and advocacy organizations around this idea (for a discussion of this activism, see Chapter 6). However, implementation even of very modest climate policies has been hampered by political actors manipulating equity discourses. For instance, the National Mining Association declared the Obama administration's Clean Power Plan "political malpractice," citing the specific harms to "low-income and fixed-income families struggling to pay their energy bills" and linking the plan to cuts in education and other social spending (NMA 2016). Similar concerns about the justice dimensions of carbon pricing (Peet and Harrison 2012) and the cost incidence of energy transition technologies such as feed-in tariffs (Grosche and Schroder 2011; Nelson, Simshauser, and Kelley 2011) have repeatedly emerged during efforts to enact climate change policy. Because international climate policy depends on the willingness of domestic publics to accept any conditions they might entail, such arguments are of central importance at multiple scales.

Both morally and politically motivated concerns have drawn attention to the intersections of climate change and justice. Although often dealt with separately (and within distinct disciplines), in this book we purposefully combine them in recognition of the value of both lines of argument. This is not the world of ideal justice, but a world of deeply unbalanced power structures that we have to navigate with a range of strategies. In the next section we sketch out the main contours of these debates, as they establish a framework for exploring the potential of insights from transitional justice for the climate context. The debates are not addressed in depth here, as there are already many excellent sources dedicated to exploring each of them.

Core climate justice debates

Three dynamically integrated justice tensions lie at the heart of the climate justice tangle, all complicated by the fact that they must be navigated across space and time. These tensions revolve around the distribution of causal responsibility for GHG emissions across time and space; the scope of obligations toward those most affected by climate change; and the relationships between climate action and broader inequalities in human well-being and access to sustainable development. These tensions are integrated, making efforts to isolate them somewhat artificial, but here we briefly sketch out the primary contours of each one.

First, **global contributions to GHG concentrations are uneven across time and space**, as are the benefits that have emerged from the production of these emissions. In the early 1990s, during the first climate agreements, a handful of developed countries were responsible for the vast majority of both historical and contemporary emissions. This pattern was explicitly recognized in the original UNFCCC text, which explicitly noted the special obligations of developed countries to take the lead in addressing climate change. This recognition of uneven causal responsibility was formalized in the oft-referenced principle of 'common but differentiated responsibility and respective capabilities' (CBDR-RC).

Taking a purely historical view of GHG emissions, however, misses global shifts in industrialization and energy use. The distribution of responsibility for cumulative emissions shifted significantly between the early 1990s and the present, as a subset of emerging economies started to experience high economic growth in conjunction with increased GHG emissions. Most notably, China overtook the United States as the largest emitter per year of GHGs in 2005. By 2014 China was responsible for roughly 10 percent of total cumulative emissions since the Industrial Revolution, whereas European countries were together responsible for about 15 percent and the United States for about 25 percent. China is not the only developing country to have seen rapid emissions growth. Currently only ten countries account for about 70 percent of total cumulative emissions, five of which are commonly categorized as developing countries (WRI 2015). The general stagnation of the economies and the emission productions in many member countries of the Organisation for Economic Co-operation and Development (OECD) has resulted in a situation where it is essentially impossible to reach global emission targets without action in developing countries to create entirely new low-carbon development pathways. This does not negate the fact that cumulative atmospheric emissions and the resultant climate change remain predominantly tied to historical and current patterns of production and consumption in the global North.

The desire for strong collective action and a minimization of historical responsibility fed into the universal design of the Paris Agreement. Taking a step away from historically informed readings of CBDR-RC, the Paris Agreement is structured around universal obligations to address climate change. Although the agreement is seen "in light of CBDR-RC and national circumstances," all countries face obligations, but can self-differentiate these depending on their domestic situations. Historical responsibility is only obliquely invoked by references to CBDR-RC in the Preamble and the Convention more generally (UNFCCC 2015). Countries may refer to historical responsibility or any other reflections on the equity of their efforts in their nationally determined contributions (NDCs) moving forward, but this is not mandatory. Indeed, very few countries refer to historical emissions, but instead demonstrate their national circumstances by referring to their share of current global emissions, per capita emissions, or climate vulnerability (Winkler et al. 2017).

Historical responsibility has been an extraordinarily difficult topic to navigate in the climate context because it is riddled with complications. For instance, a common source of debate is the long time horizon of historical emissions and the fact that those who emitted many of them did not know they were causing harm (Posner and Weisbach 2010; Kingston 2014; Zellentin 2015). Even in informal, off-the-record conversations some of the most equity-sympathetic European negotiators cannot accept that there are moral obligations to pay for harms stemming from deeply historical (i.e., 'ignorance era') emissions. Similarly, the difficulty of clearly attributing harms to specific emissions has been a consistent challenge, particularly for those who equate compensation with liability (Adler 2007; Weisbach 2011). This argument has two parts to it. First is the complication that because all emissions mix globally and then interact with other Earth systems, it is very hard to clearly attribute specific harms to specific emissions. Second, as the exact people who emitted historical emissions are long dead, who is to bear responsibility for their actions? This last question becomes particularly complicated if the emissions themselves are not the dominant focus, but the benefits they created are (Sunstein 2015). How do we even start to understand the full scope of benefits over time when many of these were diffuse and created in conjunction with other processes, including colonization (Ram-Bhandary 2015)?

We do not seek to answer the normative questions of what exactly there is historical responsibility for, or where it ends.[4] Instead we focus on this as a source of deep political tension and are interested in productive pathways forward in light of such tensions. Politically speaking, generating the depth of solidarity and collective momentum required to adequately address climate impacts will require the integration of the perceptions and concerns of all those involved. How can we cooperate in a substantially less-than-optimal world, and one in which responsibility is ambiguous, diffuse, and complicated? The murkiness of the climate context is, as we discuss in more depth later, one of the reasons we propose looking at how transitional justice processes have dealt with similarly complex situations. And, as illustrated by the Sikh example earlier, there may be multiple pathways for dealing with hard-to-pin-down notions of responsibility.

The second major justice pressure in the climate context emerges from the fact that **climate impacts are not going to be experienced uniformly** around the world. Not only do climate impacts themselves vary significantly by location, but people also have differential vulnerabilities and abilities to manage these impacts. Generally speaking, those with the least resources, many of whom contributed the fewest GHGs, are also often those most likely to be harmed by climate change. Although awareness of climate impacts has always been present in global negotiations, early negotiations revolved largely around mitigation[5] actions (Schipper 2006).

As a result of developments in climate science and documentation of climate impacts, there is currently a much richer understanding of the scope of climate impacts and their potential to harm individuals and communities, and in some cases – such as the low-lying island states – entire countries.[6] Meanwhile, the majority of states parties to the UNFCCC identify as developing countries, many of which are likely to face significant climate impacts but have limited resources to protect their citizens. Increased awareness, combined with substantial national interests, has facilitated the inclusion of adaptation[7] – and to some extent loss and damage[8] – within the global climate policy context. For instance, in 2014 the Green Climate Fund declared its intent to aim for a 50/50 split between mitigation and adaptation in its portfolio (GCF 2014).

One of recent acknowledgments of the importance of climate impacts in the negotiations is the inclusion of a Global Goal for Adaptation in the Paris Agreement. There have been multiple calls to include a global adaptation goal (AILAC and Mexico 2014; Africa Group and Sudan 2014), based on critiques that implementation of adaptation efforts has "been rather patchy, opportunistic and philanthropic in nature, rather than being delivered as obligations" (Ngwadla and El-Bakri 2016: 2). Asserting a global goal for adaptation stresses the global nature of obligations to protect people from harm: because the causes are global, the resulting obligation extends beyond normal governmental responsibilities toward their citizens and is also global. This argument affirms the importance of a global scope of justice even when efforts to address harm must themselves be rooted in local particularities.

The growing recognition that there will be some loss and damage – essentially what we are calling 'harm' – even with existing mitigation and adaptation efforts is a second way in which justice-based claims about climate impacts have emerged in the negotiations and in the literature. In 2014 the Warsaw International Mechanism for Loss and Damage was established, and after some tense negotiations loss and damage was allocated its own section of the Paris Agreement (see Chapter 2 for more on this). As with the global goal for adaptation, securing a place for recognition of these harms reflects the moral claim that there are globally rooted obligations toward those who will be most intensely affected by climate change, regardless of location or direct causal connections.

The third source of justice tensions interacts with and sets the scene for both of the other ones. Inequality characterizes society at the global and national levels (Milanovic 2012). **Inequality within and across states shapes how climate impacts will be felt and what strategies are possible** to mitigate or adapt to climate change. Climate change could also undermine human development gains either by diverting resources into climate mitigation or adaption from other essential areas, or by eroding social, ecological, or economic systems depended upon by communities.

Concerns that climate change, and climate action, could deepen inequities of human development are rooted in the original text of the UNFCCC. The Preamble strongly declares the importance of both sustainable development and climate change, and Principle 4 articulates that

> the Parties have a right to, and should, promote sustainable development. Policies and measures to protect the climate system against human-induced change should be appropriate for the specific conditions of each Party and should be integrated with national development programs, taking into account that economic development is essential for adopting measures to address climate change.
>
> (UNFCCC 1992)

As expressed by the principles of CBDR-RC, limited capacity in the form of unmet human development needs can inhibit many forms of climate action, particularly those that may require up-front investments. Simultaneously, climate change presents an additional layer of danger to already threatened lives for those facing human development needs (Beg et al. 2002). The severity of harm from climate impacts depends on a number of pre-existing factors, all of which are also implicated in uneven access to human development (IPCC 2014).

Inequalities in human development precede the immediate climate challenge, and yet are implicated in many of the very same processes giving rise to climate change, including industrialization and colonialism. As Pope Francis has argued, an "'ecological debt' exists, particularly between the global north and south, connected to commercial imbalances with effects on the environment, and the disproportionate use of natural resources by certain countries over long periods of time" (Pope Francis 2015: para. 51). Similarly, whereas explicit discussions of colonialism have been muted in official negotiations, with some exceptions,[9] acknowledgment of colonialism as part of the climate change challenge has been acknowledged in civil society climate justice mobilizing (see Chapter 6).

For many, it is unhelpful to link climate change to these broader dynamics of inequality. This theme emerged repeatedly in the workshops we organized to discuss the initial ideas for this book. A common concern was that the UNFCCC cannot, and should not, be expected to deal with the full gamut of human development inequalities or address the long shadows of colonialism. The argument was that the institution is already being pushed to capacity and that expanding this discussion would shrink already narrow margins for cooperation. For others in the workshops, it was nonsensical to talk about climate change and justice without rooting such discussions in awareness of both of these issues, although they recognized that the capacity for climate negotiations per se to address them is limited. Either way, it was widely acknowledged that human development had to be included in any meaningful discussion about how to move forward with climate action.

Global efforts to address climate change sit at the confluence of these three justice debates in the climate context. Building a pathway capable of facilitating extremely rapid efforts to reduce GHG emissions and sufficient and appropriate actions capable of protecting people from harm through climate impacts is the global climate regime's central challenge. Moreover, in recognition of pre-existing and interconnected inequalities, these actions must not harm those who are already struggling, and ideally would work to diminish rather than exacerbate inequality generally.

The Paris Agreement is the most recent institutional attempt to resolve the tensions in these justice debates. Core aspects of the agreement include NDCs in which each party articulates the range of climate action to which it can commit (i.e., self-differentiation), increased transparency mechanisms through which state actions can be compared and tracked, and continued recognition of the need for support for adaptation and loss and damage (including the establishment of a global goal for adaptation). Importantly, the Agreement also features a regular cycle of review focused not only on individual party contributions but also on the global level. The global stocktake offers an opportunity for reflection on global progress toward the objectives of the Convention (UNFCCC 2015). The Agreement is widely perceived to be the best possible under the circumstances by many of those involved in its negotiation (Dimitrov 2016; Rajamani 2016). It explicitly includes provisions that address all of mitigation, adaptation, and loss and damage, in addition to initiating a range of institutions for facilitating them (some of which we return to in Chapter 2). Each party is responsible for determining what it can and cannot do, and there is no enforcement other than peer pressure.

For some, the universal, self-differentiated, and wide 'package' approach effectively solved this balancing act. For others, self-differentiation and the lack of explicit acknowledgment of historical responsibility eroded the Paris Agreement's capacity to generate the depth of solidarity adequate action would require. In a world characterized by differences imbricated with a variety of historically rooted injustices, excluding historical responsibility from the agreement – or folding it into the adage that everyone ought to do what they can – can be seen as mute acceptance of structural inequality (Okereke and Coventry 2016). As Manfred Berg and Bernd Schaefer remind us, "calls to let bygones be bygones and to look toward the future certainly have long since been standard rhetorical features in the discourse of denial and evasion" (Berg and Schaefer 2008: 9).

Despite the aspirations toward universality, solidarity, and collective action manifest in the Paris Agreement, climate justice debates are likely to remain contentious for at least two reasons. First, the continued inadequacy of mitigation action is steadily increasing the potential for harms from climate impacts, predominantly experienced by those who have contributed little to the problem and who are already facing ongoing development challenges. Second, the urgency of global mitigation and the shifting locus of the production of emissions have resulted in mounting pressure for mitigation action by countries with increasing emissions, despite human development challenges. As representatives of the Third World Network argue, "it can be expected that developed countries will pile pressure on developing countries, especially on emerging economies, and will try to shift or avoid their obligations" (Raman 2016: 22). Those countries with low historical emissions are unlikely to acquiesce to sharply increasing mitigation obligations without protest. How could an adequate depth of solidarity and mutual action be achieved in light of these conflicts?

We suggest that examining transitional justice processes, like the Canadian TRC, provides useful lessons about how solidarity can be built – or eroded – in the face of deep justice conflicts. The Sikh statement of acknowledgment that this chapter starts with illustrates the possibility of a range of alternative pathways for navigating complex or diffuse forms of responsibility, indirect notions of harm (which are nonetheless profound), and the broader and more nuanced aspects of trying to generate or deepen a sense of unity or solidarity. Although we will pick up on the concrete strategies currently being used in the climate context to address justice conflicts in Chapter 2, we first introduce transitional justice theory and practice.

Justice in transition

The UN defines transitional justice as "the full range of processes and mechanisms associated with a society's attempt to come to terms with a legacy of large-scale past abuses, in order to ensure accountability, serve justice and achieve reconciliation" (United Nations 2004: 8). Transitional justice is thus both a conceptual framework and a set of mechanisms that have come to be used around the world to redress harms that occurred in the past, as well as to address their repercussions in the present and for the future. As suggested in our introduction, the overarching aims of transitional justice are many and wide ranging.

Transitional justice is intended to facilitate a shift toward a more just regime; help create a durable peace after periods of political violence and armed conflict; increase solidarity and promote reconciliation in divided societies; and create an environment in which past harms are addressed and new harms are more difficult to inflict. It seeks to do this by ensuring that those responsible for past harms are held to account; generating an authoritative record of these harms and their causes; providing remedies to those most affected; and reforming institutions to signal a regime change and to help prevent further harms. One of the more implicit (and perhaps idealistic) aims of the field – embodied by the engagement between the TRC and the Sikh community in Canada – is that by raising awareness of the depth and extent of past harms, transitional justice will make it harder for those not directly affected by the harms to close their eyes to what happened, and that it will push them to take some responsibility for ensuring such harms do not happen again.

In practice, transitional justice is characterized by the following set of mechanisms, which individually have specific mandates and short time frames but usually are implemented in combination as part of a longer-term process:

- **Amnesty,** or impunity from prosecution or other form of punishment. This can be a blanket amnesty for all actors and harms, a limited amnesty for specific actors or harms, or a conditional amnesty, usually granted in exchange for disclosing the details of past crimes. Amnesty is commonly de jure, meaning granted by law, although it is also often de facto, meaning effectively granted through lack of action. Although amnesty is widely used, international norms increasingly work against amnesties for grave harms. For this reason, it often is not listed as a transitional justice mechanism per se.
- **Prosecutions,** or individual criminal accountability. Prosecutions have been launched through the permanent International Criminal Court, the ad hoc International Criminal Tribunals for Rwanda and the former Yugoslavia, hybrid courts that combine international and domestic law and actors, and national courts on the territory where abuses were committed or via universal jurisdiction for abuses committed elsewhere. In some cases, individual accountability has been pursued through indigenous, traditional, or community-based mechanisms that have been adapted to deal with mass harms. In addition, individual accountability has been pursued via civil litigation and through international, regional, and domestic human rights mechanisms, some of which have also been used to establish the responsibility of states and nonstate actors for past harms.
- **Truth commissions,** or ad hoc and temporary commissions of inquiry on specific harms inflicted within a specific period. Truth commissions investigate past harms and seek to generate an 'authoritative record' of how and why they occurred, who was responsible, and the impact they had on those

most affected. Run by states, by subnational governmental bodies, as international or bilateral initiatives, and/or by civil society, they may have public or closed hearings, make general statements concerning responsibility or print detailed lists of perpetrators' names, and rely on publicly accessible documents or use subpoenas to uncover classified evidence, among other options.

- **Reparations** for those affected by past harms. These may be individual or collective, and be either material (e.g., cash payments, the building of a school or community center) or symbolic (e.g., public apologies, memorials). Broadly defined, reparations may comprise restitution, compensation, rehabilitation, satisfaction, and guarantees of nonrecurrence. Although predominantly provided in the form of intrastate administrative programs, there are examples of interstate and other forms of reparations.
- **Institutional reform**, through changes to existing institutions and/or the establishment of new institutions. These reforms are intended to promote accountability for past harms, create an environment where new harms are prevented or made difficult to commit, and signal the human rights values of the new regime through public-sector retraining and changes to government programs (e.g., education). This may include vetting of officials complicit in past abuses.

Describing transitional justice in terms of this set, or toolbox, of mechanisms implies that it is primarily a technical endeavor that is bound to succeed if the mechanisms are implemented 'correctly.' In fact, the field has a number of objectives that are not always easy to reconcile (Bell 2008). In addition to the aims identified by the United Nations (UN) in its definition – ensuring accountability for past harms, justice for those most affected by these harms, and solidarity through individual and collective reconciliation – transitional justice is used to promote conflict resolution and peace building; facilitate nation building after transition; legitimize new regimes; ensure political liberalization and the rule of law; and push developments in international human rights, humanitarian, and criminal law (Teitel 2005). These various objectives have their origins in the historical factors that shaped transitional justice into a discrete field, but that also make it a continually evolving and contested one.

Whereas some see the field's roots in repeating cycles of "trials, purges, and reparations" since antiquity (Elster 2004: 1), transitional justice is widely thought to have emerged from developments in international norms that followed World War I and became established through international treaty and customary law in the aftermath of World War II (Teitel 2000). These norms involve states' obligations to each other as part of an 'international community' and to individuals on their territory, as reflected in international human rights law and international humanitarian law. They were also influenced by Allied efforts to establish responsibility for World War II atrocities through a combination of state and individual accountability. In addition to highlighting states' obligations to each other and to victims by imposing interstate reparations on Germany and Japan, the Allies pursued individual accountability of state agents through the Nuremberg and Tokyo trials, which later shaped international criminal law (Fletcher 2015).

Transitional justice as we understand it today emerged in the 1980s and 1990s, through the political transitions from authoritarianism in Latin America and Eastern Europe. It thus accompanied and facilitated the wave of democratization that occurred after the fall of the Berlin Wall. The decline of leftist movements and thought in the post–Cold War period gave rise to a renewed global interest in human rights and their role in promoting liberal democracy. This shift came with a focus on rapid legal-institutional reform over theories of long-term socio-economic 'modernization' and a move from structural analyses of social change to an emphasis on agency and choice (Arthur 2009). The influence of human rights and contemporary liberal democratic theory on transitional justice can be seen in the field's prioritization of individual rights – particularly civil and political rights – and of states' obligations to individuals, in combination with support for a set of national-level reforms that promote political (and economic) liberalization and the establishment of rule of law.

These are still the main drivers of the field, although transitional justice mechanisms are now used not only in contexts emerging from authoritarianism but also in states emerging from civil war, in countries where regime change is unlikely to occur any time soon, and in long-standing democracies, which has brought up its own challenges. As transitional justice became a go-to solution in contexts seeking to address past harms, it gave rise to a number of debates that relate to its diverse objectives and often revolve around tensions between the backward- and forward-looking aims of the field. A discussion of some of these debates and the lessons they bore is useful, as they involve justice tensions similar to those in the climate context. As the literature on transitional justice is vast, we focus here on the debates regarding whether justice or peace is the priority and how this relates to retributive and restorative justice approaches, as well as how to reconcile the demands and needs of those most affected by past harms with the other aims of transitional justice.

Because transitional justice draws heavily on international law, many actors, particularly influential legal experts, highlight its accountability aims and have used the field to further develop international legal regimes and mechanisms, as well as the way they are adapted at the national level. Yet the aims of transitional justice go beyond legal accountability; they include assisting divided societies to resolve their conflicts and build solidarity, while creating an environment where engaging in renewed conflict and abuses is rendered more difficult. Because insistence on legal accountability can jeopardize conflict resolution in contexts where complicit actors hold political and social sway, transitional justice actors debated whether peace building or accountability should come first. This so-called 'peace versus justice' debate pointed to another tension in the field: that between retributive justice and restorative justice. Whereas retributive approaches focus on punishing those responsible for harms in order to deter others from engaging in future harms, restorative approaches focus on rebuilding societies and integrating those responsible for past harms into communities in order to promote a more unified future (Sriram and Pillay 2010). Some commentators have discussed the field's prioritization of retribution through legal accountability as a Eurocentric norm imposed by transitional justice actors in the global North (Okello et al. 2012).

These tensions proved fruitful for the field, yielding a number of lessons. First, they highlighted that justice in any type of transition is a political and politicized process, with various actors using the opportunity to promote their own approach to both transition and to transitional justice. Second, they showed that, because it is politicized, justice in transition is a highly contextualized process, which requires tailored measures rather than a one-size-fits-all approach. Third, they indicated that transition is not an event but rather a long-term process influenced by political, social, and economic shifts at the community, national, regional, and international levels, which do not function in isolation from each other. Finally, because transition is long term, transitional justice is generally not limited to a short period but rather occurs through various and multiple measures over time in response to shifts in political will and social mobilization. Ultimately, neither retributive nor restorative approaches need be prioritized, as a transitional justice process can integrate both into a range of different measures implemented over time, depending on the context (Roht-Arriaza and Mariezcurrena 2006).

A question that has been more difficult to resolve has been the extent to which transitional justice serves those most affected by past harms. Victims of large-scale abuses are at the center of transitional justice mechanisms, serving as witnesses, testimony givers, and purported beneficiaries in prosecutions, truth commissions, reparations programs, and institutional reforms, and thereby legitimizing transitional processes and new regimes with their participation and moral authority. Yet in many cases the narrow mandates of transitional justice mechanisms have served to sideline and even revictimize those most affected – for example, with the small number of successful prosecutions in international courts, the lack of new information turned up by truth commissions, the inadequacy of reparations and their implementation, and the preference for incremental reforms over social transformation that addresses the historical injustices and ongoing structural inequalities often at the root of conflict (e.g., Chapman and Merwe 2008). The experiences of those most affected in such situations highlight the unequal power relations, both national and global, that inform any policy-level process.

Acknowledging the politicized nature of transitional justice and the way it is used to pursue diverse and often conflicting interests, transitional justice actors have highlighted the need for the participation (beyond consultation) of those most affected in the design and implementation of these mechanisms. Participatory and inclusive approaches are central to efforts to contextualize transitional justice, bringing the local into this global field, eschewing blanket 'top-down' efforts in favor of locally relevant 'bottom-up' initiatives, and foregrounding the knowledge and solutions of those most affected (Okello et al. 2012; McEvoy and McGregor 2008; Lundy and McGovern 2006).

The historical roots of transitional justice and the many debates they have produced come up repeatedly in this book. It is important to remember that transitional justice is still an evolving field based on ambiguous but weighty concepts – transition, justice, accountability, reconciliation. It is continually being deployed and shaped by actors with very different interests and aims, ranging from former perpetrators to new regimes, international agencies, legal experts, human rights nongovernmental organizations (NGOs), and victims' groups. Given this reality, transitional justice should not be romanticized or idealized, on the one hand, and its mechanisms should not be treated as technical measures that can simply be grafted onto new contexts, on the other. Nonetheless, the field represents a set of dynamic concepts and mechanisms that, if carefully and inclusively applied, may help promote repair for the past and solidarity for the future.

Perhaps the greatest lesson of transitional justice is the speed with which it effected shifts in international norms, particularly in terms of accountability and reparations. By the early 2000s, transitional justice had normalized prosecutions of those most responsible for mass harms, as well as the expectation that new regimes – which were not complicit in past harms and whose citizens largely did not directly commit abuses (although they may have been passive beneficiaries) – would find the resources necessary to provide reparations to those harmed by the previous regime. Transitional justice demonstrates the power of norm entrepreneurship and the possibility of profound shifts in international and national responses to injustices.

Transitional justice in the climate context?

At first glance drawing an analogy between climate change and transitional justice may seem outrageous. Although deep-seated and intense for those immediately engaged, the justice conflicts at the heart of climate negotiations present an altogether different kind of challenge – or do they? We suggest the contexts share six structural similarities so core to the conflicts in each that transitional justice experiences could be used as a source of insight for the climate context. These similarities include their inherent need to navigate tensions between backward-oriented claims of justice and forward-oriented calls for solidarity; the associated existence of hurting stalemates and forced interdependencies; contested and limited justiciability; the presence of profound and diverse losses; and unavoidable power imbalances and a need for political deal-making.

The first core structural tension shared by the two contexts is the **need to look backward to move forward**. Transitional justice efforts sit at the intersection of a divided past and desires for a more unified future (Zartman and Kremeniuk 2005). In these contexts actors are grappling with the profound challenge of trying to manage deeply rooted injustices while building a collective future that acknowledges but is not unraveled by the past. As former President Ricardo Lagos of Chile argued with regard to that country's transition, "No hay mañana sin ayer" (There is no tomorrow without a yesterday) (Lira 2008).

We argue that the climate change context is similarly characterized by tensions between needing to address justice claims rooted in past actions and building a framework adequate for motivating and supporting forward-oriented action. As discussed earlier, historical responsibility has been a highly contentious issue on its own but is even more difficult when juxtaposed with the depth of mitigation needs now understood. Mitigation adequate for avoiding serious impacts on vulnerable populations – including the low-lying islands, mountainous regions, and other highly vulnerable communities – will almost certainly have to include mitigation efforts even from countries that have not historically been high emitters.

The challenge in both transitional justice and the climate context is how to go about addressing these inherent tensions. Transitional justice fundamentally stems from the recognition that historically rooted claims cannot simply be ignored if the regime wishes to build long-term legitimacy. However, there have also been long-standing concerns that pushing justice for past climate harms could alienate states parties attempting to find a functional compromise. This line of thinking led the prominent American scholar Cass Sunstein (and others) to argue that "the developing world shouldn't aim for justice. The goal is to avert a global climate change disaster" (Sunstein 2015).

More recent transitional justice work is less concerned with a 'peace versus justice' trade-off because it recognizes that forward-oriented peace and backward-oriented justice are repeatedly negotiated through a transitional process. The open question this framing asks is: What kinds of arrangements will facilitate a regime's need to deal with its past, while also building the kind of future that is needed to enable human dignity for all? We suggest that finding these sweet spots is one of the defining challenges for the climate regime, as it has always been in transitional justice contexts.

A second core structural similarity between the two fields is the existence of a **hurting stalemate and forced interdependency**. Hurting stalemates emerge when all various actors' well-being is entwined and the costs of conflict become sufficiently high that everyone desires a better relationship and wishes to avoid even worse outcomes from continued conflict. If actors experiencing a conflict did not have to continue to engage with each other, it is imaginable that each could go their own way and simply avoid the past. However, in most transitional justice contexts all actors have some form of interdependency that requires them to reckon with each other's actions and claims.

Unsurprisingly parties often need a 'hurting stalemate' in order to generate political will to participate in peace or transitional justice processes (Zartman 2001). Those who have suffered injustices may be called upon to de-emphasize some of their claims or find ways of co-existing with those responsible without having fully received justice for their harms. Simultaneously, those who are most responsible for harms may be uninterested in compromise unless they are also concerned that their interests are being hurt without it. Although power imbalances run throughout these processes (see later), often resulting in less justice than may be desired, even powerful actors in a truly hurting stalemate may have to accept more accountability for past actions than they would desire.

Usually physical proximity and daily intimacy between groups is the core source of interdependence that makes hurting stalemates sufficient to motivate some kind of transitional justice process. For example, in cases such as Timor-Leste and Rwanda, violence between sides literally erupted within villages. In other cases the interdependency is less locally situated but tightly bound at the national level. For instance, in both Canada and New Zealand the desire for increased national unity and some form of reconciliation between indigenous and settler populations drove their transitional justice efforts at the state level.

Interdependency looks different in the climate context because it extends beyond national boundaries and may not be immediately visible in daily decision making. However, although the intensity of harms varies (in part due to existing patterns of wealth), in a globalized economic and social system in which people themselves are mobile, increasing climate impacts in one place necessarily have implications for other places. For example, evidence suggests that the recent conflict in Syria, which led not only to profound harm in situ but also to significant forced migration, was exacerbated by climate change–related extreme drought (Gleick 2014; Kelley et al. 2015). This is a poster-child case of how localized climate impacts can have global implications in an interdependent world.

Moreover, no population is fully immune to the pressures emerging from a global carbon budget.[10] Because of the scale of mitigation efforts required to achieve a 2°C or 1.5°C world, no country can address climate change alone, and because increasing proportions of emissions are now emerging from developing countries, emission reductions in developed countries alone would be insufficient.

The climate context is characterized by unavoidable interdependency. As argued elsewhere (Klinsky 2017), failed climate policy will result in losses for all parties. After three decades of negotiations, justice debates remain largely unchanged, and the consequences of failed collective action are set to intensify. This situation bears the essential qualities of a hurting stalemate.

The third structural similarity between the climate change and transitional justice contexts emerges from the challenges they pose to existing legal institutions. **Contested and limited justiciability** is a central component of transitional justice experience. Although many transitional justice processes have legal components (see Chapter 3), legal approaches are an imperfect fit with the claims involved and the long-term needs of transitions. Specifically, legal systems struggle with complex, diffuse, or shared responsibility for harms; systemic forms of oppression are not easily addressed through individual trials or sentencing; and quite often the legal system in the context in question simply does not have the resources or institutional capacity to handle the scale of claims it would need to if trials were used as the only mechanism for justice.

These challenges are amply illustrated in multiple cases. For example, South Africa chose to establish its TRC partially because pursuing criminal justice for all cases would have overwhelmed the justice system and because the link between specific victims and perpetrators was often difficult to prove legally (Van Zyl 2000). As a result of missing evidence (often destroyed by the previous regime) or abuses occurring through multiple chains of command, it was not always possible to identify a single person as the ultimate cause of a particular harm. In addition, all harms had to be interpreted against the context of apartheid, in which harms were regularly perpetrated and often within the legal bounds of the state. Loosening the requirement of direct causation allowed the South African TRC to acknowledge victims of structural, generalized violence without having to identify single perpetrators for particular crimes or demand that they compensate individual victims (Goldstone 2000). Although it came with its own drawbacks, this strategy had the dual advantages of acknowledging more victims than would otherwise have been possible and of focusing attention on the institutional shifts required to prevent further abuses.

A related challenge to the sheer capacity of courts has been the range of responsibility within systems of discrimination or oppression. Distinctions between the person giving orders and the person carrying out orders as part of their professional role must routinely be engaged with in transitional justice processes. Depending on the system, prosecutions of every person engaged in oppression could overstretch the legal system and impose enormous burdens on the entire society. One solution has been to distinguish among perpetrators and use prosecutions sparingly. For instance, the Colombian transitional justice process combined legal threats with greater leniency for those who participated in truth telling in order to obtain the greatest coverage without overburdening an already insufficient legal system (Guembe and Olea 2006). Such arrangements acknowledge that although legal systems are a powerful tool, alone they are a poor fit for seeking justice in contexts of systemic and diffuse harms.

Many mismatches between the capabilities of legal systems and the justice issues in transitions resonate with those seen in the climate context. Climate civil litigation (criminal litigation has not been largely pursued) has faced several persistent challenges (see Chapter 2). For instance, achieving standing in courts has been difficult due to the complex causal linkages between those who have emitted GHGs and those suffering climate harms. As in transitional justice, where direct evidence linking clearly identified victims with a single perpetrator who committed a violation may be scant despite systemic oppression, complex causality has been a major challenge for climate litigation. Similarly, if justice for all instances of climate harm were pursued through the courts, it would quickly overwhelm legal capacity. Several other complications are linked to the limited fit between the legal system and the climate context, including the difficulty of identifying discrete 'victims' and 'perpetrators' and the ambiguous nature of the harms. As discussed in Chapter 4, harm is a subjective experience distinct from actual climate impacts. This adds a level of complexity to efforts to use legal approaches to address climate harms.

Both the climate context and transitional justice context challenge the boundaries of existing legal institutions and norms. It is useful to consider how transitional justice challenges to the legal system have contributed to the evolution of moral and legal norms. Current legal resources are insufficient in the climate context, but legal institutions and moral norms change. Moreover, even imperfect uses of the legal system can create pressures that facilitate the use of other mechanisms.

Experience of **profound and diverse harms** is the fourth structural similarity between the climate and transitional justice contexts. Transitional justice processes attempt to address individual and collective experiences of harm, often identified through a human rights framework, from violence or oppression in the context of efforts to also (re)build a nation or some sense of greater solidarity. These harms vary significantly, and some of them are profound: the loss of life, loss of social cohesion and connection, and, in some cases, cultural genocide. On top of and connecting to these are economic or material losses such as the destruction of individual or collective property. Against this diversity individuals and communities must determine for themselves what these harms mean and what, if any, kinds of reparation could address them.

Harms from climate change can similarly be profound and diverse. A human rights frame is increasingly used in the climate case (see Chapter 2) to communicate the depth of possible harm. Proponents have argued that climate change could result in violations of a number of human rights, including the right to life. Commonly referred to as 'loss and damage,' in this book we use the term 'climate harms' to encompass the myriad experiences of actual loss triggered by climate impacts. These climate-induced harms are similar to those experienced in the transitional justice context because they may have both economic and noneconomic components, and may be individual or collective. As discussed in Chapter 4, transitional justice experiences with reparations for diverse losses may provide some useful insights for ways of managing and categorizing the diversity of harms currently existing or likely to emerge as climate change intensifies.

One of the potential differences between harms in the two contexts is the explicitly evolving nature of climate harm. The full scope of climate impacts is likely only beginning to be understood, and attempting any full reckoning with harms emerging from them now would be premature. This being said, many harms evolve. Andrew Woolford notes in the context of efforts to understand indigenous cultural loss following colonization that the nature of harm changes its contours over time (Woolford 2006). Recognition of the potential for harms to change over time has been built into some transitional justice efforts. For instance, institutional reforms are often designed to reduce the likelihood that future harms will emerge in recognition that many of them are embedded in broad systems not immediately addressed through other mechanisms.

The fifth similarity is that unavoidable **power imbalances** characterize both the climate change and the transitional justice context. Transitional justice measures are necessarily mired in the political processes of their context. In some cases elites who were intimately engaged in committing abuses are still in power, and in other cases they may not be. In situations where elites retain resources they can use to influence others, transitional justice processes are vulnerable to co-optation. Resistance by elites may be driven by concerns about retribution or by recognition that the new arrangement will require reductions in their privileges.

This political reality is shared in the climate context. The global context is characterized by vast disparities in economic and technological power (Roberts and Parks 2006). Any agreement that acknowledges historically situated injustices and paves the way for future cooperation will have to provide some relief from retributive justice for actors with historical responsibility while also addressing existing harms and providing strong and believable commitments to nonrecurrence. Neither the transitional justice nor the climate context offers space for ideal justice. In both the political landscape suggests that a rough justice arrangement is far more likely to be achieved, although even this is by no means guaranteed.

Finally, both contexts are characterized by debates about what is needed to achieve some level of peaceful coexistence: **incremental reform or transformation?** Durable arrangements need a believable vision of an improved future. In the early years of transitional justice (and in mainstream approaches today) institutional reforms were relied upon to signal a regime's commitment to change and to establishing new institutional foundations for society. Over time there has been increased interest in the potential for more transformative approaches based in community needs and nonhegemonic worldviews.

Discussions about the scope of transformation are occurring in both the transitional justice and climate change contexts. In the transitional justice context there have been long-standing critiques that institutionally focused changes fail to adequately address the conditions underpinning oppression and violence (Gready and Robins 2014; Fourlas 2015). Continued frustrations in South Africa due to ongoing socioeconomic disparities despite the official end of apartheid illustrate the dangers of incomplete transformational efforts (Zuern 2011). Similarly, the climate context has seen steady critiques that the current rule-based approach to regulation and climate policy is insufficient in the face of the problem. For some this challenge requires nothing less than the transformation of global production and consumption patterns, or of the global social order more generally. Although the term 'transformation' is used broadly – and even was for a short time a criterion in the Green Climate Fund – the focus in most policy circles is one of incrementalism toward a system that essentially runs much like the one we have today, but with more human well-being and fewer emissions. We return to this tension in particular in Chapter 6.

Across these points of structural similarity there are differences between the transitional justice and climate change contexts. To what extent should these differences disqualify examination of transitional justice as a viable source of inspiration for the climate context? We argue that although climate change pushes transitional justice measures to their boundaries, by no means does it overstretch them beyond utility.

One contention potentially lodged against this analogy would be that transitional justice processes usually occur at the state level, whereas the climate context is explicitly global. However, this argument fails to reflect the diversity of the field. Transitional justice processes have included interstate measures, and a variety of processes have emerged at other scales based on what units of society are most central to the specific conflict. For instance, in Rwanda, which faces a situation where atrocities were committed by neighbors who continue to live in the same villages, as well as pressing humanitarian and development challenges, and a limited national infrastructure, the state instituted the *Gacaca* courts – community-based, court-like measures designed to address specific local harms within a national program of such efforts. This design choice managed an overstretched judicial system and national infrastructure and aimed to facilitate acts of repair within the context most immediately relevant to those involved (Longman 2006). Similarly, in recognition that conflicts commonly have transnational elements, others have pointed out that 'zones of impunity' are created when national (largely legal) processes exclude transnational elements of conflict or harm and have suggested that regional considerations may need to be integrated into transitional justice practice (Sriram and Ross 2007).

The appropriate scale for a process ultimately stems from the structure of the harms, institutions, and relationships of the particular context. In the climate context, absolute interdependencies across national boundaries suggest that the global level could be the appropriate scale for framing repair. Moreover, transitional justice practices may also need to evolve to better respond to intersections between local contexts and climate impacts. As Megan Bradley has argued, egregious responses to natural disasters can be seen through a transitional justice lens (Bradley 2017). More fully integrating transitional justice practice with awareness of intensifying climate impacts at the local scale may be an important direction for the field generally.

Intentionality potentially presents a second point of difference between the two contexts. Transitional justice tends to focus on intentional human rights violations, but climate harms are not intentional and are not part of a targeted program of oppression. Nor, however, are they entirely accidental or unforeseen. Starting at least in the 1990s with the development of the UNFCCC there has been wide recognition of the link between emissions and climate harms, but emissions have continued largely unabated. Accordingly, climate harms emerge from within a structure of political and material global inequalities which facilitates the separation of actions from acknowledgment of their consequences for decision makers at all scales. Over time this separation and inequality result in the normalization of decisions to continue high rates of emissions, despite recognition of likely harms to those whose human rights are most likely to be quashed through climate impacts.

This structural normalization of harm is reminiscent of a subset of transitional justice cases found in settler colonial contexts (e.g., Canada, Australia, New Zealand), in which colonial ideologies often included attempts to morally 'improve' indigenous populations, which are now seen as acts of oppression and which continue to shape diffuse and systematic discrimination. The fact that those responsible often did not see their actions as intentionally harmful (much less illegal) has not prevented the pursuit of transitional justice processes across generations in countries such as Canada and New Zealand. These resulting processes do not excuse actions based on claims that harms were unintentional but do take a nonliability-based approach to responsibility. In addition, they serve as reminders that notions of legal and moral harm change and that these shifts can be, and have been, incorporated into transitional justice processes. For instance, the Canadian TRC report states, "Reconciliation is not an Aboriginal problem; it is a Canadian one. Virtually all aspects of Canadian society may need to be reconsidered" (TRC of Canada 2015: vi). It lists specific actions aimed at a wide range of actors (including many nonstate actors) to facilitate the institutional, legal, cultural, and ideological changes required by reconciliation. This effort can be seen as an attempt to challenge the normalization of the structures underpinning harms.

Finally, transitional justice discourse has at times constructed a binary of 'victims' deserving of reparation and 'perpetrators' subject to accountability. In contrast, the notion of victims or perpetrators is rarely used in the climate context. It is undeniable that climate harms will be profound for some people. People in the small island developing states (SIDS), mountainous regions, the Arctic, and other exceptionally vulnerable regions will almost definitely face significant climate impacts, some of which at least are likely to result in serious harm. However, although the UNFCCC's recognition of "those that are particularly vulnerable to the adverse effects of climate change" features prominently in the Preamble and throughout the Paris Agreement (UNFCCC 2015), neither the term 'victim' nor the term 'perpetrator' appears.

For some, 'victimhood' fails to acknowledge the depth of resilience and agency that front-line communities are exhibiting in the face of climate impacts (UNESCO 2017). For others, the complexity of the climate context does not resolve easily into binaries of innocence and guilt. Many of those vulnerable to climate impacts also contributed to emissions, and many continue to face human development challenges. For instance, it has been suggested that if countries were given obligations based only on past emissions, some would fare poorly, as such obligations would likely exceed their capacity, triggering another form of injustice (Den Elzen and Schaeffer 2002). Moreover, significant complications are inherent in attempting to identify specific perpetrators in a situation where the connection between actions and harms is spread across time and space and mediated by myriad biophysical processes.

These conceptual complications are not unique to climate change, however. Transitional justice processes, including those in Peru, Colombia, and Northern Ireland, have also had to deal with individuals who do not fall neatly into categories of innocent and responsible. In the Colombian situation extended periods of state and nonstate violence resulted in multiple cases of individuals who were both harmed by and committed abuses. Similarly, debates about who should be included in reparations in Northern Ireland centered in part on how to deal with losses to the families of those who had been directly engaged in violent acts and who had died in the conflict (Moffett 2016). Noting that many forms of conflict "do not lend themselves to superficial distinctions of innocent victims and guilty perpetrators" (115), Luke Moffett argues for reparation processes that recognize the possibility of people both experiencing and contributing to harm. As we discuss in the later chapters, we propose an approach to the climate context that acknowledges the complexity of the situation by focusing on nonpunitive reparations in conjunction with approaches to responsibility and institutional reform that are not bound by the confines of legal liability.

Pushing the boundaries of both fields

One concern we have faced throughout this project is whether we are over-stretching the concept of transitional justice by attempting to use it to examine climate change. Identifying the limits and reasonable expectations of transitional justice has been a sustained area of investigation and debate among practitioners and scholars. For instance, some have argued for a more expansive approach to transitional justice that ranges from deeper engagement with economic, social, and cultural rights to efforts at social transformation through redistribution and community-based, participatory processes (see Chapter 6). Such attempts have raised concerns that by broadening transitional justice past its traditional focus on civil and political rights violations that occurred within a specific period of conflict, transitional justice will attempt to be all things to all people and thus lose its ability to contribute meaningfully in these particular situations (McAu-liffe 2017). There is also a concern that efforts to expand transitional justice create a situation where it cannot hope to succeed. Processes weighted down with vastly unrealistic expectations could backfire or collapse, resulting in even less just outcomes than what might have been secured with a more modest framework for transition.

Although we are sensitive to the concern that we are stretching transitional justice theory and practice, we think that the climate context is sufficiently struc-turally similar to transitional contexts that lessons learned elsewhere could pro-vide useful insights. Using analogies to solve problems is a time-tested strategy because it can help provide a point of reflection and generate creative problem solving (Clement 1988; Bonnardel 2000). We examine climate change through the lens of transitional justice for both of these reasons. Can we learn anything new about the dynamics of the justice debates in climate change by looking at them as a type of transitional justice problem? Can insights from transitional justice experiences help us see potential solutions or scope unforeseen roadblocks? Throughout this book our goal is to do precisely this: to look at a now well-established problem with new eyes.

However, efforts to address justice tensions in the climate context are not new. Before we can ask how transitional justice might be useful in this arena and look at ways we can push the climate regime beyond its current boundaries, we must first step back and examine the scope of strategies people have already tried to apply in the climate context. We turn to this task next, in Chapter 2.

Notes

1 Philosophical literature on climate justice has a long tradition. Useful starting places include: (Shue 1992; Jamieson 2001; Gardiner 2004; Caney 2005, 2009; E. A. Page 2007).
2 Rumors of this statement spread immediately among the nongovernmental organiza-tion observers and Party negotiators at COP17 in 2011, which is where the first author became aware of it. Because it was declared during a negotiation for which no transcript is available, it cannot be proven without doubt. However, it is notable that no equity

or justice language is in the Durban Platform in accordance with long-standing United States interests, and this statement has been broadly attributed to Todd Stern. See also (Pickering, Vanderheiden, and Miller 2012).

3 Although the terms 'developed' and 'developing' are problematic, we are using them in this book because the terms are central in the UNFCCC texts and negotiation process.

4 Historical responsibility is a substantial subfield of climate ethics. Some of the commentators who have worked on these issues include (Zellentin 2015; Shue 2009; Duus-Otterström 2014; Caney 2005; Edward A. Page 2012).

5 'Mitigation' in the climate context refers to efforts to reduce GHG emissions.

6 Instead of listing any particular sources for this trend we point to the Working Group II report of the Fifth Assessment Report of the Intergovernmental Panel on Climate Change. This report presents sobering and widespread documentation of the growing understanding of the linkages between climate impacts and people's concrete experiences of harm on the ground (IPCC 2014).

7 'Adaptation' in the climate context refers to efforts to protect people from being harmed by climate change impacts. This is a wide category of action and could include anything from increasing social security nets to infrastructure projects.

8 'Loss and damage' in the climate context typically refers to the actual harms experienced by people if they are not adequately protected from climate impacts.

9 There have been a number of prominent references to colonialism in the negotiation process. For instance, Anil Agarwal and Sunita Narain's (1991) seminal paper on the justice dimensions of the international climate change negotiations refers to climate change as a case of 'environmental colonialism.' Similarly, Bolivia has explicitly argued that the accumulation of emissions in the atmosphere is part and parcel of colonialism and neocolonialism. From this perspective historical emissions "configure a climate colonialism expressed through the control of atmospheric space" (Bolivia 2015: 2).

10 The global carbon budget is the total amount of atmospheric space for emissions available if we wish to stay below a particular threshold of global climate change.

References

Adler, Matthew D. 2007. "Corrective Justice and Liability for Global Warming." *University of Pennsylvania Law Review* 155(6): 1859–67.

Africa Group, and Sudan. 2014. "Proposal from the African Group on Draft Elements on Finance Under the ADP Lima Elements on Climate Finance." UNFCCC http://www4.unfccc.int/submissions/Lists/OSPSubmissionUpload/106_99_130621901867637690-AGN%20ADP%20Paper.pdf.

Agarwal, Anil, and Sunita Narain. 1991. *Global Warming in an Unequal World*. New Delhi: Centre for Science and Environment.

AILAC, and Mexico. 2014. "Adaptation in the ADP: Joint Submission of AILAC and Mexico." UNFCCC http://www4.unfccc.int/submissions/Lists/OSPSubmissionUpl oad/39_99_130581311840849856-Adaptation%20Submission%20AILAC-Mexico%20vf.pdf.

Arthur, Paige. 2009. "How 'Transitions' Reshaped Human Rights: A Conceptual History of Transitional Justice." *Human Rights Quarterly* 31: 321–67.

BASIC Experts. 2011. "Equitable Access to Sustainable Development: Contribution to the Body of Scientific Knowledge." Beijing, Brasilia, Cape Town, and Mumbai: BASIC Expert Group.

Beg, Noreen, Jan Corfee Morlot, Ogunlade Davidson, Yaw Afrane-Okesse, Lwazikazi Tyani, Fatima Denton, and Youba Sokona. 2002. "Linkages between Climate Change and Sustainable Development." *Climate Policy* 2(2–3): 129–44.

Bell, Christine. 2008. "Transitional Justice, Interdisciplinarity and the State of the 'Field' or 'Non-Field.'" *International Journal of Transitional Justice* 3(1): 5–27.

Berg, Manfred, and Bernd Schaefer, eds. 2008. *Historical Justice in International Perspective: How Societies Are Trying to Right the Wrongs of the Past*. Cambridge: Cambridge University Press.

Bolivia. 2015. "Intended Nationally Determined Contribution From the Plurinational State of Bolivia." UNFCCC www4.unfccc.int/submissions/INDC/Published%20 Documents/Bolivia/1/INDC-Bolivia-english.pdf.

Bonnardel, Nathalie. 2000. "Towards Understanding and Supporting Creativity in Design: Analogies in a Constrained Cognitive Environment." *Knowledge-Based Systems* 13(7–8): 505–13.

Bradley, Megan. 2017. "More than Misfortune: Recognizing Natural Disasters as a Concern for Transitional Justice." *International Journal of Transitional Justice* 11(3): 400–20.

Brown, Donald. 2003. "The Importance of Expressly Examining Global Warming Policy Issues Through an Ethical Prism." *Global Environmental Change* 13: 229–34.

Byrd, Robert, and Chuck Hagel. 1997. "Senate Resolution 98." 105th Congress of the Senate of the United States. https://www.congress.gov/bill/105th-congress/ senate-resolution/98.

Caney, Simon. 2005. "Cosmopolitan Justice, Responsibility, and Global Climate Change." *Leiden Journal of International Law* 18(4): 747–75.

Caney, Simon. 2009. "Climate Change, Human Rights and Moral Thresholds." In *Human Rights and Climate Change*, edited by Stephen Humphreys, 69–90. Cambridge: Cambridge University Press.

Chapman, Audrey R., and Hugo van der Merwe, eds. 2008. *Truth and Reconciliation in South Africa: Did the TRC Deliver?* Philadelphia, PA: University of Pennsylvania Press.

Clement, John. 1988. "Observed Methods for Generating Analogies in Scientific Problem Solving." *Cognitive Science* 12(4): 563–86.

Den Elzen, Michel, and Michiel Schaeffer. 2002. "Responsibility for Past and Future Global Warming: Uncertainties in Attributing Anthropogenic Climate Change." *Climatic Change* 54(1–2): 29–73.

Dimitrov, Radoslav S. 2016. "The Paris Agreement on Climate Change: Behind Closed Doors." *Global Environmental Politics* 16(3): 1–11.

Duus-Otterström, Göran. 2014. "The Problem of Past Emissions and Intergenerational Debts." *Critical Review of International Social and Political Philosophy* 17(4): 448–69.

Elster, Jon. 2004. *Closing the Books: Transitional Justice in Historical Perspective*. Cambridge: Cambridge University Press.

Fletcher, Laurel E. 2015. "A Wolf in Sheep's Clothing? Transitional Justice and the Effacement of State Accountability for International Crimes." *Fordham International Law Journal* 39: 447–532.

Fourlas, George N. 2015. "No Future Without Transition: A Critique of Liberal Peace." *International Journal of Transitional Justice* 9(1): 109–26.

Gardiner, Stephen M. 2004. "Ethics and Global Climate Change." *Ethics* 114(3): 555–600.

GCF. 2014. "Decisions of the Board." *Green Climate Fund, Sixth Meeting of the Board, 19–21 February 2014, Bali, Indonesia*.

Gleick, Peter H. 2014. "Water, Drought, Climate Change, and Conflict in Syria." *Weather, Climate, and Society* 6(3): 331–40.

Goldstone, Richard. 2000. "Foreword." In *Looking Back, Reaching Forward*, edited by Charles Villa-Vicencio and Wilhelm Verwoerd, viii–xiii. Cape Town: University of Cape Town.

Gready, Paul, and Simon Robins. 2014. "From Transitional to Transformative Justice: A New Agenda for Practice." *International Journal of Transitional Justice* 8(3): 339–61.

Grosche, Peter, and Carsten Schroder. 2011. "On the Redistributive Effects of Germany's Feed-in Tariff." *Economics Working Paper, No. 2011, 07*, Christian-Albrechts-Universitat Kiel, Department of Economics. www.econstor.eu/bitstream/10419/49291/1/665791 33X.pdf.

Guembe, Maria Jose, and Helena Olea. 2006. "No Justice, No Peace: Discussion of a Legal Framework Regarding the Demobilization of Non-State Armed Groups in Colombia." In *Transitional Justice in the Twenty-First Century: Beyond Truth versus Justice*, edited by Naomi Roht-Arriaza and Javier Mariezcurrena, 120–42. Cambridge: Cambridge University Press.

IPCC. 2014. "Summary for Policy Makers." In *Climate Change 2014: Impacts, Adaptation, and Vulnerability. Art A: Global and Sectoral Aspects. Contribution of Working Group II to the Fifth Assessment Report of the Intergovernmental Panel on Climate Change*, edited by C. B Field, D. J. Barros, K. J. Dokken, K. J. Mach, M. D. Mastrandrea, T. E. Bilir, and M. Chatterjee. Cambridge: Cambridge University Press.

Jamieson, Dale. 2001. "Climate Change and Global Environmental Justice." In *Changing the Atmosphere: Expert Knowledge and Environmental Governance*, edited by Clark Miller and Paul Edwards, 287–307. Cambridge, MA: MIT Press.

Kelley, Colin P., Shahrzad Mohtadi, Mark A. Cane, Richard Seager, and Yochanan Kushnir. 2015. "Climate Change in the Fertile Crescent and Implications of the Recent Syrian Drought." *Proceedings of the National Academy of Sciences* 112(11): 3241–46.

Kingston, Ewan. 2014. "Climate Justice and Temporally Remote Emissions." *Social Theory and Practice* 40(2): 281–303.

Klinsky, Sonja. 2017. "An Initial Scoping of Transitional Justice for Global Climate Governance." *Climate Policy*: 1–14.

Lira, Elizabeth. 2008. "The Reparations Policy for Human Rights Violations in Chile." In The Handbook of Reparations, edited by Pablo De Greiff, 55–101. Oxford: Oxford University Press.

Longman, Timothy. 2006. "Justice at the Grassroots? Gacaca Trials in Rwanda." In *Transitional Justice in the Twenty-First Century: Beyond Truth versus Justice*, edited by Naomi Roht-Arriaza and Javier Mariezcurrena, 206–28. Cambridge: Cambridge University Press.

Lundy, Patricia, and Mark McGovern. 2006. "Participation, Truth and Partiality: Participatory Action Research, Community-Based Truth-Telling and Post-Conflict Transition in Northern Ireland." *Sociology* 40(1): 71–88.

McAuliffe, Padraig. 2017. *Transformative Transitional Justice and the Malleability of Post-Conflict States*. Cheltenham: Edward Elgar Publishing.

McEvoy, Kieran, and Lorna McGregor, eds. 2008. *Transitional Justice From Below: Grassroots Activism and the Struggle for Change*. Oxford: Hart Publishing.

Milanovic, Branko. 2012. "Global Income Inequality by the Numbers in History and Now: An Overview." *World Bank Development Research Group: Poverty and Inequality Team.* http://elibrary.worldbank.org/doi/pdf/10.1596/1813-9450-6259.

Moffett, Luke. 2016. "Reparations for 'Guilty Victims': Navigating Complex Identities of Victim-Perpetrators in Reparation Mechanisms." *International Journal of Transitional Justice* 10(1): 146–67.

Müller, Benito. 2001. "Fair Compromise in a Morally Complex World: The Allocation of Greenhouse Gas Emission Permits Between Industrialized and Developing Countries." *EV30*. Oxford: Oxford Institute for Energy Studies.

Nelson, Tim, Paul Simshauser, and Simon Kelley. 2011. "Australian Residential Solar Feed-in Tariffs: Industry Stimulus or Regressive Form of Taxation?" September. http://search.informit.com.au/documentSummary;dn=507147507129574;res=IELBUS.

Ngwadla, Xolisa, and Samah El-Bakri. 2016. "The Global Goal for Adaptation under the Paris Agreement: Putting Ideas Into Action." *CDKN*. https://cdkn.org/wp-content/uploads/2016/11/Global-adaptation-goals-paper.pdf.

NMA. 2016. "White House Economists Commit Political Malpractice to Keep Coal in Ground." *National Mining Association*. www.nma.org/index.php/press-releases-2013/2574-white-house-economists-commit-political-malpractice-to-keep-coal-in-ground.

Okello, Moses Chrispus, Chris Dolan, Undine Whande, Nokukhanya Mncwabe, and Stephen Oola, eds. 2012. *Where Law Meets Reality: Forging African Transitional Justice*. Cape Town: Pambazuka Press.

Okereke, Chukwumerije, and Philip Coventry. 2016. "Climate Justice and the International Regime: Before, During, and After Paris: Climate Justice and the International Regime." *Wiley Interdisciplinary Reviews: Climate Change*, July.

Page, Edward A. 2007. "Fairness on the Day after Tomorrow: Justice, Reciprocity and Global Climate Change." *Political Studies* 55(1): 225–42.

Page, Edward A. 2012. "Give It Up for Climate Change: A Defence of the Beneficiary Pays Principle." *International Theory* 4(2): 300–30.

Peet, Chelsea, and Kathryn Harrison. 2012. "Historical Legacies and Policy Reform: Diverse Regional Reactions to British Columbia's Carbon Tax." *BC Studies* 173(Spring): 97–122.

Pickering, Jonathan, Steve Vanderheiden, and Seumas Miller. 2012. "'If Equity's In, We're Out': Scope for Fairness in the Next Global Climate Agreement." *Ethics & International Affairs* 26(4): 423–43.

Pope Francis. 2015. "Encyclical Letter Laudato Si' of the Holy Father Francis on Care for Our Common Home." The Holy See. http://w2.vatican.va/content/francesco/en/encyclicals/documents/papa-francesco_20150524_enciclica-laudato-si.html.

Posner, Eric A., and David Weisbach. 2010. *Climate Change Justice*. Princeton, NJ: Princeton University Press.

Rajamani, Lavanya. 2016. "Ambition and Differentiation in the 2015 Paris Agreement: Interpretative Possibilities and Underlying Politics." *International & Comparative Law Quarterly* 65(2): 493–514.

Raman, Meenakshi. 2016. "The Climate Change Battle in Paris: An Updated Analysis of the Paris COP21 and the Paris Agreement." *Third World Network*. www.twn.my/title2/climate/doc/Meenabriefingpaper.pdf.

Ram-Bhandary, Rishikesh. 2015. "The Hurdle of Climate Reparations." *Global Policy*. www.globalpolicyjournal.com/blog/16/10/2015/hurdle-climate-reparations.

Roberts, Timmons, and Bradely Parks. 2006. *A Climate of Injustice: Global Inequality, North–South Politics, and Climate Policy*. Cambridge, MA: MIT Press.

Roht-Arriaza, Naomi, and Javier Mariezcurrena, eds. 2006. *Transitional Justice in the Twenty-First Century: Beyond Truth Versus Justice*. 1st edition. Cambridge: Cambridge University Press.

Schipper, E. Lisa F. 2006. "Conceptual History of Adaptation in the UNFCCC Process." *Review of European Community & International Environmental Law* 15(1): 82–92.

Shue, Henry. 1992. "The Unavoidability of Justice." In *The International Politics of the Environment: Actors, Interests and Institutions*, edited by Andrea Hurrell and Benedict Kingsbury, 373–97. Oxford: Clarendon Press.

Shue, Henry. 2009. "Historical Responsibility: Accountability for the Results of Actions Taken." *SBSTA, UNFCCC, Technical Briefing at the Sixth Session of the Adhoc Working Group on Long-Term Cooperative Action Under the Convention.* http://unfccc.int/files/meetings/ad_hoc_working_groups/lca/application/pdf/1_shue_rev.pdf.

Sriram, Chandra Lekha, and Suren Pillay, eds. 2010. *Peace Versus Justice? The Dilemmas of Transitional Justice in Africa.* Scottsville: University of Kwa-Zulu Natal.

Sriram, Chandra Lekha, and Amy Ross. 2007. "Geographies of Crime and Justice: Contemporary Transitional Justice and the Creation of 'Zones of Impunity.'" *International Journal of Transitional Justice* 1(1): 45–65.

Sunstein, Cass R. 2015. "Climate 'Reparations' for Poor Nations? Not so Fast." *Bloomberg View* (blog). www.bloomberg.com/view/articles/2015-09-29/climate-reparations-for-poor-nations-not-so-fast.

Teitel, Ruti. 2000. *Transitional Justice.* Oxford: Oxford University Press.

Teitel, Ruti. 2005. "The Law and Politics of Contemporary Transitional Justice." *Cornell International Law Journal* 38: 837–62.

TRC of Canada. 2015. "Honoring the Truth, Reconciling for the Future." *Truth and Reconciliation Commission of Canada.* www.trc.ca/websites/trcinstitution/File/2015/Honouring_the_Truth_Reconciling_for_the_Future_July_23_2015.pdf.

UNESCO. 2017 Climate Change Frontlines. http://www.climatefrontlines.org.

UNFCCC. 1992. "United Nations Framework Convention on Climate Change." http://unfccc.int/resource/docs/convkp/conveng.pdf.

UNFCCC. 2015. "The Paris Agreement." http://unfccc.int/resource/docs/2015/cop21/eng/l09r01.pdf.

United Nations. 2004. "The Rule of Law and Transitional Justice in Conflict and Post-Conflict Societies: Report of the Secretary-General." http://www.un.org/ruleoflaw/files/2004%20report.pdf.

Van Zyl, Paul. 2000. "Justice Without Punishment: Guaranteeing Human Rights in Transitional Societies." In *Looking Back, Reaching Forward*, edited by Charles Villa-Vicencio and Wilhelm Verwoerd, 42–57. Cape Town: University of Cape Town.

Weisbach, David. 2011. "Negligence, Strict Liability, and Responsibility for Climate Change." *Iowa Law Review* 97: 521–66.

Winkler, Harald, Niklas Höhne, Guy Cunliffe, Takeshi Kuramochi, Amanda April, and Maria Jose de Villafranca Casas. 2017. "Countries Start to Explain How Their Climate Contributions Are Fair: More Rigour Needed." *International Environmental Agreements: Politics, Law and Economics.*

Woolford, Andrew. 2006. *Between Justice and Certainty: Treaty Making in British Columbia.* Vancouver: University of British Columbia Press.

WRI. 2015. "CAIT Climate Data Explorer." *World Resources Institute.* http://cait.wri.org/equity.

WSO. 2013. "It Matters: The Legacy of Residential Schools." *World Sikh Organization.* www.worldsikh.org.

Zartman, I. William. 2001. "The Timing of Peace Initiatives: Hurting Stalemates and Ripe Moments." *Global Review of Ethnopolitics* 1(1): 8–18.

Zartman, I. William, and Viktor Aleksandrovich Kremeniuk, eds. 2005. *Peace Versus Justice: Negotiating Forward- and Backward-Looking Outcomes.* Lanham, MD: Rowman and Littlefield.

Zellentin, Alexa. 2015. "Compensation for Historical Emissions and Excusable Ignorance." *Journal of Applied Philosophy* 32(3): 258–74.

Zuern, Elke. 2011. *The Politics of Necessity: Community Organizing and Democracy in South Africa.* 1st edition. Madison, WI: University of Wisconsin Press.

2 Classic strategies for managing climate justice dilemmas

Debates about the intersection of justice and climate change are not new, they are not going away any time soon, and it is entirely possible that they will deepen as both mitigation pressure and the need to respond to climate impacts intensify. As with any effort to propose a new way of thinking about a suite of challenges, before we can offer any thoughtful proposals about how to address these issues, we must first understand what is being done and has been tried. How have various actors tried to address climate justice tensions? What is the current state of these efforts? And what are the strengths and limitations of each of these strategies? In this chapter we pause to reflect on the state of the art of four broad strategies to address, or at least manage, tensions about climate justice.

We suggest that in the international climate arena these four strategies are 1) using fair burden share rules to allocate international effort; 2) advocating for green economic shifts that avoid the issue of justice by promising win-win opportunities; 3) using legal approaches to seek redress and push regulatory reforms; and 4) grassroots organizing around the core concept of climate justice to push for a variety of more fundamental shifts in social, cultural, and economic life. We briefly summarize how each of these strategies has contributed to efforts to manage climate justice debates and reflect on their strengths and limitations in the face of the depth of the challenge. We ask: Where are these strategies taking us, and is this where we want to go?

Fair burden sharing

It is hard to overstate the extent to which 'fair burden sharing' has been used as a core strategy to address climate justice dilemmas. Starting with the UNFCCC, the notion of 'burdens' has been foundational to this strategy. For instance, the Convention explicitly lays out that developing countries' abilities to develop must not be impeded by climate action and that developed countries are intended to take the lead on addressing climate change. In recognition of the burden of this task, fair allocation of it was immediately a topic of consideration at the core of the UNFCCC. Most commonly, these debates center around interpretations of a core principle of the Convention, that climate action should be taken in accordance "with equity and common but differentiated responsibility and respective capabilities." Although the original Convention and the resulting texts have never laid out formalized principles for burden sharing, trying to determine what exactly CBDR-RC means for individual states in relation to global goals has been one of – if not the – dominant approaches to resolving justice tensions at the international level. Efforts to formalize and bring clarity to fair burden sharing in international climate change policy started in the 1990s (Agarwal and Narain 1991; Groenenberg, Blok, and van der Sluijs 2004; Meyer 2000; Tonn 2003) and have been ongoing.

Due to the centrality of this issue, it is unsurprising that the literature on fair burden sharing is diverse in terms of the ways in which core ideas such as 'responsibility' are defined and the particular mechanisms needed to ensure it (Baer et al. 2009; Chakravarty et al. 2009; Groenenberg, Blok, and van der Sluijs 2004; Ott et al. 2004; Pan 2003; Winkler et al. 2011; Klinsky and Dowlatabadi 2009). This diversity also comes from the inherently complex and political nature of the climate change problem. Interests and justice claims are often intermingled, and parties have different – and multiple – interests. Simultaneously, there are numerous ways to interpret the norms and parameters of 'global' society in the climate change context, which has implications for policy approaches at the international level. For instance, cosmopolitan ethicists have argued for a global application of distributive justice in the climate context (Moellendorf 2002; Singer 2006), whereas others have argued that distributive justice per se is an inappropriate frame because of the intergovernmental nature of global climate policy (Posner and Sunstein 2007). Finally, even when policy proposals use similar principles, they may operationalize them differently (Höhne, den Elzen, and Escalante 2013). For example, the idea of causal responsibility is ubiquitous in international climate policy proposals but has multiple interpretations (Klinsky and Dowlatabadi 2009).

In this chapter we are concerned less with the exact proposals made in the fair burden sharing literature and more with how viewing global climate action through this lens works. How have these arguments been made, and what can and can't they accomplish in the face of the climate justice debates articulated in Chapter 1? Despite their diversity in terms of the actual approach they take to burden sharing, fair burden sharing policy proposals share structural similarities that facilitate their examination as a strategy of engagement. These structural elements include a normative component, burden sharing rules, and motivations for addressing fairness explicitly.

Proposals about how countries ought to share the burden of climate policy action are consistently normative because they are visions of what the global policy arena should look like, not what it does look like, although questions of feasibility shape many proposals (e.g., Bosetti and Frankel 2012). Fair burden sharing proposals typically identify who should be involved, the goals that climate policy should endeavor to reach, and specific implementation options. For example, in Paul Baer, Sivan Kartha, and Tom Athanasiou's Greenhouse Development Rights (GDR) approach, countries are the primary actors, and the goal is climate stabilization without impingement on human development. In this case countries' climate mitigation obligations are determined by a combination of their historical emissions and their ability to absorb the costs of mitigation action (Baer et al. 2009). Regardless of the specific proposal, one of the primary contributions of this strategy has been to demand more careful articulations of particular normative claims: What is responsibility and how ought we to measure it? What kinds of rights – such as development rights in the GDR – ought we to have?

Fair burden sharing proposals also typically suggest standardized rules for dividing climate change burdens or ancillary resources, such as atmospheric space. Some proposals include mathematical formalizations (Baer et al. 2009; Chakravarty et al. 2009; Tonn 2003), whereas others do not (Ott et al. 2004). Both approaches feature rules for transparently differentiating parties' rights and obligations. Standardized rules – either mathematically expressed or not – have been used as a strategy for highlighting the tensions between subjective notions of fairness, which may be closely tied to self-interest, and objective notions of justice, which in theory are more systemically rooted. For instance, in 2011 experts from Brazil, South Africa, India, and China (BASIC) put forth mathematically generated articulations of what fair burden sharing rules would look like if these types of uniform considerations were used to guide global action (BASIC Experts 2011). In these particular cases, this formalization strongly drew attention to the extent to which the global carbon budget has already been largely consumed through emissions from the global North (Winkler et al. 2011).

Finally, burden sharing approaches have argued that it is important to have an explicit discussion of equity in the global climate regime. Three primary reasons for why articulations of equity are important in the climate context have emerged from this literature. First, states are unlikely to agree to arrangements that do not resonate with their perceptions of fairness. As Ambuj Sagar and Tariq Banuri argue, "protection of the global climate system requires buy-in from all countries, and options that are deemed to be inequitable are unlikely to be sustainable in the long run" (1999: 513). Explicitly including considerations of fairness when designing or proposing a policy framework can be a politically strategic act for increasing the chances that the proposal will be accepted as the basis for a global deal.

Second, there is a global norm and legal precedent for including CBDR-RC and equity in any global agreement (Winkler and Rajamani 2014). As mentioned, CBDR-RC is widely accepted as a central component of the Convention, and proposals for a global climate regime that do not include it would immediately raise questions for some. Crafting proposals that resonate with existing language can signal constructive engagement, and may increase the chances that proposals – or aspects of them – are incorporated into agreements. In the face of urgency, and after two (going on three) decades of institutional investment, the global community has internal incentives to build on existing structures, despite their limitations.

Third, because climate change policy necessarily raises justice questions, explicitly seeking to craft a just policy has moral support (Brown 2003; Shue 1999). There is an unavoidable moral argument to be made here: because we know that justice tensions necessarily characterize these policy contexts, it would be unconscionable to exclude analyses of fair burden sharing from consideration. Similarly, it has been argued that using reasoned principles as the basis for decision making is a superior alternative to pure power politics in the climate context due to the potentially devastating consequences and profound power imbalances at play (BASIC Experts 2011). Some evidence suggests that the moral arguments available to SIDS have accorded them negotiating influence beyond their size (Deitelhoff and Wallbott 2012).

For all of these reasons fair burden sharing has become a major, if not the dominant, discourse in UNFCCC-focused discussions of the justice dimensions of climate policy. In several cases fair burden sharing arguments have been used as negotiating blocks to try to shape the global regime. For instance, the Africa Group has argued that the burden of global climate action should include mitigation and adaptation commitments, along with a discussion of finance and technology, and that countries' allocations should be determined though a "principle based reference framework" that would compare country efforts with one another and against their capacities, and with the scope of global needs (Swaziland 2012).[1] In the Paris Agreement, self-differentiation of country commitments tends to run counter to formalized fair burden sharing arrangements. However, aspects of the fair burden sharing discourse continue to shape the negotiations. For instance, countries are encouraged (although not required) to justify why their NDCs should be considered equitable, a task which inherently encourages countries to engage these arguments. To date these justifications have been uneven and, for many, deeply unsatisfactory (Winkler et al. 2017), but this component is built into the Agreement. In addition, countries are explicitly called upon to consider equity during the global stocktake.[2] It is unclear how, exactly, countries should include equity in the stocktake, but fair burden sharing is likely to continue to play a central role in these discussions. Meanwhile, in the absence of a clear direction for equity in the Paris Agreement, several civil society groups focused on the UNFCCC have stepped in to propose their own forms of 'equity review' built explicitly on the notion of fair burden sharing (Civil Society Equity Review 2017).

Potential limitations of a fair burden sharing approach

Despite the arguments for explicitly considering burden sharing, this strategy does have limitations. Dependence on equity rhetoric that starts from the presumption of zero-sum burden sharing could harden oppositional positions. Conflicts involving moral claims can become entrenched to the point of intractability. The potential for fairness disputes to lead to stalemates is demonstrated by juxtaposing insistence on actions by developing countries. For instance, the Byrd-Hagel Resolution, unanimously passed by the Senate (Byrd and Hagel 1997), explicitly states that the United States will not participate in any global agreement until all countries, including the large developing countries, face equivalent obligations. The government argues that otherwise the agreement would be unfair to the United

States economy. Similarly, Canada insisted on requiring 'fair and comprehensive' commitments from all countries before withdrawing from the Kyoto Protocol (Canada 2011). In contrast, when the experts from the BASIC countries released their joint proposals for global climate actions, historical responsibility for emissions was a central determinant of future emission allocations in every single one of them (BASIC Experts 2011). In a global regime in which country contributions must be approved domestically, fair burden sharing can set up a dynamic of impossible stalemates. It is notable that when President Donald Trump signaled his intent to withdraw from the Paris Agreement he explicitly used arguments about fairness six times in a fifteen-minute speech (Trump 2017).

In addition, fair burden sharing may merely relocate conflicts to technical discussions. All proposals involving the formalization of burden sharing rules depend on metrics to differentiate countries. This process of operationalization involves a series of decisions (see Muller and Mahadeva 2013 for a particularly good discussion of this), each of which has political implications. Tensions about metrics have already been seen in debates about which year to use as the basis for historical responsibility (Den Elzen et al. 2005; Höhne and Blok 2005). It is not possible to have a clear proposal about fair burden sharing without engaging in technical debates about the merits and demerits of various options for measuring ambiguous factors such as responsibility or capability. However, the risks of a movement toward technical debates are that technical debates about metrics may not resolve equity conflicts, and that such a move could reduce the transparency and inclusivity of these discussions because participation would require greater technical knowledge. The details of calculating metrics and deciding which data sources to use become complicated and quickly raise the bar to entry. The fairest burden sharing arrangement in the world is not actually fair if the majority of the people affected by it may not have the resources to fully understand it.

Questions about how demanding moral action should be before it is 'overdemanding' also raise challenges for fair burden sharing (Murphy 1993). How much effort is enough, and how should feasibility be determined? Actors will presumably (and have already done so) invoke evidence that supports the view of feasibility that most suits their interests, which may or may not satisfy others' idea of fair burden sharing. A chief insight from work on the social psychology of justice is that if parties in a dispute feel that the other is using justice rhetoric purely for tactical purposes, this can deepen the conflict (Mikula and Wenzel 2000). The risk of demanding more than can be achieved domestically is that it can polarize parties and reduce the likelihood that they hear each other's legitimate claims.

Finally, with the exception of a small number of proposals that include subnational differentiation (Baer et al. 2009; Chakravarty et al. 2009), the majority of proposals for burden sharing focus on the state. However, greater involvement of nonstate actors, including the private sector, may be needed, if only to generate the funds and actions required. Without better integration of nonstate actors, burden sharing could contribute to a negotiation framework that systematically overlooks alternative strategies, sources of funding, and mitigation options.

Overall, fair burden sharing has been an absolutely crucial part of global discussions about climate justice, and it will likely remain central, even though self-differentiation in the Paris Agreement is in tension with it. However, because of its limitations fair burden sharing alone is unlikely to be a sufficient strategy to support the depth and speed of climate action needed in terms of reducing GHGs and responding to impacts.

Green growth

The term 'green growth' may not, at first glance, be associated with justice debates, but we suggest that it represents a second major strategy that has been, and could be, used to deal with these tensions. The idea of sustainable economic development is foundational in international climate policy. The chapeau of the Convention recognizes "that all countries, especially developing countries, need access to resources required to achieve sustainable social and economic development" (UNFCCC 1992). Recently, discussions about the potential of 'green growth' to achieve economic, social, and environmental well-being have become pronounced. A recent review identified over eighty reports and policy documents published since 2009 by international and national organizations promoting 'green growth' or the 'green economy' (UNDESA 2012). Similarly, 'green economy' was one of the two themes of the UN Conference on Sustainable Development (Rio+20), and it has been explicitly targeted as a strategy for addressing core global challenges, including climate change (UNCSD 2011).

Although a range of definitions exist for green growth or green economy (see UNDESA 2012 or Huberty et al. 2011 for reviews), the core idea is that there can be positive synergies between environmental integrity and economic growth. This is illustrated in a joint report of the World Bank and the People's Republic of China:

> Green development is based on three key concepts: economic growth can be decoupled from rising greenhouse gas emissions and environmental degradation; the process of "going green" can itself be a source of growth; and "going green" is part of a virtuous circle that is mutually reinforcing with growth.
> (World Bank and People's Republic of China 2012: 217)

It is argued that these synergies are needed because conventional economic systems have created market failures that have improperly (if at all) incorporated ecological costs into economic systems and have resulted in nonoptimal structures (Hallegatte et al. 2012; Toman 2012). By incorporating ecological considerations into understandings of economic well-being, it is possible to create economic systems that are closer to an optimal design and that create long-term growth which does not exceed ecological limits. In theory this type of growth may or may not translate into increases in purely financial metrics such as gross domestic product (GDP), but it would increase well-being, which includes the direct and indirect benefits of sustained environmental integrity. From this perspective one need not think exclusively about climate action as a burden; instead green growth holds out the promise that climate action can be achieved while generating benefits for the people, companies, and countries pursing it.

In parallel with policy discourse highlighting green growth, technological developments – such as in solar photovoltaics, wind energy, and information technology – are fueling attention to this paradigm as evidence mounts that many traditionally 'dirty' activities, such as energy production, could be effectively 'greened' without reducing their ability to provide improvements in well-being. For example, the International Energy Agency (2011) – an organization known for its conservative, rather sober analyses – suggests that the most cost-effective strategy for electrification in 70 percent of rural, remote areas would be through off-grid or micro-grid systems, more than 90 percent of which would be through renewables. Due to the importance of electrification for a range of human needs (Sustainable Energy for All 2012), renewable electrification would be an example of 'green growth' that promises well-being improvements without increasing environmental harms. These types of developments would be absolutely crucial for meeting climate action goals and yet have the enormous benefit of being motivated not by regulatory pressure, but by the self-interest of a huge diversity of actors across society.

However, as Huberty and colleagues (2011) have noted, proponents vary in their perceptions of the depth of transformation that green growth requires or produces. For some, green growth is merely the claim that economic and ecological well-being are not *necessarily* in conflict with one another and that correcting market failures can be a means of reconciling them. For others, green growth presents an opportunity for a 'green growth revolution' in which protecting the environment creates economic growth through changes to employment, innovation, and other spinoffs of these activities (Huberty et al. 2011). Either way, green growth proponents suggest that economic systems can reduce negative environmental consequences while generating human development and/or economic benefits. We return to conversations about the transformative potential of green growth in Chapter 6.

Unlocking climate action through green growth?

From a climate negotiation perspective, it is not only the content of calls for green growth that are of interest but also the logics behind attention to the concept. The rapid increase of interest in green growth raises hopes that it could address the very negotiating impasses highlighted as problematic in the strategy of fair burden sharing (Zhang and Shi 2014). Two logics underpin these hopes.

First, if it is possible to pursue economic well-being while protecting ecological resources, or better yet, to use climate mitigation actions to drive economic growth, then the trade-offs between domestic mitigation costs and global ecological well-being are eliminated. As a Costa Rican negotiator articulated, "we want ambition [in reducing emissions] to be framed in terms of self-interest" (Cavelier-Adarve 2012). Similarly, in its major report on domestic economic policy China argues that a "new race toward green development is now being played out in the global economy, with significant benefits accruing to early movers" (World Bank and People's Republic of China 2012: 218), thus providing an incentive for China to develop its own economy in a 'green' way. The key messaging line from a major report released by the Global Commission for the Economy and Climate, a self-appointed group of high-ranking economists and policy makers from a range of governments and organizations, is this: "Countries at all income levels have the opportunity to build lasting economic growth and at the same time reduce the immense risk of climate change" (Global Commission on the Economy and Climate 2014). Following the wisdom that all politics is local, one avenue of support for the strategy of green growth is the hope that it could erode or reverse domestic opposition to climate policy due to its promise for economic well-being. Considering that any global climate policy agreement rests on the ability of each country to garner domestic approval for its international position, the potential for green growth to provide win-wins domestically is a major advantage.

Second, green growth provides an avenue for the private sector to be more involved in climate change action. If economic growth and ecological protection could be combined, it would present profit incentives for the private sector at all scales. Addressing climate change mitigation and adaptation will require substantial amounts of financing, quite possibly far beyond anything that could be provided through public-sector financing alone. Green growth could create an avenue by which the financial, technical, and innovation-oriented resources of the private sector could be leveraged and directed toward climate action. For example, currently less than 0.04 percent of the global bond market is 'green,' but if this increased to even 0.12 percent it would be equivalent to $100 billion (Clapp 2014).

Both of these arguments point to the potential of a green growth strategy to alter the zero-sum framework that may be contributing to the lack of global action. Genuine alignment of economic and ecological interests would fundamentally transform global negotiations and create incentives for deeper and faster actions by all parties. From this perspective green growth is a potential strategy for dealing with climate justice tensions: if there is no burden to allocate, then countries can instead focus on the forward-oriented task of realigning their economies to take advantage of these new opportunities. This is a far more palatable approach to resolving justice tensions than fair burden sharing is for many – although not all – countries.

Limitations of a green growth strategy for climate policy

Despite these logics, there are several limitations to relying on green growth as an engine for climate action and as a response to negotiation impasses. To start with, there are many definitions of green growth. Although ambiguities in the definition could facilitate engagement among a wider set of actors, as has been argued for terms like 'sustainable development' (Robinson 2004), the risk is that green growth ceases to mean anything, becomes too thin to effectively mobilize genuine change, or disguises a lack of real action. As Brown and colleagues argue in their review of green economy discourse, "competing interpretations of the green economy nevertheless remain as a major point of fracture in the international community" (Brown et al. 2014: 248). Suspiciousness of a thin concept could increase distrust, especially of those who feel that the green growth narrative is being imposed on them. Such distrust has already been voiced. For instance, in the aftermath of Rio+20, the Green Economy Coalition, largely composed of NGOs and research institutions, warned:

> We must also ensure that green growth is inclusive with clear ambitions for equity and poverty reduction. Without these principles and qualifiers, the suspicions that a Green Economy means little more than 'green wash', or will commoditise nature, or will impose rules from the top down, or lacks ambition on social development, will only flourish and come true.
> (Greenfield and Benson 2013: 5)

Furthermore, the green growth framework may be holding out false promise. Many have stressed that conventional economic assumptions systematically undervalue and erode ecological integrity. Scholars have argued that ideas of perpetual growth in themselves are fundamentally flawed due to physical planetary limits, at least in as far as growth is typically conceived (Daly 1991; Victor 2008). From this perspective, true 'green growth' would require a change in paradigm far beyond addressing market failures using conventional means: growth itself would need to be challenged, and few governments are willing to openly embark on pathways to zero or negative growth.

Empirical evaluations of the actual dynamics of green growth remain ambiguous. This ambiguity is partly because scholars approaching the issue from different perspectives have concentrated on different elements (Newell, Boykoff, and Boyd 2012), and partly because there are multiple subcomponents of what might constitute a green growth approach. For instance, do analyses of carbon taxes that suggest positive economic effects (Barker 2010) count under a green growth rubric? Similarly, claims that regulatory policies can increase innovation are a central subcomponent of the green growth argument, but evidence of this causal relationship remains mixed. Green growth is a complex concept with multiple causal relationships, each of which requires specific analysis, and many of which may, or may not, be examined under an explicit green growth banner.

Empirical evidence for green growth is even less crisp if inclusiveness or distributive justice is included in the concept. The mixed success of the Clean Development Mechanism (CDM) for achieving its dual mandate of development and emission reductions highlights the limitations of using a market approach to tackle distributional issues and human development in the climate context (Boyd 2009; Sutter and Parreño 2005). One of the most exhaustive examinations of the extent to which green growth can be, or is inherently, inclusive was done by the World Bank. It argued, very clearly, that although these patterns of growth could be inclusive, this was by no means a guaranteed outcome (World Bank 2012).

Finally, the political challenges facing the green growth claim remain significant. Changing political and economic systems and value propositions is tremendously difficult. Even if a society or economy might benefit in the aggregate, green growth policies necessarily change who exactly are the 'winners and losers.' All emission trading systems have faced major challenges, many of which have stemmed from their potential to shift privileges across actors in the pursuit of a greener economic structure (Ellerman, Convery, and Perthuis 2010; Klinsky 2013). Similarly, the political challenges of implementing carbon taxes – although well supported through a green growth platform – have been profound (Harrison 2010). Even in the Republic of Korea, the green growth poster child and home of the Global Green Growth Institute, the concept has been the subject of intense political debate and was promoted, rejected, and promoted again in the space of a single year, illustrating the lure of but tentative confidence in the concept (Hyon-Hee 2013a; Hyon-Hee 2013b; Kim and Thurbon 2014)

Efforts to transform the economic and energy system are clearly required, and evidence does seem to suggest that such transformations are possible (Global Commission on the Economy and Climate 2014). However, green growth is not the first time a vision of economic transformation has been offered, and past experiences have not been universally positive. Despite its potential it remains far from clear that green growth will be able to deliver what its proponents promise. One of the great strengths of the green growth strategy in the context of climate justice impasses is that it does offer a reminder of the potential for benefits and opportunities within the scope of massive change the world economy must undergo if adequate mitigation is to be achieved. However, it is essential to also remember that aggregate benefits do not translate into evenly distributed benefits. Although green growth expands the operating space for negotiations, it alone is unlikely to be able to guide us through climate justice debates.

Let's fight it in court: using the law for climate justice

The potential to use legal tools to motivate climate action has long been recognized. As early as the late 1980s experts were exploring the implications of liability for climate harms, and the 1988 Toronto Declaration cited precedents prohibiting transboundary harm as a precursor to more formal explorations of the issue (Gupta 2014). By the late 1990s in the post-Kyoto world it was becoming evident that the international process was moving so slowly and had become so contentious that it may be unable to achieve the depth of emission reductions desired. Since then the interest in climate law has steadily climbed. This interest is readily seen in the Sabin Center for Climate Change Law Database. This database contains cases both in the United States and internationally that explicitly address climate change. The first case they include was lodged in 1986. This reached a handful of cases a year until the early 2000s, when the number moved into the double digits. In 2007 there were forty-four cases, and by 2016 over a hundred annually (Sabin Centre 2017). As William Burns and Hari Osofsky note in their overview of the field, "over the course of the last few years, climate change litigation has been transformed from a creative lawyering strategy to a major force in transnational regulatory governance" (Burns and Osofsky 2011: 1). This activity has included both human rights and non–human rights approaches.

For those familiar with using legal tools as a strategy for policy making, this exponential growth is bittersweet. On the one hand, it demonstrates increased recognition of the potential power of this approach in an increasingly alarm-ing global context. Courts have long been seen as a crucial node in adjudicat-ing claims of justice and in establishing forward-oriented rules capable – one hopes – of impeding further injustices. On the other hand, litigation is expen-sive, slow, and may not always be conducted by or for those who are most vulnerable or least well off. Peter Roderick – once the legal counsel for Shell Oil, then a lawyer for Friends of the Earth UK, and then the director of the Climate Justice Programme NGO – reflected on this duality. Litigation, he writes, is "rarely better in my experience than the lesser of two evils. The substance and procedure of the law usually favours the rich. Elitist language and a mis-match of resources too often shut out those who could benefit most from jus-tice." And yet, as we enter another decade of increasing emissions and political stand-offs in multiple jurisdictions, he also acknowledges that "the ultimate justification for law is that it offers the possibility of resolving disputes without us killing each other. And there can be no bigger dispute than over the future of our planet" (Roderick 2011: ix).

This section provides a very brief overview of legal action outside the UNFCCC as a strategy for supporting action on climate change and serves as the basis for our further examination of accountability mechanisms in Chapter 3.[3] How are legal strategies being used in the context of climate action, where are its limita-tions, and what might some of its costs be?

Because we are interested in what has been learned from the strategy of using law, instead of reviewing the comparative strengths and weaknesses of different kinds of claims across possible legal resources, we divide all legal activity into two categories: human rights–based and non–human rights–based litigation. In each case we outline the major strengths, limitations, and possible directions of this type of engagement as a strategy aimed at ameliorating climate justice tensions. These observations will then serve as the basis for further thinking about how to include law within the suite of accountability measures commonly used in transi-tional justice contexts. Although transitional justice arrangements usually include a legal dimension, law is only one of several mechanisms typically integrated in this approach.

Human rights–based approaches

Explicit integration of climate change and human rights law is relatively recent, but has gained significant traction in a number of ways. In this section we outline these developments, including the OHCHR declaration that countries are obli-gated to consider human rights in the climate change context, party decisions to embed human rights in the UNFCCC process, and domestic efforts to use human rights to shape climate policy.

Within the framework of international human rights law, in which attention is focused primarily on the development of jurisprudence, the first official human rights and climate change petition was lodged in 2005 by activist Sheila Watt-Cloutier on behalf of the Inuit Circumpolar Conference and more than sixty other individuals with the Inter-American Commission on Human Rights (IACHR). The petition explicitly claimed that the United States government had failed to uphold its duties by knowingly continuing GHG emissions unabated despite threats to core rights (including life, security, movement, sustenance) of Inuit people (Watt-Cloutier 2005).

Although this petition was unsuccessful, it contributed to a growing interest in using human rights law as an alternative form of pressure for political action on climate change. In 2007 the Maldives hosted other SIDS to develop the MaléDeclaration, which explicitly argues that:

> climate change has clear and immediate implications for the full enjoyment of human rights including inter alia the right to life, the right to take part in cultural life, the right to use and enjoy property, the right to an adequate standard of living, the right to food and the right to the highest attainable standard of physical and mental health.
>
> (Maldives 2007)

The declaration further requested the Office of the United Nations High Commissioner for Human Rights (OHCHR) fully investigate the extent to which climate change could threaten human rights. In 2009 OHCHR released this study, which determined that climate change would affect human rights but did not violate them per se. The report cites three objections to seeing climate impacts as clear violations of human rights. First, it argues that it is "virtually impossible" to link particular emissions from a specific country to a concrete harm. Second, it argues that human rights losses from climate change are embedded in other processes, so it is impossible to identify the extent to which change itself is responsible for the resulting loss. And third, it argues that many climate impacts will occur in the future and that "human rights violations are normally established after the harm has occurred" (OHCHR 2009: 70).

However, the OHCHR report notes that **countries are obligated to consider human rights in their climate policy decisions**. The most obvious of these obligations is domestic: as states parties are seen as ultimately responsible for safeguarding their citizens' human rights, they could be held accountable for acts or omissions that result in human rights losses for their citizens (although, as seen in the Inuit case earlier, such a claim failed in relation to the United States). The report further identifies the possibility that "States may have an obligation to protect individuals against foreseeable threats to human rights related to climate change" (OHCHR 2009: 74), suggesting that there is some space for the recognition of human rights abuses before they occur. In addition, obligations to be nondiscriminatory in terms of assistance; to move toward the realization of economic, social, and cultural rights; and to uphold participation in decision making are noted as particularly important in the face of climate change.

The report also identifies some extraterritorial obligations, although these are less clear. In addition to highlighting the importance of global cooperation generally, and the "particular responsibility" developed countries have to assist developing countries, the report refers to economic, social, and cultural rights (ESCR) to argue that states have four additional legal obligations:

- Refrain from interfering with the enjoyment of human rights in other countries.
- Take measures to prevent third parties (i.e., private companies) over which they hold influence from interfering with the enjoyment of human rights in other countries.
- Take steps through international assistance and cooperation, depending on the availability of resources, to facilitate fulfilment of human rights in other countries, including disaster relief, emergency assistance and assistance to refugees and displaced persons.
- Ensure that human rights are given due attention in international agreements and that such agreements do not adversely impact upon human rights.

(OHCHR 2009: 86)

In 2015 the OHCHR made a submission on its perspective on human rights to the UNFCCC. This submission avoids the language of 'violation,' but reiterates that states have general obligations to prevent climate change because it will affect human rights and encourages states to use a human rights framework that emphasizes concern about individual harms (OHCHR 2015).

The extraterritorial human rights obligations described here are unclear and widely debated, in part because of their relationship to ESCR, which are already a contested category of human rights. For some scholars these limitations, and several others, are profoundly damaging to attempts to use human rights in legal strategies in the climate context. Several scholars note that the United States government in particular has been disinclined to accept ESCR in general, and has systematically refused any recognition of them as legally binding obligations (Limon 2009). Claims using these rights in a United States context are unlikely to be successful. In addition to citing the issues of complexity and the indirect attribution challenges noted by the OHCHR report and others (Bodansky 2009), Eric Posner argues that using human rights litigation would result in poor regulation due to the potential for it to be inefficient (either resulting in too much or too little deterrence) and possibly to result in regressive economic losses (Posner 2007).

However, these debates must be placed into their political context. Looking at the genesis of the OHCHR report, John Knox (2009) discusses developed countries' insistence that they do not have extraterritorial obligations regarding ESCR. Tensions about the potential for obligations to stem from violations of ESCR beyond territorial boundaries helps articulate why these countries would be worried about the possibility of litigation based on strong human rights law being used in the climate context. Where, exactly, would the limits of responsibility lie for developed countries? The desirability of being able to litigate climate change through human rights law is strongly shaped by where one sits. Even here the justice disputes between countries in the current global political order leave their mark.

Simultaneously to these developments in international human rights law, in the climate change negotiations **multiple countries explicitly cited human rights in their submissions** to the COP13, which established the Ad Hoc Working Group on Long-Term Cooperative Action, a framework designed to create what eventually became the Paris Agreement. Although human rights were not noted in this decision, several countries continued to advocate for human rights language to be included in climate negotiation texts (see Rajamani 2010 for a fuller discussion). Human rights were also included in the Preamble to the Paris Agreement (UNFCCC 2015).

Meanwhile, recent developments in domestic law have also added to the momentum of using human rights as a strategy for addressing climate change. Although not addressed through the international human rights machinery, **multiple domestic cases have made reference to human rights conventions** as part of their arguments for standing. For instance in both *Urgenda v. the Kingdom of the Netherlands* (Hofhuis, Bockwinkel, and Brand 2015) and *Verein KlimaSeniorinnen Schweiz v. Bundesrat* (Verein KlimaSeniorinnen Schweiz 2016) plaintiffs explicitly rested their arguments at least partially on their government's obligation to uphold international human rights obligations.

Legal analysis of the connection between human rights and climate change has been relatively recent, but it has gone from a fringe idea to something considered by major international human rights organizations within a handful of years. The idea has not been uncontroversial, however, and the overlapping tensions about human rights and climate change in the context of globally shared obligations could be seen to diminish the potential of thinking about climate change from a human rights perspective. After all, if those who bear obligations are systematically working to avoid accepting this discourse, a human rights framework may add little.

Nonetheless, legal analysis of human rights in the climate context is an evolving field with active attempts at developing jurisprudence. Writing about the intersections between human rights and climate change, Lavanya Rajamani (2010) usefully distinguishes between two overlapping but distinct forms of human rights discourse. The legal human rights discourse is rooted in specific legal institutions and in the accumulation of jurisprudence that has shaped our notions of what is, and is not, justiciable. From this perspective, determining whether climate change violates human rights is a legal question that rests on the interpretation of the courts over time – interpretation that rests on specific analyses of who is harmed, by which processes, and by whom. In contrast, the moral human rights discourse rests on the philosophical logic underpinning claims of universal human rights. As Derek Bell argues, such claims are "justified by moral argument rather than their instantiation in international law" (2013: 161) and stem from arguments about natural law and human dignity. These two human rights discourses are frequently in tension. Although some violations may be seen as an infraction of both moral and legal rights, others may not.

The tension between legal and moral human rights discourses can be a productive one, as moral arguments can encourage a more critical stance than developed if analysis is approached only through a legal framework (Rajamani 2010). Not only does jurisprudence shift – by design – as legal norms evolve, but several classic objections – including lack of concrete attribution and claims that climate impacts are only future oriented – are also eroded through increased scientific interrogation of attribution and the progression of climate change. This suggests that evaluation of the extent to which climate harms can be considered legal human rights violations is far from over. In fact, it may be only in its infancy. Norms, as has been demonstrated by many other human rights contexts, are not written in stone. They change, in part, through the purposeful efforts of norm entrepreneurs.

Non–human rights–based approaches

While human rights–oriented claims continue to be explored, a separate suite of legal efforts have focused on other lines of argument within domestic legal systems. We can roughly divide this activity into four strategic arguments: 1) constitutional rights and public trust doctrine; 2) climate change nuisance and negligence claims; 3) securities regulation and financial transparency; and 4) public interest litigation regarding specific governmental policy duties. We briefly outline each of these in order to illustrate how they have been used in the climate context and what some of the outcomes have been.

One of the central strategies for using law in the climate context domestically has focused specifically on **constitutional rights and public trust doctrine**. To some extent these claims resonate with the underlying arguments many use in the human rights context, despite the difference in specific bodies of law used to support them. For instance, claimants have argued that governments have failed to protect the constitutional right to life through inadequate climate action.

One of the most high-profile cases of this type is *Juliana v. the United States*, in which James Hansen (an American climate scientist well known for his climate activism), an environmental NGO, and a group of children have sued the United States government, along with several fossil fuel–producing companies and associations (including the American Petroleum Institute), for threatening the right to life, liberty, and property of the young people in the suit and future generations of Americans. Importantly, particularly in light of the complexity of causation and ambiguous aspects of harm, this case was granted standing. The judges agreed that the young people's rights are important to consider, and that there is sufficient basis for believing that climate change has the potential to infringe upon them. They noted that as the defendants had actively contributed to the problem, to deny the case a hearing would infringe on the young people's right to due process. In writing the decision to allow a trial to proceed Judge Aiken wrote,

> This action is of a different order than the typical environmental case. It alleges that defendants' [i.e., the government and the fossil fuel entities listed in the case] actions and inactions – whether or not they violate any specific statutory duty – have so profoundly damaged our home planet that they threaten plaintiffs' fundamental constitutional rights to life and liberty.
>
> (Aiken 2016: 134)

In *Juliana v. the United States* the duty of the state to protect the environment in trust was noted as a background element of constitutional rights. The explicit obligation of the government to act as trustee of the public goods required for public welfare has been explored by a number of scholars and cases. For instance, Christina Wood has argued that public trust law ought to be pursued and developed extensively in the climate context as a way around the limitations of other forms of law (Wood 2016). The challenge to public trust claims has been that courts are wary of declaring governments the trustees of the atmosphere or of acknowledging clear public rights to emission reductions based on such broad claims.

This hesitancy is illustrated in *Funk v. Wolf* (Cohn Jubelirer 2016), in which a group of citizens – mostly young people – tried to compel the Pennsylvania government to create a GHG reduction plan based on the environmental rights amendment of the state constitution. This amendment reads:

> The people have a right to clean air, pure water, and to the preservation of the natural, scenic, historic and esthetic values of the environment. Pennsylvania's public natural resources are the common property of all the people, including generations yet to come. As trustee of these resources, the Commonwealth shall conserve and maintain them for the benefit of all the people.
>
> (Pennsylvania 1968: Article 1, Section 27)

In this case the court gave the petitioners standing in part because of the provision for future generations within the environmental rights amendment and did agree that the issue was relevant for the court – both claims which the state had challenged. However, it did not compel the government to create and enact climate change regulations because it decided that although citizens may have a general right to a clean environment, they do not have the right to specific actions to be taken by the government. Designing such actions, the court decided, could only appropriately be undertaken by the General Assembly or relevant government officials. This case exemplifies the difficulty of using arguments about government obligations to act as trustee: to date defending rights to the environment has been an uphill battle even in jurisdictions that have some form of environmental rights in their constitutions.

A second common line of argument has focused on **climate change as a nuisance or harm**. In both civil and common law traditions actions that harm another – either through intention or negligence – can be subject to litigation. Tort law within the common law tradition (in which torts address specific forms of harm actors might do to one another) has long been explored as a strategy to address climate change (Grossman 2003; Kysar 2010; Lytton 2007). However, tort law is based on the core notion of a specific perpetrator harming a specific victim. The assumption that causation is direct has been repeatedly problematic when trying to use tort law in climate cases.

This was clearly illustrated in *Kivalina v. Exxon-Mobile*, in which the Alaskan village of Kivalina sued Exxon-Mobile for damages incurred by the need to relocate the village due to significant coastal erosion. Although the court was sympathetic to Kivalina, it ultimately ruled that there was insufficiently direct causation between the claimants and the defendants (United States Court of Appeals for the Ninth Circuit 2012). Reflecting on the challenges of using tort law in the climate context, Douglas Kysar wryly comments that "diffuse and disparate in origin, lagged and latticed in effect, anthropogenic greenhouse gas emissions represent the paradigmatic anti-tort, a collective action problem so pervasive and so complicated as to render at once both all of us and none of us responsible" (Kysar 2010: 2).

Although civil law does not have torts, it has a similar concept of negligence and harm. The question of negligence was central in *Urgenda Foundation v. the Kingdom of the Netherlands*, in which a Dutch court ruled that the government failed in its duty of care within the civil code by pursuing a lower emission target than it otherwise ought in light of the serious consequences of climate change. The remedy put forth by the court was for the government to develop policies that would put it on a more aggressive climate mitigation pathway (Hofhuis, Bockwinkel, and Brand 2015).

This case marked a major change in climate litigation. For the first time a court had ruled that the state's duties went beyond merely diligently implementing its existing regulations and included actively changing its policy landscape to accommodate a broader suite of obligations stemming from notions of avoiding harm.[4] At the time of writing we are aware of several copycat cases being developed in Belgium, Norway, and Portugal.

However, it is notable on this front that new computing capabilities are changing the nature of climate change evidence. Using large-scale statistical models it is now possible, in cases in which there is an adequately robust weather record, to determine whether the probabilities of extreme events has shifted due to climate change (Otto 2015). As this technology develops, it is possible that it will provide more articulate evidence in a tort case than is currently the norm. To date, tort and nuisance claims have been very rarely successful, for all the reasons mentioned earlier by Kysar. The core characteristics of climate change mean it is persistently difficult to draw direct causal relationships between acts and harms, which raises complications for these kinds of cases.

A third set of cases have focused on **securities regulation and fiduciary duties**. Relatively recent, these cases have emerged due to several oil and gas corporations' lack of transparency with shareholders about climate change risks (SEC 2016a, 2016b). Related cases have also focused on company pension plans and their lack of transparency about climate change risks. These cases are fundamentally different from the tort and public trust cases because they focus on the extent to which these corporations knew about the risks climate change posed and purposefully hid this knowledge not only from the public but also, and more to the point, from their shareholders, which could be a form of fraud punishable through securities regulations. At the time of writing these cases are ongoing. One of the interesting aspects of these cases is that they could also have a criminal component to them, if senior executives can be demonstrated to have knowingly and purposefully committed what amounts to fraud (i.e., by failing to accurately represent climate risk, they were unfairly inflating reported shareholder values). We will return to these developments in Chapter 3.

Finally, to date the majority of domestic litigation has happened in the United States and Europe, but several scholars note the potential for this to become a more significant presence in developing countries as well, particularly through **public interest litigation and government obligations**. In particular, Lin (2014) argues that India's public interest litigation tradition opens a number of avenues for effective suits to be held against that government due to either inadequate mitigation or adaptation. These cases are similar to claims about constitutional rights and public trust, but often feature arguments that governments have failed to satisfy particular obligations.

The *Leghari v. Federation of Pakistan* case provides a useful example of this type of legal action in the context of government obligations to support climate adaptation. In this case Ashgar Leghari, a farmer, successfully sued the Pakistani government for failing to implement its 2012 Climate Change Plan, which largely featured strong adaptation support country-wide (Shah 2015). As Lin (2014) also notes, despite the potential of public interest litigation, the use of legal means in developing countries' activities must be placed in their global context.

As many developing countries are concerned about being unfairly burdened by mitigation, the domestic civil society community may wish to avoid using legal means to force them to do so – at least on the mitigation front. The possibility of using such strategies to advance adaptation may be another issue, one more akin to efforts to use human rights law to protect domestic citizens. At this point it is too soon to tell how such efforts will unfold.

Overall there has been sustained interest in using a variety of legal resources to create pressure for climate policy, and these efforts are rapidly becoming more numerous. This being said, the climate context continues to push the boundaries of existing legal resources: its complexity and long causal chains challenge any kind of direct liability or nuisance claims; it represents a new line of thought in terms of human rights violations; and it presents law makers with questions for which there are few precedents. In addition, as is widely recognized, litigation is far from an ideal approach to policy making due to its expense, noncooperative nature, and incremental process. Due to these aspects, legal efforts should be seen as part of the broader policy-making process, not an alternative to it. The important component from this angle is to ask how these efforts are or could interact with other mechanisms. Based on the problems with legal approaches in the climate context, we see this as a potentially important but limited strategy. As with the other strategies discussed, it brings some important resources to the table, but alone it is unlikely to be sufficient.

From the ground up: climate justice activism

In 2009 Copenhagen was home not only to COP15 but also to KlimaForum – the People's Climate Summit. Held in central Copenhagen and supported by the Danish government, KlimaForum served as a hub for civil society to develop and articulate an alternative vision of global climate action. Working under the slogan, "System Change not Climate Change," this hub sought to mobilize vast civil society networks of people and organizations concerned not only that the UNFCCC was not generating enough climate action, but also that the types of action it was generating may not be in line with fundamental claims of justice. The People's Climate Summit featured arts installations, public direct action, seminars and teach-ins, and opportunities to strengthen civil society networks. Supported by this civic space, over 100,000 people participated in what was at the time the largest climate march ever held.[5] Both the march and the sustained presence of KlimaForum for the entire two-week duration of the COP were loud and visible reminders that the vast majority of humanity was not participating in the climate negotiations but was going to be directly affected by what transpired in them. Public mobilization and grassroots organizing marks a fourth major strategy for climate justice.

Although KlimaForum and civil society engagement around COP15 marked a watershed for mobilization around the concept of climate justice, organizing started long before this and has continued long after it. In this section we briefly look at the scope of civil society organizing for and around the concept of climate justice. Our goal is to illustrate the major contributions of this strategy and identify the major lines of argument within it.[6]

Civil society organizing

It is never clear where to start a history. Does the history of civil society mobilization around climate change and climate justice start with the environmental movement as embodied by activists in North America and Europe in the 1960s and 1970s? Does it start with the liberation movements of the 1960s, 1970s, and 1980s? Does this history start with the oil crisis and the efforts of many developing countries to negotiate a New International Economic Order (NIEO)?[7] Or does it start with the environmental justice movement in the United States, itself a rebirth of the civil rights movement when it became clear that, despite civil rights, environmental 'bads' disproportionately burdened communities of color and low-income communities?

Any one of these lines of historical analysis could be developed. As civil society organizing is rooted in the experiences of people in particular places and situations, it is unsurprising that there are multiple lines of development within climate justice mobilization. It is in fact the diversity of demands and their embeddedness in social structures that sets this strategy apart from the others: climate change justice in this perspective is about far more than the distribution of GHG emissions, legal rights, or the potential to address basic needs through new forms of economic development. Although people may disagree about what exactly has to change, the call for climate justice emerging from this activity is a call for a fundamental reimagining and reordering of society at all scales and across all dimensions.

The multiplicity of issues integrated into grassroots climate activism is well illustrated in one of the earliest articulations of climate justice. The Bali Principles of Climate Justice (ICJN 2002) were developed in 2002 during the lead-up to the Johannesburg World Summit on Sustainable Development (Rio+10). Signatories included both large environmental NGOs such as Greenpeace and Friends of the Earth and a range of grassroots organizations, including, among others, the Indigenous Information Network (Kenya), the National Alliance of People's Movements (India), and the Third World Network (global but based in Malaysia). These principles explicitly built upon the Principles of Environmental Justice that emerged in 1991 out of the United States-based People of Color Environmental Justice Leadership Summit (FNPCELS 1991).[8] As with the Environmental Justice principles, the Bali Principles were wide-ranging. The twenty-seven principles varied from establishing the "sacredness of Mother Earth, ecological unity and the interdependence of all species" (Principle 1), to "recognition of a principle of ecological debt that industrialized governments and transnational corporations owe the rest of the world as a result of their appropriation of the planet's capacity to absorb greenhouse gases" (Principle 7), to affirmation of "the right of indigenous peoples and local communities to participate effectively at every level of decision-making" (Principle 21).

Although the Bali Principles also articulated concern about the use of market-based mechanisms in climate policy, affirming that "that any market-based or technological solution to climate change, such as carbon-trading and carbon sequestration, should be subject to principles of democratic accountability, ecological sustainability and social justice" (Principle 13), resistance to market-based approaches was not central in their formation. Instead, these principles focused largely on articulating rights for current and future generations, life in general, and the Earth itself. They also stressed the historically rooted injustice manifest through the concept of "ecological debt" (Principles 7, 8, and 9).

In 2004 a separate but overlapping discourse of climate justice began to gain traction. The Durban Declaration of Carbon Trading and the Call for People's Action on Climate Change (CJN! 2004) were early documents emerging out of, and giving shape to, the Climate Justice Now! (CJN!) network. Both of these took a strongly oppositional stance to the use of carbon markets in climate action, largely due to the justice implications of increasing privatization. Stating that "through this process of creating a new commodity – carbon – the Earth's ability and capacity to support a climate conducive to life and human societies is now passing into the same corporate hands that are destroying the climate," the Durban Declaration further argues that carbon markets are "a false solution which entrenches and magnifies social inequalities."

Over time, CJN! became an increasingly strong network, and during COP13 it developed a set of principles with the intent of "building a diverse movement – locally and globally – for social, ecological and gender justice." Although opposition to carbon markets and to the fossil fuel industry remained central in this narrative, the network also explicitly picked up on notions of historical responsibility central to the Bali Principles. In its short framing statement it explicitly argued that

> rich industrialised countries have put unjustifiable pressure on Southern governments to commit to emissions reductions. At the same time, they have refused to live up to their own legal and moral obligations to radically cut emissions and support developing countries' efforts to reduce emissions and adapt to climate impacts.
>
> (CJN! 2007)

As Russell (2012) documents, during the lead-up to COP15, a group of Danish activists had also started mobilizing civil society under the moniker Climate Justice Action. The central line of focus in this organization was the need for profound shifts within social and economic systems in order to achieve deep and rapid reductions in GHGs. Initially the focus of this organizing was not historical responsibility, ecological debt, or growing inequalities, but global ecological harm broadly and its link to capitalism. As mobilization congealed toward COP15, capitalism was seen as a central challenge to climate justice. For instance, some have argued (see Russell 2012) that the first use of 'climate justice' appears in an essay published by CorpWatch entitled, "Greenhouse Gangsters vs. Climate Justice" (Bruno, Karliner, and Brotsky 1999), in which climate justice is almost exclusively tied to the need to stop fossil fuel use within a capitalistic society.

As the 2008 economic crisis rippled across the United States, Europe, and then globally, these fundamental challenges to capitalism gathered momentum. Fueled both by the disappointing outcomes in Copenhagen and global attention to the failures of capitalism generally, another civil society declaration was released in 2010 following the World People's Conference on Climate Change and the Rights of Mother Earth in Cochabamba, Bolivia. This declaration consolidated the range of claims heard thus far and even more explicitly tied the climate problem to much broader social and economic systems, calling capitalism "an imperialist system of colonization of the planet." The wide-ranging list of possible solutions to the current crises included both addressing historical debts and reimagining ways of life. For instance, one guideline within this declaration was that within the UNFCCC actions must be taken to "restore to developing countries the atmospheric space that is occupied by their greenhouse gas emissions. This implies the decolonization of the atmosphere through the reduction and absorption of their emissions."

Simultaneously, it called for "the recovery, revalorization, and strengthening of the knowledge, wisdom, and ancestral practices of Indigenous Peoples, which are armed in the thought and practices of 'living well'" (PWCCC 2010). Importantly, in this framing of the climate problem financial compensation is seen as essential but insufficient. Instead, it argues, the focus must not be only on financial compensation, but also on restorative justice, understood as the restitution of integrity to Mother Earth and all its beings.

In the years since these foundational declarations, climate justice organizing has continued to grow and has resulted in the creation of multiple substantial organizations. For instance, the Pan African Climate Justice Alliance (PACJA) is now a major force both inside and outside the UNFCCC, and the Mary Robinson Foundation for Climate Justice has played a highly visible role in advocating particularly for a human rights approach to climate justice. Similarly, several faith-based networks have emerged, including the World Council of Churches, which continue to carry language about climate justice into and around the negotiations. In some cases strong existing organizations have taken up the call to work on climate justice. An example of this is seen in the National Association for the Advancement of Colored People decision to expand their environmental justice platform to include climate justice.

Throughout this organizing effort there have been continual interactions between those on the outside of the international negotiations and those on the inside. These tensions were highlighted during the Copenhagen negotiations (Russell 2012; Chatterton, Featherstone, and Routledge 2013) and then again in Durban 2011 when once again there was an alternative People's Space hosted at the University of KwaZulu-Natal in parallel to COP17. At both of these events there were organizational disputes about the legitimacy of the UNFCCC process. For some, these negotiations had strayed so far from the core demands of justice – particularly in terms of the strong support displayed for market-based climate actions and the lack of attention to concrete reparation – that support for them in any way would represent a co-optation of justice (Russell 2012).

Others have felt that engagement within the negotiations is important and have sought to find ways of applying pressure both within and outside these spaces. For instance, the Indigenous People's Forum on Climate Change has continued to work within the UNFCCC space and has consistently worked to shape key policies – including Reducing Emissions from Deforestation and Degradation (REDD) and its variants – in an effort to protect indigenous and peasant communities from these forms of climate action (Claeys and Pugley 2017). Similarly, PACJA includes in its membership both active negotiators and representatives of NGOs, as in many situations the justice-related goals of these groups at the international level are highly correlated.

Tensions about how substantial change needs to be in order to satisfy the basic demands of justice in the climate context have run throughout public mobilization efforts and speak to the fundamental challenge of deciding which pathway to take. Is incremental change enough, or does justice really require transformation? As we discuss in Chapter 6, these tensions are far from resolved and in fact may be heightened by approaching the challenge from a transitional justice perspective. When is compromise co-optation? When have calls for justice been half-heard and only partially met, resulting in accommodations that facilitate additional exploitation and the erosion of the power of justice claims initially? Articulation of these concerns is one of the important contributions of grassroots climate justice mobilization.

Unsurprisingly, grassroots mobilization has largely, although not entirely, operated outside the UNFCCC. To some extent this has limited the ability of these movements to effect change within this, or other, institutions. However, the boundaries of the UNFCCC are highly permeable. Particularly in the global South, many people immersed within the UNFCCC process are often also in communication with, if not directly supportive of, these movements. In addition, the broad solidarity networks mobilized through such efforts mean that multiple organizations may have vertical (within country) as well as horizontal (across countries) contacts. One clear illustration of this is the Plurinational State of Bolivia, which has formalized many of the broadest claims of climate justice and attempted to integrate them into UNFCCC texts. Among other elements this has resulted in the recognition of Mother Earth in the Preamble of the Paris Agreement (UNFCCC 2015).

Although these movements may not achieve their full aims, they play a crucial role in the climate justice discussion because they are able to stress a far greater range of justice claims – many of them more fully rooted in the actual lived experiences of people – than are otherwise easily integrated into the mainstream UNFCCC process. Conceptually this work insists on the accountability of the global system to the people most affected by decisions taken at national or global levels. This provides a consistent counterpoint to the mainstream approach of separating climate change from broader processes and challenges and provides a far wider, and potentially more transformative, suite of options for the future.

Synergies among strategies

These four strategies do not encompass the entire universe of efforts to address climate justice, and separating them into four distinct narratives is somewhat artificial. Indeed, people have used legal strategies to help build the foundation for green growth options. And efforts have been made to bring the positive-sum dimensions of green growth and the potential to build capabilities into the fair burden sharing space (Klinsky et al. 2016). Overall, these strategies provide a useful roadmap as to what has already been tried.

Several of these efforts, especially fair burden sharing and legal strategies, have worked more closely with existing institutions and mechanisms and attempted to find productive and pragmatic pathways toward climate justice. The green growth approach and grassroots justice mobilizing, although diametrically opposed in many ways, are similar in reaching beyond institutional change toward more profound transformation. This transformation resides not in governments or the UNFCCC, but in the power of nonstate actors, including citizens, consumers, the private sector, and civil society broadly. We pick up on this tension between reform and transformation throughout the remainder of the book. Chapters 3, 4, and 5 focus on relatively incremental institutional responses targeted largely at the UNFCCC, and Chapter 6 returns to a discussion about transformation.

Possibly the most important message that emerges from surveying these four strategies is that each of them has a great deal to contribute, but alone none of them is likely to be adequate to the scope of the challenge we face. One of the benefits of a transitional justice approach is its recognition that addressing complex justice disputes is multifaceted. It is never about selecting one strategy over another, but rather thinking about how they can or ought to be designed so that they, over time, enable greater justice overall. It is with this integrative spirit that we now turn to examining the possibilities for using transitional justice mechanisms in the climate context, beginning with approaches to managing responsibility and accountability.

Notes

1 This articulation was built on the Equity Reference Framework championed by Xolisa Ngwadla (Ngwadla 2014; Ngwadla and Rajamani 2014).
2 The global stocktake is a collective reflection on global progress toward the goals of the Convention that takes place every five years.
3 For more in-depth discussion, see in particular Burns and Osofsky (2011) and Lord, Goldberg, and Rajamani (2012).
4 At the time of writing this case was in the appeal process.
5 In 2014 this record was broken by the People's Climate March in New York City, which was estimated to have well over 300,000 attendees. Similarly, a hundred days after Donald Trump's inauguration in 2017, a second People's Climate March in Washington, DC, attracted more than 200,000 people, in addition to spurring a large number of 'sister marches' worldwide.
6 For a comprehensive analysis of this social movement, see (Russell 2012; Chatterton, Featherstone, and Routledge 2013; Ciplet 2014).
7 The NIEO was an agenda on the international stage during the late 1970s that articulated a need for a fundamentally different economic and power relationship between developed and developing countries.
8 These 1991 principles also served as the basis for the Climate Justice Declaration emerging from the second United States-based People of Color Environmental Justice Leadership Summit in 2004 (SPCEJLS 2004). As this declaration is more focused on the domestic level, we do not discuss it in depth here.

References

Agarwal, Arun, and Sunita Narain. 1991. *Global Warming in an Unequal World*. New Delhi: Centre for Science and Environment.

Aiken, Ann. 2016. "Juliana vs United States." US District Court, D. Oregon Eugene Division. Docket Number 6:15-cv-01517-TC. https://casetext.com/case/juliana-v-united-states-1.

Baer, Paul, Tom Athanasiou, Sivan Kartha, and E. Kemp-Benedict. 2009. "Greenhouse Development Rights: A Proposal for a Fair Global Climate Treaty." *Ethics, Place & Environment* 12(3): 267–81.

Barker, Terry, and S. Serban Scrieciu. 2010. "Modelling Low Stabilization With E3MG: Towards a 'New Economics' Approach to Simulating Energy-Environment-Economy System Dynamics." *Energy Journal* 31(1): 137–64.

BASIC Experts. 2011. "Equitable Access to Sustainable Development: Contribution to the Body of Scientific Knowledge." Beijing, Brasilia, Cape Town, and Mumbai: BASIC Expert Group.

Bell, Derek. 2013. "Climate Change and Human Rights." *Wiley Interdisciplinary Reviews: Climate Change* 4(3): 159–70.

Bodansky, Daniel. 2009. "Introduction: Climate Change and Human Rights: Unpacking the Issues Symposium: International Human Rights and Climate Change." *Georgia Journal of International and Comparative Law* 38: 511–24.

Bosetti, Valentina, and Jeffrey Frankel. 2012. "Politically Feasible Emissions Targets to Attain 460 ppm CO2 Concentrations." *Review of Environmental Economics and Policy* 6(1): 86–109.

Boyd, Emily. 2009. "Governing the Clean Development Mechanism: Global Rhetoric Versus Local Realities in Carbon Sequestration Projects." *Environment and Planning A* 41(10): 2380–95.

Brown, Donald. A. 2003. "The Importance of Expressly Examining Global Warming Policy Issues Through an Ethical Prism." *Global Environmental Change* 13(4): 229–34.

Brown, Ed, Jonathan Cloke, Danielle Gent, Paul. H. Johnson, and Chloe Hill. 2014. "Green Growth or Ecological Commodification: Debating the Green Economy in the Global South." *Geografiska Annaler: Series B, Human Geography* 96(3): 245–59.

Bruno, Kenny, Joshua Karliner, and Chin Brotsky. 1999. "Greenhouse Gangsters vs Climate Justice." www.corpwatch.org/article.php?id=1048.

Burns, William, and Hari Osofsky, eds. 2011. *Adjudicating Climate Change: State, National, and International Approaches.* Cambridge: Cambridge University Press.

Byrd, Robert, and Chuck Hagel. 1997. "Senate Resolution 98." 105th Congress of the Senate of the United States. https://www.congress.gov/bill/105th-congress/senate-resolution/98.

Canada. 2011. "A Climate Change Plan for the Purposes of the Kyoto Protocol Implementation Act 2012." www.ec.gc.ca/Publications/default.asp?lang=En&n=EE4F06AE-1&xml=EE4F06AE-13EF-453B-B633-FCB3BAECEB4F&offset=3&toc=show.

Cavelier-Adarve, Isabel. 2012. "AILAC: The New Latin American 'Third Way' at UN Climate Talks." http://climatefinance.info/profiles/blogs/ailac-the-new-latin-american-third-way-at-un-climate-talks.

Chakravarty, Shoibel, Annanth Chikkatur, Heleen de Coninck, Stephen Pacala, Robert Socolow, and Massimo Tavoni. 2009. "Sharing Global CO2 Emission Reductions Among One Billion High Emitters." *Proceedings of the National Academy of Sciences* 106(29): 11884–88.

Chatterton, Paul, David Featherstone, and Paul Routledge. 2013. "Articulating Climate Justice in Copenhagen: Antagonism, the Commons, and Solidarity." *Antipode* 45(3): 602–20.

Ciplet, David. 2014. "Contesting Climate Injustice: Transnational Advocacy Network Struggles for Rights in UN Climate Politics." *Global Environmental Politics* 14(4): 75–96.

Civil Society Equity Review. 2017. "Equity and the Ambition Ratchet: Towards a Meaningful 2018 Facilitative Dialogue." http://civilsocietyreview.org/wp-content/uploads/2017/11/CSO_Report_COP23_Equity_and_the_Ambition_Ratchet_SCREEN.pdf.

Claeys, Priscilla, and Deborah Pugley. 2017. "Peasant and Indigenous Transnational Social Movements Engaging With Climate Justice." *Canadian Journal of Development Studies/Revue canadienne d'études du développement* 38(3): 325–40.

Clapp, Crista. 2014. "Climate Finance: Capitalising on Green Investment Trends." In *The Way Forward in International Climate Policy: Key Issues and New Ideas 2014*, edited by H. de Coninck, R. Lorch, and A. Sagar, 44–48. London: Climate and Development Knowledge Network and Climate Strategies.

CJN! 2004. "Climate Justice Now! A Call for People's Action against Climate Change." http://climatejustice.blogspot.com/2004_11_23_archive.html.

CJN! 2007. "Climate Justice Now! Principles." https://lists.riseup.net/www/info/cjn.

Cohn Jubelirer, Renee. 2016. "Funk vs Wolf." Pennsylvania Commonwealth Court. Docket Number 467 M.D. 2015.

Daly, Herman E. 1991. *Steady-State Economics*, 2nd edition. Washington, DC: Island Press.

Deitelhoff, N., and L. Wallbott. 2012. "Beyond Soft Balancing: Small States and Coalition-Building in the ICC and Climate Negotiations." *Cambridge Review of International Affairs* 25(3): 345–66.

Den Elzen, M., J. Fuglestvedt, N. Hohne, C. Trudinger, J. Lowe, B. Matthews, and B. Romstad. 2005. "Analysing Countries' Contribution to Climate Change: Scientific and Policy-related Choices." *Environmental Science & Policy* 8(6): 614–36.

Ellerman, A. D., F. J. Convery, and C. de Perthuis. 2010. *Pricing Carbon*. Cambridge: Cambridge University Press.

FNPCELS (First National People of Color Environmental Leadership Summit). 1991. "Principles of Environmental Justice." www.ejnet.org/ej/principles.html.

Global Commission on the Economy and Climate. 2014. "Better Growth, Better Climate: The New Climate Economy Report." http://newclimateeconomy.net.

Greenfield, O., and E. Benson. 2013. "Building the Big Picture for a Green Economy." *UNEP Perspectives* (Issue 9). www.unep.org/civil-society/Portals/24105/documents/perspectives/ENVIRONMENT_PAPERS_DISCUSSION_9.pdf.

Groenenberg, H., K. Blok, and J. van der Sluijs. 2004. "Global Triptych: A Bottom-up Approach for the Differentiation of Commitments Under the Climate Convention." *Climate Policy* 4(2): 153–75.

Grossman, D. A. 2003. "Warming Up to a Not-So-Radical Idea: Tort-Based Climate Change Litigation." *Columbia Journal of Environmental Law* 28: 1.

Gupta, J. 2014. *The History of Global Climate Governance*. Cambridge University Press. www.amazon.com/History-Global-Climate-Governance/dp/1107040515.

Hallegatte, S., G. Heal, M. Fay, and D. Treguer. 2012. "From Growth to Green Growth: A Framework." *National Bureau of Economic Research*. www.nber.org/papers/w17841.

Harrison, K. 2010. "The Comparative Politics of Carbon Taxation." *Annual Review of Law and Social Science* 6(1): 507–29.

Hofhuis, H. F. M., J. W. Bockwinkel, and I. Brand. 2015. "Urgenda Foundation vs Kingdom of the Netherlands." Docket Number C/09/456689 / HA ZA 13-1396. Hague District Court. http://www.urgenda.nl/documents/VerdictDistrictCourt-UrgendavStaat-24.06.2015.pdf

Höhne, Niklas, and Kornelis Blok. 2005. "Calculating Historical Contributions to Climate Change: Discussing the 'Brazilian Proposal.'" *Climatic Change* 71(1–2): 141–73.

Höhne, N., M. den Elzen, and D. Escalante. 2013. "Regional GHG Reduction Targets Based on Effort Sharing: A Comparison of Studies." *Climate Policy* 14(1): 122–47.

Huberty, Mark, Huan Gao, Juliana Mandell, John Zysman, Nina Kelsey, Jacob Riiskjaer Norgard, and Jeremey Pilsaar. 2011. *Green Growth: From Religion to Reality*. Berkeley: Roundtable on the International Economy.

Hyon-Hee, Shin. 2013a. "Korea Eyes Era of 'Green Growth 2.0.'" *The Korea Herald*, 10 November. www.koreaherald.com/view.php?ud=20131110000342.

Hyon-Hee, Shin. 2013b. "South Korea Ditching Green Growth." *The Korea Herald*, 30 March. www.asianewsnet.net/South-Korea-ditching-green-growth-44753.html.

ICJN (International Climate Justice Network) 2002. "Bali Principles of Climate Justice." www.indiaresource.org/issues/energycc/2003/baliprinciples.html.

IEA. 2011. *World Energy Outlook 2011: Energy for All – Financing Access for the Poor*. www.iea.org/media/weowebsite/energydevelopment/weo2011_energy_for_all.pdf.

Kim, Song Young, and Elizabeth Thurbon. 2014. "Green Growth: Rebooted in South Korea, Booted Out in Australia." *The Conversation*. http://theconversation.com/green-growth-rebooted-in-south-korea-booted-out-in-australia-22243.

Klinsky, Sonja. 2013. "Bottom-up Policy Lessons Emerging from the Western Climate Initiative's Development Challenges." *Climate Policy* 13(2): 143–69.

Klinsky, Sonja, and Hadi Dowlatabadi. 2009. "Conceptualizations of Justice in Climate Policy." *Climate Policy* 9: 88–108.

Klinsky, Sonja, David Waskow, Eliza Northrop, and Wendy Bevins. 2016. "Operationalizing Equity and Supporting Ambition: Identifying a More Robust Approach to 'Respective Capabilities.'" *Climate and Development*: 1–11.

Knox, John. 2009. "Linking Human Rights and Climate Change at the United Nations Symposium." *Harvard Environmental Law Review* 33: 477–98.

Kysar, Douglas. 2010. *What Climate Change Can Do About Tort Law*. New York: Social Science Research Network.

Limon, Marc. 2009. "Human Rights and Climate Change: Constructing a Case for Political Action Symposium." *Harvard Environmental Law Review* 33: 439–76.

Lin, Jolene. 2014. "Litigating Climate Change in Asia." *Climate Law* 4(1–2): 140–9.

Lord, Richard, Silke Goldberg, and Lavanja Rajamani. 2012. *Climate Change Liability: Transnational Law and Practice*. Cambridge: Cambridge University Press.

Lytton, Timothy. 2007. "Using Tort Litigation to Enhance Regulatory Policy Making: Evaluating Climate-Change Litigation of Lessons from Gun-Industry and Clergy-Sexual-Abuse Lawsuits." *Texas Law Review* 86: 1837.

Maldives. 2007. "Male' Declaration on the Human Dimension of Global Climate Change." www.ciel.org/Publications/Male_Declaration_Nov07.pdf.

Meyer, Audre 2000. *Contraction & Convergence: The Global Solution to Climate Change*. Totnes: Green Books for the Schumacher Society.

Mikula, Gerold, and Michael Wenzel. 2000. "Justice and Social Conflict." *International Journal of Psychology* 35(2): 126–35.

Moellendorf, Darrel. 2002. *Cosmopolitan Justice*. Boulder, CO: Westview Press.

Muller, Benito, and Lavan Mahadeva. 2013. "The Oxford Approach: Operationalizing the UNFCCC Principle of 'Respective Capabilities.'" Oxford Institute of Energy Studies. https://www.oxfordenergy.org/publications/the-oxford-approach-operationalizing-the-unfccc-principle-of-respective-capabilities.

Murphy, Liam. 1993. "The Demands of Beneficence." *Philosophy & Public Affairs* 22(4): 267–92.

Newell, Peter, Max Boykoff, and Emily Boyd, eds. 2012. *The New Carbon Economy: Constitution, Governance and Contestation.* 1st edition. Chichester: Wiley-Blackwell.

Ngwadla, Xolisa. 2014. "An Operational Framework for Equity in the 2015 Agreement." *Climate Policy* 14(1): 8–16.

Ngwadla, Xolisa, and Lavanya Rajamani. 2014. "Operationalising an Equity Reference Framework in the Climate Change Regime: Legal and Technical Perspectives." Cape Town: Mitigation Action Plans and Scenarios (MAPS).

OHCHR. 2009. "Report of the Office of the United Nations High Commissioner for Human Rights on the Relationship between Climate Change and Human Rights." https://documents-dds-ny.un.org/doc/UNDOC/GEN/G09/103/44/PDF/G0910344.pdf?OpenElement.

OHCHR. 2015. "Understanding Human Rights and Climate Change Submission by OHCHR to the 21st Conference of Parties to the UNFCCC," 27 November. www.ohchr.org/EN/Issues/HRAndClimateChange/Pages/HRCAction.aspx.

Ott, Hermann, Harald Winkler, Bernd Brouns, Sivan Kartha, M.J. Mace, Saleemul Huq, and Yasuko Kameyama. 2004. "South-North Dialogue on Equity in the Greenhouse: A Proposal for an Adequate and Equitable Global Climate Agreement." www.erc.uct.ac.za/Research/publications/04Ott-etal-SouthNorthDiaLogue.pdf.

Otto, Fredereike. 2015. "Climate Change: Attribution of Extreme Weather." *Nature Geoscience* 8(8).

Pan, Jiahua. 2003. "Commitment to Human Development Goals with Low Emissions: An Alternative to Emissions Caps for Post-Kyoto from a Developing Country Perspective." *Research Centre for Sustainable Development, Chinese Academy of Social Sciences.* www.fni.no/post2012/panjiahua_paper_draft.pdf.

Pennsylvania. 1968. "Constitution of the Commonwealth of Pennsylvania." State of Pennsylvania. http://www.legis.state.pa.us/WU01/LI/LI/CT/HTM/00/00.htm.

Posner, Eric. 2007. *Climate Change and International Human Rights Litigation: A Critical Appraisal.* Rochester: Social Science Research Network.

Posner, Eric, and Cass Sunstein. 2007. "Climate Change Justice." *Georgetown Law Journal* 96: 1565.

PWCCC. 2010. "People's Agreement on Climate Change and the Rights of Mother Earth: Final Declaration of the World People's Conference on Climate Change and the Rights of Mother Earth." *World People's Conference on Climate Change and the Rights of Mother Earth.* Cochabamba, Bolivia. https://pwccc.wordpress.com/support.

Rajamani, Lavanya. 2010. "The Increasing Currency and Relevance of Rights-Based Perspectives in the International Negotiations on Climate Change." *Journal of Environmental Law* 22(3): 391–429.

Robinson, John. 2004. "Squaring the Circle? Some Thoughts on the Idea of Sustainable Development." *Ecological Economics* 48(4): 369–84.

Roderick, Peter. 2011. "Forward." In *Adjudicating Climate Change: State, National, and International Approaches*, edited by W. C. G. Burns and H. M. Osofsky. Cambridge: Cambridge University Press.

Russell, Bertie. 2012. "Interrogating the Post-Political: The Case of Radical Climate and Climate Justice Movements." http://etheses.whiterose.ac.uk/3348/1/Completed_Thesis_-_B_Russell.pdf.

Sabin Centre. 2017. "Climate Litigation Database." http://columbiaclimatelaw.com/.

Sagar, Ambuj, and Tariq Banuri. 1999. "In Fairness to Current Generations: Lost Voices in the Climate Debate." *Energy Policy* 27: 509–14.

SEC (Securities and Exchange Commission). 2016a. "Rule 14a-8 No-Action Request to SEC from Chevron Corp. Regarding Shareholder Proposal Submitted by Hermes Equity Ownership Services and UMC Benefit Board, Inc."

SEC (Securities and Exchange Commission). 2016b. "Rule 14a-8 No-Action Request to SEC from Exxon Mobil Corp. Regarding Shareholder Proposal Submitted by As You Sow et al." Securities and Exchange Commission. http://blogs2.law.columbia.edu/climate-change-litigation/wp-content/uploads/sites/16/case-documents/2016/20160323_docket-na_letter-1.pdf.

Shah, Syed Mansour Ali. 2015. "Leghari vs Federation of Pakistan." http://blogs2.law.columbia.edu/climate-change-litigation/wp-content/uploads/sites/16/non-us-case-documents/2015/20150404_2015-W.P.-No.-25501201_decision-1.pdf.

Shue, Henry. 1999. "Global Environment and International Inequality." *International Affairs* 75(3): 531–45.

Singer, Peter. 2006. "Ethics and Climate Change." *Environmental Values* 15(3): 415–22.

SPCEJLS (Second People of Color Environmental Justice Leadership Summit). 2004. "The Climate Justice Declaration." www.emeac.org/2014/11/climate-justice-declaration.html.

Sustainable Energy for All. 2012. "Sustainable Energy for All: A Framework for Action." *The Secretary-General's High-level Group on Sustainable Energy for All.* www.se4all.org/wp-content/uploads/2013/09/SE_for_All_-_Framework_for_Action_FINAL.pdf.

Sutter, Christopher, and Juan Carlos Parreño. 2005. "Does the Current Clean Development Mechanism Deliver Its Sustainable Development Claim?" *Hamburg Institute of International Economics*, June 2007.

Swaziland. 2012. "Submission by Swaziland on Behalf of the Africa Group on the Vision, Ambition and Principle Under the ADP." https://unfccc.int/files/meetings/ad_hoc_working_groups/kp/application/pdf/adp_africangroup_050912.pdf.

Toman, Michael. 2012. "'Green Growth': An Exploratory Review." *The World Bank Development Research Group: Environment and Energy Team.* http://elibrary.worldbank.org/docserver/download/6067.pdf?expires=1368127291&id=id&accname=guest&checksum=24500261021E72A025C10368456B349B.

Tonn, Bruce. 2003. "An Equity First, Risk-Based Framework for Managing Global Climate Change." *Global Environmental Change* 13(4): 295–306.

Trump, Donald. 2017. "Statement by President Trump on the Paris Climate Accord." www.whitehouse.gov/the-press-office/2017/06/01/statement-president-trump-paris-climate-accord.

UNCSD. 2011. "Rio +20 United Nations Conference on Sustainable Development Objective and Themes." www.uncsd2012.org/objectiveandthemes.html.

UNDESA. 2012. "A Guidebook to the Green Economy." www.uncsd2012.org/content/documents/528Green%20Economy%20Guidebook_100912_FINAL.pdf.

UNFCCC. 1992. "United Nations Framework Convention on Climate Change." http://unfccc.int/resource/docs/convkp/conveng.pdf.

UNFCCC. 2015. "The Paris Agreement." http://unfccc.int/resource/docs/2015/cop21/eng/l09r01.pdf.

United States Court of Appeals for the Ninth Circuit. 2012. "Native Village of Kivalina, City of Kivalina vs Exxon Mobile." http://cdn.ca9.uscourts.gov/datastore/opinions/2012/09/25/09-17490.pdf.

Verein KlimaSeniorinnen Schweiz. 2016. "Request to Stop Omissions in Climate Protection: Petition Submitted to European Commission on Human Rights." http://blogs2.law.columbia.edu/climate-change-litigation/wp-content/uploads/sites/16/non-us-case-documents/2016/20161025_3585_petition-1.pdf.

Victor, Peter. 2008. *Managing without Growth: Slower by Design, Not Disaster*. Cheltenham: Edward Elgar Publishing.

Watt-Cloutier, Sheila. 2005. "Petition for the Inter American Commission on Human Rights Seeking Relief from Violations Resulting from Global Warming Caused by Acts and Omissions of the United States." www.inuitcircumpolar.com/uploads/3/0/5/4/30542564/finalpetitionicc.pdf.

Winkler, Harald, Niklas Höhne, Guy Cunliffe, Takeshi Kuramochi, Amanda April, and Maria Jose de Villafranca. Casas. 2017. "Countries Start to Explain How their Climate Contributions Are Fair: More Rigour Needed." *International Environmental Agreements: Politics, Law and Economics*. www.readcube.com/articles/10.1007/s10784-017-9381-x.

Winkler, Harald, T. Jayaraman, Jiahua. Pan, Adraiano Santihago de Oliveira, Yongsheng Zhang, Girish Sant, Jose Domingoa Gonzalez Miguez, Thapelo Letete, Andrew Marquand, and Stephen Raubenheimer. 2011. *Equitable Access to Sustainable Development: A Paper by Experts from BASIC Countries*. Beijing, Brasilia, Cape Town, Mumbai: BASIC Expert Group.

Winkler, Harald, and Lavanya Rajamani. 2014. "CBDR&RC in a Regime Applicable to All." *Climate Policy* 14(1): 102–21.

Wood, Mary Christina. 2016. "Nature's Trust: Environmental Law for a New Ecological Age." *Integrated Environmental Assessment & Management* 12(1): 206–208.

World Bank. 2012. "Inclusive Green Growth: The Pathway to Sustainable Development." http://siteresources.worldbank.org/EXTSDNET/Resources/Inclusive_Green_Growth_May_2012.pdf.

World Bank, and People's Republic of China. 2012. *China 2030: Building a Modern, Harmonious, and Creative Society*. Washington, DC: Development Research Centre of the State Council, the People's Republic of China and World Bank.

Zhang, Yong-Sheng, and He-Ling Shi. 2014. "From Burden-Sharing to Opportunity-Sharing: Unlocking the Climate Negotiations." *Climate Policy* 14(1): 63–81.

3 Managing responsibility
Amnesty, legal accountability, and truth recovery

Any agreement about justice must deal with responsibility. Even if some acts might ultimately be forgiven, it would be nonsensical to expect a true resolution of the debates if all notions of responsibility were ignored or excluded from discussion. The climate context is no exception, and responsibility and accountability for both the past and for contributing to an improved future have been central to climate debates. Responsibility, for instance, is embedded in the principle of states' 'common but differentiated responsibilities,' which is used both in the Convention and in subsequent texts, including the Paris Agreement. CBDR is broadly taken as recognition that the differences in responsibility for contributing to climate change must be part of an equitable division of efforts to deal with it.

As we discussed in Chapter 1, responsibility is a crucial issue because a relatively small number of countries, representing a minority of the world's population, are responsible for emitting the vast majority of cumulative global emissions to date. Yet this pattern of accumulated emissions is shifting as a number of emerging economies have started to use more fossil energy. For instance, in 1992 developing countries were immediately responsible for roughly 34 percent of industrial greenhouse gas emissions. By 2011, when the Durban Platform was negotiated, these countries were responsible for 58 percent of industrial emissions (WRI 2015). By 2007 China had become the single largest emitter, although China's per capita emissions remain at roughly a third of those in the United States. Broadly speaking, emissions are expected to continue to grow in developing countries, largely driven by increasing energy demand. At the same time, the role of nonstate actors in terms of responsibility is being increasingly recognized. For instance, Richard Heede and his team attribute roughly 60 percent of global emissions to only ninety multinational companies (Heede 2014), raising questions about how best to include the accountability of such actors in any discussion of responsibility.

Debates about responsibility have heightened as the costs of climate impacts become more concrete. How will these costs be borne, and how will responsibility factor in? To date sensitivity about liability has been extremely high, but claims for justice are not going to disappear as communities face the loss of life, infrastructure, economic viability, and natural resources even if powerful actors would far prefer to avoid discussing liability.

These debates, particularly about how to handle historical responsibility and liability for harm within a rapidly changing global context, have been difficult to navigate. In this chapter we consider what the climate context could learn from transitional justice approaches to responsibility. We first discuss a range of transitional justice measures, namely amnesty, individual criminal responsibility, legal state and corporate responsibility, and truth commissions. We then return to the international climate negotiations to interrogate how such mechanisms could be used in this context. We suggest that amnesties, legal action, and truth commissions all have something to offer the climate context but would need to be used in concert. As in many transitional justice contexts, the question here is not which mechanism to use, but how the outcomes of one can facilitate others. Moreover, as we discuss in the subsequent chapters, the core challenge of the climate context cannot be solved through responsibility measures alone, even if they are crucial.

Managing responsibility in the transitional justice context

One of the main debates that shaped transitional justice in the 1980s and 1990s, which continues to be a reference point as the field evolves, is whether to pursue peace or justice first. In the transitions from authoritarianism to democracy in Latin America and Eastern Europe, the previous regimes still held significant sway, politically, institutionally, and socially. Policy makers found that pursuing accountability for past harms carried the risk of keeping representatives of the old regime from the negotiating table in the short term, and of alienating its supporters in the long term – to the extent that social solidarity and the prevention of future harms appeared under threat. Although international human rights, humanitarian, and criminal law oblige states to investigate past harms and provide redress to those most affected, and to provide norms and tools for prosecutions of individuals deemed most responsible, the political realities of these transitions appeared to call for compromise. Policy makers often fell back on the centuries-old practice of providing amnesty from liability for past harms. In addition to promising an end to conflict, amnesty – which comes from the Ancient Greek for 'forgetfulness' – implies wiping the slate clean in order to move on from past harms.

In recent years, however, amnesties have been challenged by international and local stakeholders not only for countering international law but also, more importantly, for not responding to the needs and demands of those most affected by past harms. These more recent calls position the needs of those affected as more pressing than the political concerns of policy makers. Policy makers have accordingly responded to calls for retributive justice by exploring restorative justice options. They sought to establish responsibility and ensure accountability without overt punishment through prosecutions. In some cases they sought to bypass institutions, particularly courts, compromised under the old regime. State-run truth-seeking and truth-telling processes proved a popular solution to this problem, and truth commissions emerged as a defining mechanism of transitional justice. Although they largely focus on individual responsibility for past harms, truth commissions, like reparations and institutional reform, also demonstrate the responsibility of the state for redressing and preventing harms. They embody the backward- and forward-looking aims of transitional justice, linking efforts to create a better future to redress for past harms.

The debate over peace versus justice became less urgent as transitional justice practice developed and lessons were learned. It is now clear that transitions are long-term processes and that amnesties, truth commissions, prosecutions, and other mechanisms for establishing and managing responsibility can occur simultaneously, at different times, and in various sequences, depending on shifting norms, political will, and social mobilization. This section provides a brief overview of each responsibility mechanism and different ways they have been conceptualized and implemented in the transitional justice context before the chapter turns to possible applications of each in the climate context.

Amnesty

In transitional justice, amnesty is discussed and applied in several ways (Mallinder 2008; Lessa and Payne 2012). **Blanket amnesty** refers to cases where all individuals implicated in past harms are exempted from prosecution and other forms of retributive punishment. Policy makers have used this approach in cases where powerful actors threaten a peaceful transition. For example, Lebanon adopted a blanket amnesty at the close of its fifteen-year civil war to bring the warring parties to the negotiating table. In Brazil, the military dictatorship enacted a blanket amnesty law to allow activists in exile back into the country, but mainly to protect itself from future prosecutions as it became clear that a transition would occur.

Limited amnesty, meanwhile, refers to cases where only those deemed most responsible for past abuses or responsible for gross human rights violations are held to account, whereas others are granted amnesty. This approach was used in Colombia, for example, primarily because the justice system would have been overloaded by the number of cases to investigate and prosecute. A specific form of limited amnesty is 'conditional amnesty,' where individuals are offered the option of amnesty on the condition of 'giving back' in some way. In South Africa, the Truth and Reconciliation Commission oversaw this process, evaluating amnesty applications based on how much the applicants disclosed about abuses they perpetrated and the extent to which these abuses were politically motivated and proportional to their political goals. In Colombia, perpetrators, including of gross violations in some cases, are granted amnesty by a special court if they disclose and acknowledge their abuses and propose a valid individual or collective reparation plan for those they harmed.

Amnesty by definition is enacted by legislation. It is a legal, or **de jure**, measure adopted to prevent prosecutions at the domestic level. Transitional justice actors often use the term **de facto amnesty** to refer to cases where impunity prevails despite efforts to account for past abuses. This term covers a wide range of cases. For example, it may refer to cases where an amnesty law is adopted but does not specify which crimes are included and so is difficult to implement, as occurred in Côte d'Ivoire. It may also refer to cases where national authorities do not pursue accountability measures despite having the means, as occurred in post-apartheid South Africa with the National Prosecuting Authority deciding not to put former apartheid functionaries on trial and successive state presidents attempting to pardon perpetrators without using transparent processes or involving those most affected by the harms. As such, de facto amnesty may occur during or well after a political transition. In a sense, de jure amnesty is preferable to de facto amnesty, as it is a legal acknowledgment that harm was done even in its attempt to ensure impunity.

As is often the case with transitional justice measures, the norms concerning amnesty have changed over the past thirty years. Whereas domestic policy makers frequently adopted blanket or various forms of limited amnesty in the early days of transitional justice, the norm is increasingly that amnesty is not granted for gross violations. Lisa Laplante (2008a) notes that this shift is due to developments in international human rights law, particularly rulings against amnesty laws by regional human rights bodies such as the Inter-American Court of Human Rights (IACtHR), which base their findings on states' obligation to investigate and punish abuses and to provide justice to those affected. Although such obligations could be read to apply to all abuses, they are in the main being applied in cases of gross abuses and particularly to individuals deemed most responsible for these violations. Laplante argues that the increasing tendency for domestic policy makers not only to annul old amnesty laws but also to incorporate criminal investigations into the mandate of truth commissions and other mechanisms is a sign that amnesties are less accepted at both the international and national levels.

The proponents of amnesty are not always perpetrators and others complicit in abuses under authoritarian regimes or in armed conflicts. Actors as diverse as peace builders working with parties who refuse to negotiate peace agreements without guarantees of impunity, members of communities where different sides were caught up in conflict and are both perpetrators and victims of abuses, and policy makers coping with political upheavals during and after transitional processes may see amnesty as a viable solution in politically complex transitional contexts (Mallinder 2007). For this reason, amnesty continues to be a feature of transitional justice.

Nonetheless, three decades of transitional justice practice have shown that amnesties can be socially divisive and damaging in the long term, entrenching a culture of impunity and eventually undermining the domestic and international legitimacy of transitional regimes. In addition, as the field becomes more responsive to the needs and demands of those most affected by harms, transitional justice actors view the victims' sacrifice entailed in amnesties as too high a cost. In this context, policy makers have begun carefully weighing the costs and benefits of various types of amnesty in relation to the political-historical specificities of their contexts and in light of evidence from other transitional contexts that amnesties can be short-lived and often are replaced by other accountability measures, both restorative and retributive (Lessa and Payne 2012). Focusing on retributive measures, the next section presents an overview of individual criminal responsibility in its various manifestations, followed by a discussion of efforts to ensure state and corporate responsibility using legal means.

Individual prosecutions

Ruti Teitel (2000) notes that, in the popular imagination, transitional justice is associated with punishing perpetrators through trials, mainly because transitional justice as a field in its own right emerged from efforts to hold Nazis accountable after World War II. Although the positive impact of individual criminal accountability, like that of transitional justice generally, has been difficult to prove (Duggan 2010), the idea is that prosecutions establish individual responsibility, generate a record of the events and motivations behind past abuses, give those affected an opportunity to engage with those responsible, demonstrate that the new regime does not tolerate abuses, increase trust in legal institutions and the rule of law, and deter people from engaging in future abuses.

Prosecutions in the transitional justice context draw on developments in international law since the 1940s, specifically the increasing acceptance of international human rights and humanitarian law, and of legal sanctions against individual perpetrators through international criminal law. Given the relative rarity of domestic prosecutions during transition, mainly due to political reasons but also resource and capacity constraints facing local courts, the focus in the 1980s and 1990s was on creating **international criminal tribunals**. The aim was to build international justice norms in order to assist with the domestication of international law at a later date. The early 1990s saw the establishment of the ad hoc, temporary International Criminal Tribunals for the former Yugoslavia (ongoing) and Rwanda (closed in 2015). This movement culminated in the establishment of the permanent International Criminal Court (ICC) in The Hague in 2002.

The ICC prosecutes individuals accused of genocide, crimes against humanity, and war crimes (crimes of aggression are still a pending category). The court's jurisdiction covers crimes committed on the territory of states parties to the ICC's Rome Statute, or by nationals of states parties on other territories, after the date those states ratified the treaty. It also covers cases referred by an individual state or the UN Security Council. In addition to ensuring due process for the accused, the ICC adopted an innovative approach in offering victims the opportunity to participate in proceedings and present their views before the court; providing victims with access to counseling, protection, and legal support; and implementing reparations orders through an independent Trust Fund for Victims. As such, the court includes elements of both retributive and restorative justice. The ICC, like all international criminal accountability efforts, is financed through contributions from member states that are based on countries' incomes, as well as voluntary donations from states, international organizations and agencies, nongovernmental organizations, charitable foundations, and other actors.

Although hailed for promoting international accountability norms, the ICC has faced a range of criticisms, including for being too slow and expensive, successfully prosecuting very few individuals, relying on other actors' political will to apprehend suspects, holding proceedings far from those most affected by harms, failing to adequately ensure victim protection and participation, serving neocolonial and geopolitical interests by pursuing cases primarily in Africa, and promoting a westernized and one-size-fits-all conception of justice. The ICC is also hampered by its temporal jurisdiction, where abuses committed before 2002, or before a state party ratifies the treaty, are not covered (Bosco 2014). The court is continually evolving, however, as suggested by its recent announcement – potentially relevant to the climate context – that it will consider mass crimes that are caused by or result in environmental destruction and illegal exploitation of natural resources or dispossession of land (Office of the Prosecutor 2016).

In response to the shortcomings of international criminal tribunals noted earlier, particularly their inaccessibility to those most affected by harms, some states have chosen to establish internationalized or **hybrid courts** on their own territory, often in concert with the UN or with a regional body such as the African Union. Hybrid courts are independent, ad hoc institutions with limited time frames. Examples include the Special Court for Sierra Leone, the Extraordinary Chambers in the Courts of Cambodia, and the Special Panels for Serious Crimes in Timor-Leste. Relying on a combination of international and domestic law as well as staff, these courts are intended to ensure the domestication of international law, to build the capacity of the national legal system, and to block local 'spoilers' from undermining proceedings, while also costing less, focusing on a particular situation, and being more responsive to local issues than international tribunals. Hybrid courts face many of the same criticisms as the international tribunals, in addition to challenges relating to local political will, for example, in terms of sensitivities around the types of abuses and time period they should cover and local authorities' ability and willingness to apprehend suspects (Williams 2016).

Some states have established special chambers within their judicial systems that address abuses of international law and could be considered a form of hybrid court, such as the Specialist Chambers for Kosovo. Other states have pursued prosecutions against those accused of gross abuses through regular **domestic courts**, as has been the case across Latin America. Significantly, prosecutions in domestic courts can occur during or after political transition, as well as in cases where political transition has not occurred but the current regime is signaling its commitment to international norms. The domestication of treaty and customary international law by states is a central aim of transitional justice, and all of the international and internationalized courts established to date have positioned themselves as complementary to national jurisdictions, rather than as a replacement. Ultimately, international laws and norms are being developed in order to promote states' obligation to investigate and prosecute individuals responsible for grave abuses (Ellis 2014; Stahn and Zeidy 2011). A noteworthy trend at the international and domestic levels is a growing focus on economic crimes, where individuals are prosecuted for corruption and associated crimes committed alongside gross abuses and are often ordered to pay reparations from their illicit gains.

As more states integrate international law into their legislation, national courts are increasingly empowered to exercise **universal jurisdiction** over crimes under international law, which originally referred to crimes such as piracy but now also refers to genocide, crimes against humanity, and war crimes. The extent of their powers in this regard depends on their legislation, and some states may prosecute nationals of any state for crimes committed on any territory, whereas others may only prosecute their own nationals or crimes committed on their territory or against their nationals. In 2012, 163 of the 193 UN member states could exercise universal jurisdiction over one or more international crimes (Amnesty International 2012). Although universal jurisdiction has been implemented in a number of cases, such as several high-profile cases in Spain against former senior officials of Latin American dictatorships, most countries have chosen not to exercise universal jurisdiction because the legislation is inadequate or political will is lacking. In a parallel development, since the 1980s, several victims have used the United States Alien Tort Statute, a relatively obscure 1789 federal law, to bring civil suits against individuals who committed human rights abuses outside United States territory.

In cases where the national justice system has been undermined by civil war or complicity with a repressive regime, and where specific indigenous or community-based conflict resolution measures are culturally accepted, states have sought to adapt **indigenous justice mechanisms** to addressing gross abuses. This approach has proven useful in cases where the sheer number of cases would overwhelm an already struggling domestic system. Some indigenous mechanisms are justice oriented and have a retributive focus, such as the state-run *Gacaca* courts in Rwanda, and others are more restorative and focused on reintegration, such as the community-based *Mato Oput* process in northern Uganda. Although the extent to which such mechanisms ensure individual accountability is contested, these diverse practices offer the benefit of being locally relevant and more accessible to those most affected by harms (Huyse and Salter 2008).

Transitional justice prioritizes individual responsibility; however, grave abuses are usually committed under the aegis of a powerful entity, most frequently a state, but also corporations. The next section outlines attempts to ensure legal accountability for abuses sponsored by these actors.

State and corporate accountability

Individual criminal accountability as a central focus in transitional contexts is a fairly recent phenomenon. As Fletcher (2015) demonstrates, after World War II, the Allies pursued both individual accountability and state responsibility. They linked Germany's and Japan's terms of surrender to reparations, institutional reform, and other state accountability mechanisms, in addition to holding individuals to account through the Nuremberg and Tokyo trials. The focus on individual responsibility is due primarily to a normative shift away from punishing states (and the populations they represent) toward a post–Cold War individuation of both responsibility (of perpetrators) and suffering (of victims) popularized through human rights discourse (Mutua 2001). Although states' obligations to their and other states' populations have increased over time, there is still no cohesive legal basis for state responsibility among the various strands of international law relevant to transitional justice, namely international human rights, humanitarian, and criminal law (Fletcher 2015).

To date, legal state responsibility for abuses addressed by transitional justice is promoted largely by **regional human rights bodies** in Europe, the Americas, and Africa. Particularly active examples are the IACHT and IACtHR. These bodies are guided by treaties between sovereign states and by the norms of customary international law. Typically, individuals, groups, organizations, and member states may bring a complaint before a regional human rights body if they have exhausted domestic legal means. This body can instruct a member state to address, prevent, and redress harms caused by the state, by state agents, or by the state's failure to prevent abuses. New regimes are equally responsible for the abuses of old regimes as for their own.

Another avenue for promoting state responsibility is the **United Nations human rights machinery**, centered around the Human Rights Council, which works in cooperation with OHCHR; a number of human rights treaty bodies (e.g., the Committee on Economic, Social and Cultural Rights and the Committee of the Rights of the Child); and various committees, rapporteurs, and working groups. The Human Rights Council can undertake a confidential investigation of complaints brought by individuals, groups, and organizations concerning gross human rights abuses allegedly committed by any state member of the UN in cases where domestic remedies have been exhausted. The International Court of Justice (ICJ), which addresses only cases against UN member states brought by other states, has supported the UN human rights machinery and made rulings on human rights issues in a small but increasing number of cases. Although the decisions and rulings of these regional and international bodies are binding, states choose whether and to which extent to implement them, in the face of pressure ranging from media shaming to trade sanctions and even withheld development aid (Johns 2015).

In 2005, UN member states also adopted the principle of the **responsibility to protect** (R2P) their populations from genocide, war crimes, ethnic cleansing, and crimes against humanity. R2P consists of three pillars: each state's responsibility to protect its population from these grave abuses, all states' responsibility to assist each other in doing so, and states' responsibility to take appropriate collective action against a state that fails to protect its population, including through direct intervention. Although R2P has been used inconsistently and is markedly politicized, it is a new tool in efforts to hold states responsible for upholding international norms.

In light of the role domestic, multinational, and transnational corporations have played in committing, supporting, or failing to prevent gross abuses on their own or in cooperation with states and nonstate groups, transitional justice actors have also attempted to develop legal norms around **corporate accountability**. Given the general lack of international and often national means for ensuring corporate criminal liability, and states' reluctance to apply such legal provisions, most of the literature on corporate accountability centers on UN and regional human rights instruments and norms. It examines the UN's work on the issue, which culminated in its 2011 Guiding Principles on Business and Human Rights, as well as various regional and national norms around corporate responsibility, such as the OECD Guidelines for Multinational Enterprises, with a focus on preventing abuses and providing reparations when they have occurred. Although these norms are based on states' responsibility to protect human rights and corporations' responsibility to respect them, the UN is currently in the process of considering a binding treaty on human rights and business that would oblige multinational and transnational corporations to protect rights. Another avenue for establishing corporate accountability has been civil litigation against corporations using domestic laws in their host countries or their countries of origin, as well as the Alien Tort Statute that allows non-nationals to bring a tort action in the United States for abuses of international law. A well-known example of the latter is the litigation brought by apartheid victims against corporations they claim were complicit in supporting the abuses of the South African apartheid regime (Michalowski 2013).

Although these attempts to establish legal state and corporate responsibility for past abuses have had limited success and face substantial legal and political limitations, they represent innovative efforts by transitional justice and other actors to build international accountability norms. They should be seen as complementary to efforts to ensure individual criminal accountability. The constraints implicit in pursuing any form of legal accountability, however, have resulted in the rise of the truth commission as a quasi-legal approach to countering impunity. Truth commissions are a middle ground between amnesty and prosecution or litigation. They are also based on principles of restorative justice, shifting the focus from punishment of those responsible for abuses to acknowledgment of those most affected and repair of divided societies. Truth commissions are one of the main and increasingly used mechanisms of transitional justice.

Truth commissions

Truth commissions are ad hoc, temporary commissions of inquiry that investigate documented and undocumented abuses, generate an authoritative and undeniable record of patterns of abuses that occurred within a certain time period, and disseminate their findings in an effort to redress harms and prevent abuses from recurring. Transitional justice actors refer to these commissions as truth-recovery or truth-seeking bodies, highlighting their investigative side, and as truth-telling bodies, foregrounding the testimonies of those most affected by harms. Using a restorative rather than a retributive approach, these commissions may announce that they are pursuing ambitious aims beyond truth recovery, such as promoting reconciliation in a divided society, seeking justice for those most affected, and fostering healing for wounded individuals and collectives. They also usually signal, both domestically and internationally, a new regime's break with past abuses and commitment to a new democratic order characterized by rule of law. They are thus often nation building projects that serve to legitimize new regimes (Daly 2008).

As truth commissions are generally established by legislation or decree, they tend to be official mechanisms run by the state, although they may also be provincial and even municipal initiatives. In a few cases where the state is unable or unwilling to establish a truth commission, or where an official truth commission is compromised by political interests, civil society formations have initiated their own either alternative or supplementary commissions. For example, the Catholic Church in Guatemala established the Recovery of Historical Memory project to fill gaps left by the official Commission for Historical Clarification. Most domestic truth commissions operate during or after political transitions from authoritarianism and war to democracy. As transitional justice becomes a norm, however, truth commissions have been established in countries that have not yet undergone regime change, as with Togo's Truth, Justice and Reconciliation Commission. They have also been established in long-standing democracies, as is the case with Canada's TRC.[1]

In some cases, truth commissions are international or bilateral institutions. For example, the UN has ensured that peace agreements it sponsors include a provision for a truth commission, as with the Commission on the Truth for El Salvador, or a UN body has set up a truth commission itself, as with the Commission for Reception, Truth, and Reconciliation in Timor-Leste. Regional bodies, such as the European Union or the African Union, have also played this role (at times in concert with the UN), as in the case of the International Commission on Kidnapped and Other Missing Persons for Macedonia. In addition, a state may establish a truth commission to examine abuses committed in other territories, as was the case with the Swedish government forming the Independent International Commission on Kosovo, in which civil society–based commissioners from around the world examined abuses by both local and international armed forces. Finally, an example of a bilateral truth commission is the Commission on Truth and Friendship, established by Indonesia and Timor-Leste to examine abuses committed during Timor-Leste's independence referendum (Freeman 2006).

Truth commissions usually have a mandate to investigate patterns of gross abuses committed within a specific time period, although in a few cases a commission has focused on a particular event, as with the Greensboro Truth Commission's examination of a 1979 anti-supremacist rally in the United States. Truth commissions typically cover a wide range of abuses, from extrajudicial killings to forced displacement, although some have looked into a specific violation, as in the instance of Algeria's Ad Hoc Inquiry Commission in Charge of the Question of Disappearances. Although they may cover a wide range of harms, these harms tend to be civil and political rights violations, particularly of bodily integrity, with the result that social, economic, and cultural abuses are often sidelined. A few commissions have specifically investigated socioeconomic harms and economic crimes, for example, with the Kenyan Truth, Justice, and Reconciliation's focus on land grabbing and, more recently, the Brazilian National Truth Commission's focus on corporate complicity with the overthrown military dictatorship.

Commissioner selection may occur by appointment through a closed process or by nomination through a public process, with varying degrees of transparency. Commissioners may be local, international, or a mix, depending on the context. Although they are meant to be independent and unbiased, they usually represent a broad spectrum of political and other interests.

In their investigations, some commissions rely on information in the public domain, particularly documentation of abuses gathered by civil society, and others have power of subpoena to gain access to confidential information. With regard to testimony, commissions may have closed hearings, in order to protect those giving testimony, or public hearings, in order to broaden their impact through the media and particularly to give those most affected the opportunity to share their experiences. Participation is voluntary, although some commissions, such as the South African Truth and Reconciliation Commission, use incentives like the possibility of amnesty to encourage perpetrators to come forward. Truth commissions engage primarily with victims and alleged perpetrators; however, the South African commission was also innovative in holding public 'institutional hearings' to examine collaboration with the apartheid regime of institutions and groups as diverse as business and labor, the legal profession, the health sector, the media, religious communities, political parties, and the armed forces.

In their final reports, commissions may make general statements regarding responsibility – for example, showing that state actors were responsible for a certain percentage of violations – or they may release lists of perpetrators' names. Final reports present the commission's findings and make nonbinding recommendations for addressing past abuses, including through accountability measures, reparations, and institutional reforms. They attempt to place civil-political rights abuses in historical context, which allows them to discuss socioeconomic harms and their links to historical and structural injustices. These reports are sometimes summarized in more accessible documents, such as short reports or comic books, which may later be used for educational purposes. Truth commissions are funded by national treasuries and by donations from governmental donors, intergovernmental organizations, charitable foundations, and nongovernmental organizations (Hayner 2010).

As this brief summary suggests, truth commissions are shaped by their contexts, especially by the extent of both political will and social mobilization around dealing with the past. They can be used to deflect accountability and maintain the status quo as much as to establish responsibility for past harms, check future abuses, and spur public conversation about social change. Truth commissions have been critiqued for following the biases of mainstream human rights discourse in prioritizing civil and political rights abuses over economic, social, and cultural rights violations. In the same vein, they are said to individualize both responsibility and suffering, and to obscure the historical injustices and structural inequalities that enabled past abuses, and often allow abuses to continue (Mutua 2001). Critics question the extent and depth of the information commissions are able to gather given their constrained time frames (usually a couple of years) and limited human and financial resources, and even what 'truth' could mean given the power dynamics involved in the construction of history in divided societies (Daly 2008). Truth commissions' claims of effecting reconciliation and healing are questioned, and in some cases they are said to revictimize victims by not meeting their expectations while reviving old traumas (Chapman and van der Merwe 2008).

Despite these criticisms, truth commissions are now a go-to solution in transitional contexts and a staple of transitional justice. Each new commission presents an opportunity to learn from previous commissions and improve practice. For example, an increasing number of truth commissions include addressing socioeconomic abuses in their mandates, as in the case of Kenya's Truth, Justice and Reconciliation Commission focus on land issues. Others have sought to foreground the historical nature of abuses and the way they continue to affect the present, such as Peru's Truth and Reconciliation Commission and Tunisia's Truth and Dignity Commission. Many also attempt to be more victim centered, having learned from the South African TRC to foreground the participation, needs, and demands of those most affected by past harms, rather than primarily ensuring due process for perpetrators. These developments may signal a slow shift away from a narrow, legalistic approach toward a more transformative approach in the practice of truth commissions (Gready and Robins 2014).

The way truth commissions are designed and implemented is evolving, as are all measures designed to establish and promote responsibility for past harms. Moreover, many transitional justice processes have integrated aspects of all of these mechanisms depending on the situation. It is in this spirit that we now turn to the climate context. Considering its unique characteristics, what relevance might any of these approaches for managing responsibility in transitional justice processes have – either singly or in concert – for managing the tensions about responsibility in the climate justice context?

Applying responsibility measures in the climate context

Responsibility mechanisms from the transitional justice framework can be used for a variety of purposes. For instance, some prosecution efforts have been motivated by the desire to punish particular individuals and/or deter others from engaging in certain acts. In other situations prosecutions have been used primarily as a threat to motivate engagement with other transitional justice mechanisms, particularly truth commissions. In this section we consider what three mechanisms aimed at dealing with responsibility – amnesties, legal accountability, and truth commissions – might offer the climate context both individually and in combination.

Amnesty

Amnesties are widely used in transitional justice contexts. One database suggests that 420 amnesty processes have been used since World War II (Mallinder 2007). However as discussed earlier, a number of lessons have accumulated through the inclusion of amnesties in transitional justice processes which has led to changing norms about when to use and how to design them. Whereas blanket amnesties were once commonly used, many of the newer amnesties are limited or conditional, and typically are rooted in some legal process. Such shifts have been motivated by concerns about blanket amnesties' longevity and effects on long-term regime legitimacy.

Even with these alterations, the underlying logic of amnesties stems from the political and psychological challenges of building some form of solidarity or unity after a period of violence. In the transitional justice context amnesties have often emerged from a political interest in providing protection for actors who could otherwise 'spoil' a compromise, the costs of legal prosecution, and the opportunity costs of alienating those with essential skills or resources in transition periods. Combining them with other mechanisms has been one way of creating incentives for otherwise recalcitrant actors to cooperate with broader processes. All these political reasons for using amnesties resonate in the climate context.

For example, many actors (state and nonstate) that produce high emissions also hold the political, financial, and technological capabilities needed for effective global climate action. These actors are the least interested in a strong accountability system in terms of responsibility for past emissions. As in the transitional justice context, limited or conditional amnesties in the climate context can be used to partially shield those who would otherwise subvert justice processes entirely in exchange for their cooperation in other elements of an agreement. Another similarity between the two contexts is that it would be hard to develop a justice approach that addresses each discrete contribution to climate change. Many transitional justice processes have dealt with systemic and diffuse harms in part by pursuing only selective prosecutions. Sometimes these prosecutions are accompanied by formal amnesties for all others who might have otherwise been prosecuted, but quite often the selectivity of this process results in less transparent de facto amnesties, frequently for those less severely implicated in the harm.

Both descriptive and normative questions emerge from the observation of the similarities across the climate and transitional justice contexts. Descriptively we might predict that based on these similarities, amnesties are likely to be politically attractive in the climate context, possibly irresistible. Normatively we might ask whether or not using amnesties will further the goals of addressing historical justice while also creating solidarity for forward-oriented collective action.

To some extent the descriptive question has been answered. The climate regime has already started to use amnesties, although without framing them as such, for precisely the reasons indicated earlier. This is most visible in the Paris Agreement in two ways. First, CBDR-RC was softened with the addition of "in light of national circumstances," which highlights capacity limitations rather than differential responsibility. Moreover, national contributions to mitigation efforts are entirely voluntary, with no requirement for any acknowledgment of responsibility for current or cumulative emissions. Second, several developed countries insisted on protection from legal liability for past emissions in exchange for including loss and damage as a separate article in the Agreement. Specifically, the paragraph states that "Article 8 of the Agreement does not involve or provide a basis for any liability or compensation" (UNFCCC 2015a). Although this text does not void all efforts to seek liability for damages, it does prohibit the use of developed countries' recognition of loss and damage (i.e., through their willingness to create a separate article for loss and damage in the Paris Agreement) as an implicit agreement that they caused harm or accept the validity of any compensatory claims. Essentially, both these aspects of the Paris Agreement represent a trade-off of liability for commitment to forward-oriented support. In this sense the Paris Agreement is built around a form of limited amnesty accompanied by other mechanisms, including commitments to nonrecurrence or reparations.

Due to the depth of fear about the costs of compensation or liability (particularly as the severity of climate impacts becomes more apparent) among precisely those countries that have the resources to contribute to reparations or other forms of climate action, it seems very likely that attempts to limit or absolve accountability for historical emissions will continue. These efforts will be led by developed countries but, as responsibility for accumulated emissions shifts, other state and nonstate actors are also likely to start becoming nervous about accountability. In addition, for some countries – such as Brazil or China – it is possible that fully satisfying the demands of historical justice could be more expensive than they can afford in light of their human development needs (Höhne and Blok 2005). In such circumstances it seems almost inevitable that amnesty in some form will continue to feature in the climate context.

In order to answer the normative question of whether we *ought* to use amnesty, we need to balance its political draw with the risks it poses. The first risk is that without being explicitly accompanied by sufficient reparations or reforms, amnesties can undermine solidarity and delegitimize the new regime. In the transitional context, for example, the amnesties granted during Mozambique's transitional justice process may have fueled the resurgence of violence and undermined the transition government in the long run (Igreja 2015). Amnesties granted to Argentinian elites during early reforms were eventually overturned as international accountability norms changed, in part, through purposeful efforts by human rights organizations (Engstrom and Pereira 2012).

Such lessons highlight the pattern that although amnesty may be essential in one political context, it can leave a new regime fragile in the face of evolving norms or incomplete manifestations of remorse and change. As norms change regarding how we understand climate harms, it is entirely possible that there will be less tolerance for the failure of international or domestic actors to hold those responsible to account. In addition, creating a situation in which powerful actors are seen to have caused harm with impunity is not conducive to facilitating the depth of emission reductions needed, as these reductions almost necessarily will have to come from countries that have not historically been high emitters, and may also face significant climate impacts.

The second risk is that amnesties are vulnerable to elite co-optation which can rapidly erode their legitimacy, and that of any regime built upon them. Efforts to ensure transparency and due process in the design and application of amnesties may be particularly important if they are to be seen as legitimate. De jure amnesties are typically seen as preferable to de facto ones for precisely these reasons. For example, in her assessment of the ICC's engagement with amnesties, Mallinder (2007) compares the utility of individual amnesties granted through transparent processes to blanket amnesties or those divorced from reparations. She argues that amnesties have been helpful in long-term efforts to rebuild societies only when *actions are identified, actors named, and their responsibility and eligibility for amnesty transparently decided.* The real value of amnesty from this perspective is not so much that it legitimizes forgetting, but that it provides a formal way of acknowledging harm and uses it to build trust in the new regime.

Transitional justice experiences suggest that amnesties are likely to remain a central part of the negotiation of accountability in the climate context due to their political appeal. However, there are better and worse ways of using this tool from the perspective of honoring justice claims and promoting long-term legitimacy. We suggest that both of these lessons ought to be integrated into a process of acknowledgment designed to offer an alternative pathway for productively linking reprieve from full historical responsibility with reparations and forward-oriented commitments.

The first lesson is that amnesties must be limited and purposeful. A blanket amnesty on past emissions is not a viable option if long-term legitimacy is sought for the new regime. Similarly, de facto amnesty through systematically sidelining or avoiding all claims of responsibility is also a high-risk strategy that could undermine aspirations for solidarity and collective action.

Accordingly, in the **process of acknowledgment** we are proposing states seeking amnesty should explicitly identify what they are asking to be forgiven in a public process. This could be done through NDCs or through some other iterative process tied to the global stocktake. Switzerland provides a useful example here. In its NDC it explicitly identified its historical responsibility (Switzerland 2015). This precedent could be built and expanded upon. Countries could be required to report their historical emissions and choose to propose which portion of these emissions they would like the global community to forgive or exclude from further accounts of responsibility.

As countries with few cumulative emissions would have little to ask forgiveness for, they would presumably wait to present such requests until their cumulative emissions were at a level at which they could start to feel pressure from other measures such as legal accountability mechanisms or civil society organizing. Establishing a transparent and dynamic process for openly discussing and deciding on requests for amnesty would at first be difficult, but could prove to be a long-term and dynamic institution capable of facilitating further integration of high emitters as this category evolves. This process would be more akin to the acknowledgment of harm seen in truth commissions than the admission of guilt in legal processes. The goal would be to offer a pathway for historical emissions to be formally forgiven without rendering justice claims invisible.

The second lesson is that amnesties must be accompanied by other mechanisms, as is the case with conditional amnesties. To the extent that responsibility for historical emissions is downplayed, formally forgiven, or protected through legal means, these forms of amnesty must be accompanied by substantive reparations (see Chapter 4) and commitments to nonrecurrence (see Chapter 5). When articulating their responsibility and requesting which portion of historical emissions they would like to be absolved of responsibility for in the process of acknowledgment, each country would also commit to reparations (in the form of supporting adaptation or loss and damage) and to nonrecurrence (in the form of mitigation action and ongoing support for addressing human vulnerability to climate change). The central tension here would be driven by increased pressure on historical emitters – possibly by legal means – and by awareness of the need to broaden and deepen collective action. It is to one of these forms of mechanism we now turn. What role might prosecution or litigation play in the climate context?

Prosecution and litigation

In the transitional justice context legal remedies have primarily used a suite of human rights–based resources and focused on both individuals and collectives. Legal remedy has also played a consistent role in efforts to address climate justice, but as discussed, has faced a number of limitations (see Chapter 2). However, despite differences in the types of cases pursued in the transitional justice and climate contexts, the two share several structural similarities. Specifically, the systemic nature of harms and the breadth of collective responsibility in both situations push the limits of domestic and international law conceptually and pragmatically. Moreover, even where institutions would in theory have the conceptual resources to deal with claims, attempting to address all justice claims could easily overwhelm these institutions. We suggest that transitional justice experiences with legal remedy offer both general and specific insights for efforts to pursue accountability in the climate context.

The first general insight from transitional justice is that legal resources are not fixed, but are continually being developed as understandings of harm and justice evolve. Over time, the purposeful development of norms and institutions has effectively changed how we think about human rights abuses and what legitimate governance looks like. As these norms and institutions have deepened, civil society has been able to use them to apply pressure on governments (and, in places, on corporations or other nonstate actors) even when immediate prosecution is not likely or possible.

A second insight is that legal remedy alone is inadequate and inefficient. The costs of pursuing trials and developing adequate evidence for all those involved in diffuse, collective, and large-scale harms are substantial. Moreover, although they can be symbolically important, trials alone may not help victims and, without longer-lasting reforms, are unlikely to provide sufficient deterrence to guarantee nonrecurrence.

Accordingly, the majority of transitional justice processes have focused on prosecutions for only the most grievous offenders or those for whom prosecution may send the most powerful messages. Taking this insight seriously suggests that we might wish to think about the potential for criminal prosecution aimed at powerful individuals who can be said to have held extraordinary responsibility for climate harms. It also draws attention to the need to pursue strategies for holding collective entities – such as corporations and states – to account.

In this chapter we focus explicitly on exploring relatively novel legal pathways. As described in Chapter 2, multiple efforts are already underway globally to pursue a wide range of climate litigation. Much of this is domestic, and we fully expect that such efforts will continue and are likely to be strengthened as the understanding of climate science develops (including the ability to probabilistically attribute harms to climate change). Simultaneously, as we discuss in Chapter 5, enhancement of domestic legal resources could be one of the long-term reforms countries might consider as part of their commitment to nonrecurrence. Here we reflect on the innovation of legal institutions shown in transitional justice and imagine how this could be harnessed in the climate context.

Individual prosecutions

To date the majority of efforts to use legal remedies in the climate context have not focused on legal accountability for individuals. Although specific people have been named in a number of climate lawsuits, these suits are typically lodged against the state or particular departments for failing to fulfill some obligation. This pattern stands in contrast to the transitional justice context in which the twentieth century saw the development of particular institutions capable of holding individuals accountable. We see two possible pathways for developing mechanisms capable of holding individuals accountable for contributing to climate harms: 1) individual prosecutions for extraordinary forms of responsibility and 2) using fraud and fiduciary duty obligations to hold individuals to account.

As human rights and climate change norms continue to develop, it is possible that particularly **grievous individual actions** could start to be framed as crimes against humanity. Just as in transitional justice contexts, such mechanisms would focus on unusually powerful individuals who can be shown to have purposefully taken, or failed to take, actions that resulted in significant intensification of climate harms. Such individuals would necessarily have to be in control of significant resources (financial or political) and be shown to have used their personal authority to purposefully derail climate action.

Although this premise may seem far-fetched, consider the actions of Donald Trump in the context of global climate efforts. Almost immediately after becoming president of the United States Trump unilaterally used his presidential authority – against the recommendations of many of his advisors (including his secretary of state) and against public opinion – to write executive orders that undid a number of climate policies in the United States (Trump 2017a), indicated his intent to withdraw from the Paris Agreement (Trump 2017b), and stopped all contributions to the Green Climate Fund and a variety of other international mechanisms designed to assist and cooperate with developing countries in the context of climate change. It is not impossible that these types of actions could come to be seen as a form of human rights violation.

Once framed as human rights violations, there are two possible ways that grievous individual actions could be prosecuted. First, just as international human rights norms have resulted in the domestication of human rights laws, so, too, could international framing of such actions as 'crimes' build sufficient political pressure to **create domestic legal frameworks** to address this. It is possible to imagine a future in which public pressure is sufficiently high that governments may wish to demonstrate their legitimacy and leadership in the climate context by allowing or facilitating prosecutions for individuals who have wielded unusual levels of power to impede climate action.

The second, related pathway would be to **seek standing within the ICC** in light of its recent acknowledgment of environmental crimes. Although climate change is not listed as one of these crimes, the ICC's mandate of complementarity is specifically designed to prevent impunity for crimes that may not be punished through other courts. The ability of the ICC to address such claims would depend on the development of domestic legal frameworks to accommodate these kinds of crimes. Seeking to develop this capacity of the ICC would appear to be a potentially smoother pathway than developing a distinctly new legal entity. Some have suggested the need for an International Environmental Court (IBA 2013). However, if these crimes could be accommodated within the ICC, such efforts may not be required.

A second strategy for holding individuals accountable in the climate context is **fiduciary duty and fraud mechanisms**. This strategy is already being developed, albeit indirectly, through investigations in the United States that suggest large fossil fuel companies purposefully failed to inform their shareholders of their vulnerability to climate risks (including financial risks of potential climate policy). Failing to properly inform shareholders of these risks would be a form of fraud because it would artificially inflate the value of stocks. A variety of such cases are currently in development in the United States, most notably against Exxon-Mobil (SEC 2016b), although Chevron was also instructed to accept a shareholder proposal that would require it to provide more detailed information about its investment risks linked to climate change (SEC 2016a).

Cases focused on inadequate transparency about climate change investment risks could either be framed as individual or corporate accountability strategies, as the line of culpability between corporations and their top executives in such situations is ambiguous. The potential for liability for such acts to be a deterrent could be significant, at least if attached to particular high-level individuals within the company. As one former oil executive has mentioned informally, "jail time plays havoc with your golf handicap for years, not to mention your social calendar."[2] This strategy is quite different from the human rights approach discussed earlier, but is one that is already underway and that, if successful, could significantly change how accountability for purposefully impeding climate action or misleading economic decision makers in the face of this issue is addressed.

State and corporate accountability

Increasing the legal accountability of corporations and states for human rights violations and environmental harm is an area in which the transitional justice and climate justice communities could support one another. In neither context are legal resources for collective accountability well developed, and the underlying institutional requirements could be relatively similar. We look at three possible strategies within this category: 1) continuing to use regional human rights bodies to hold states accountable for human rights obligations; 2) developing stronger international norms and legal resources for holding corporations accountable; and 3) using the International Court of Justice (ICJ).

Appealing to **regional human rights bodies** and using conventional human rights law is one strategy commonly used in transitional justice practice to hold states accountable that has already started to be used in the climate change context, although this remains in its early stages and has had limited success. The first human rights petition filed by the Inuit to the IACHR in 2005 (Watt-Cloutier 2005) has been followed by others. For instance in 2016 a group of elderly Swiss women filed a complaint with the European Commission on Human Rights arguing, among other things, that Switzerland was failing to protect their right to life, health, and physical integrity as protected by the European Convention on Human Rights (Verein KlimaSeniorinnen Schweiz 2016). In the Inuit case the petition was granted, but this has not resulted in any actions by the American government at whom it was aimed. Several other cases have made reference to international human rights law but were domestic cases, primarily being fought on legal grounds of constitutional (not human) rights (see Chapter 2).

In addition to the use of conventional human rights machinery, several innovations have been generating increased interest. The first of these has been the effort to **expand the interpretation of human rights violations**. Notably, efforts to seek justice for human rights abuses within transitional justice have expanded from civil and political rights to consider economic, social, and cultural rights (Laplante 2008b; Gready and Robins 2014) as well as rights threatened by environmental disaster and government responses to these (Bradley 2017). Here we see the potential for mutual evolution of legal understandings of what constitutes a justiciable violation of human rights with our notions of climate accountability. Broadening notions of justiciability extends beyond the UNFCCC: it much more centrally revolves around shifting ideas of human rights norms, domestic willingness to acknowledge such human rights claims, and the abilities of the international human rights machinery to generate accountability for them.

A second line of increased interest has revolved around long-standing **international treaties** that obligate states to protect citizens from human rights abuses by a third party. Recognition of the complexity of global supply chains, the difficulty of holding transnational corporations to account when legal obligations vary by jurisdiction, and the potential distance between victims and corporate decision making triggered efforts to develop some kind of international agreement on business and human rights in the early 2000s.

These concerns led to the broad adoption of the *UN Guiding Principles on Business and Human Rights* in 2011. The foundational principle of this agreement is that

> states must protect against human rights abuse within their territory and/or jurisdiction by third parties, including business enterprises. This requires taking appropriate steps to prevent, investigate, punish and redress such abuse through effective policies, legislation, regulations and adjudication.
>
> (United Nations 2011)

Despite widespread support, the Guiding Principles are voluntary, and multiple groups have argued that a stronger legal framework is needed to seek justice for human rights violations committed by corporate actors. For example, over 600 organizations have joined the Treaty Alliance, which is explicitly focused on providing a civil society voice on this issue (Treaty Alliance 2016). One option currently being debated at the UN level is the possibility of strengthening the Guiding Principles – which currently operate using only the existing human rights machinery – by creating a new, legally binding treaty. In 2013 Ecuador called for an internationally binding treaty on human rights and business, and in 2015 an official working group was established to investigate the options for such a treaty.

Several options have repeatedly surfaced as possibilities for creating such a body (EPRS 2017). For instance, one option might be to hold corporations themselves responsible under international law. A second pathway might be for states parties to such a treaty to promise to hold corporations based in their territory accountable for human rights abuses. Either of these arrangements could include some form of international reporting and monitoring mechanism. One suggestion has been that an arrangement similar to the ICC be designed specifically to work on corporate accountability. Some have suggested that an international redress mechanism is also needed both to hear victims' claims and to award damages. Finally, another option might be for states to agree formally to support each other by sharing evidence and other legal resources in cases in which transnational corporations seek to avoid accountability (for a summary of all of these options see De Schutter 2016).

Considering that some of the multinational corporations of most interest for a range of human rights violations are also the largest fossil fuel corporations,[3] working to strengthen legal resources capable of applying pressure to corporate actors is an obvious point of overlap between the transitional justice, human rights, and climate justice legal communities. It is imaginable, for instance, that countries could include commitments to either the Guiding Principles or to an emergent international treaty on business and human rights as part of their NDCs over time. Such commitments could also be integrated into efforts focused on the design of mechanisms such as the burgeoning Sustainable Development Mechanism (SDM) (see Chapter 6).

The third accountability strategy could involve the **International Court of Justice**, which explicitly addresses debates among states and may be the body to approach for managing transboundary harms. Indeed, the idea of requesting an opinion from the ICJ is not a new one. The state of Palau has long been considering requesting that the ICJ give an opinion on states' obligation not to damage others through the production of GHGs (Kysar 2013). This opinion would not necessarily mandate any repair, but it would provide an open forum for acknowledging harm and could set the scene for further interstate legal claims. Such an opinion would also provide a basis for discussing emissions as a factual matter of transboundary harm, which could then be referred to in the political process. For instance, the UNFCCC could be requested to 'take note' of this opinion without having to take on the work of determining responsibility for past harms itself. An added benefit of this strategy is that the ICJ is already in existence and so would not require substantial institutional development in the short term.

However, the complexity of the climate case could pose a significant hurdle to the effective use of the ICJ. Disentangling historical emissions and climate harms will necessarily require substantial technical and subject-specific expertise that is considerably outside the usual scope of jurists serving the ICJ. In addition, the ICJ has jurisdiction only over states. Nonstate actors, including corporations, civil society, and subnational governing institutions, have become increasingly central in climate governance. For this reason, although getting an ICJ opinion would add significant weight to the broader strategy of changing norms about acceptable climate action and responsibility for harm, this strategy should not be expected to result in immediate acts of repair or new commitments to nonrecurrence.

Overall transitional justice contexts are characterized by power imbalances, and some actors may be isolated from the harms that would otherwise drive a hurting stalemate. Developing the capacity to pursue justice through the legal system can generate pressure on powerful actors who would otherwise avoid participation in collective action. This line of logic follows directly from transitional justice experience. It is the tension created through threats to use the legal system and the desire for protection from this that would be useful when paired with amnesties as described earlier.

However, legal action should be seen as one among a suite of resources for managing the justice tensions within the climate context. Regardless of the importance of continued efforts to create and use legal resources in the climate context, there are going to be harms which continue to elude this form of accountability, and there are going to be trade-offs in terms of the resources required for this pathway. It is for precisely such reasons that truth commissions offer some potential utility in the climate context.

Truth commissions

As discussed earlier, truth commissions have become a common component of transitional justice processes (ICTJ 2008). Truth commissions can bolster a regime's legitimacy by breaking with or publicly addressing the past, create opportunities for reconciliation, develop recommendations for actions to prevent further harm, and address elements of harm not covered within judicial processes. Like other transitional justice mechanisms, truth commissions alone are unlikely to be successful, and without accompanying actions, they can alienate supporters.

As with all of the other transitional justice mechanisms, the design and implementation of truth commissions has changed over time and across contexts. This provides a breadth of possible design ideas to consider when contemplating how to use this mechanism in the climate context. We suggest that three primary design elements need to be considered when evaluating how truth commissions could be used as inspiration. These are 1) which institutional bodies should establish a commission and who the commissioners would be; 2) what data the commissions would assess and where these would come from; and 3) what kind of outcomes would be produced and how these would be delivered. These decisions are not entirely independent of one another, but we briefly discuss the possible options for each before suggesting several possible formats for a truth commission–like process in the climate context.

Institutions and commissioners

The institutional base for truth commissions has varied significantly depending on context. Although most truth commissions are established by states, they have been created by a range of actors depending on each particular context, so that they may be state run, local (municipal, provincial), international (e.g., UN or regional), or civil society run.

There are two imaginable scales for a truth commission process in the climate context. The first would be site-specific efforts following devastation from a climate-related extreme event. Although current science makes it difficult to attribute single events to climate change, attribution science is rapidly changing. This opens up a range of possibilities for expanding existing practices of post-disaster debriefing to include consideration of climate impacts and to link local effects with global processes and responsibilities. The goal of a truth commission–like process post-disaster would be to identify the role of climate change in creating harm and to assess the appropriateness and sufficiency of adaptation and harm-reduction actions. This type of commission could also feed into efforts to document on-the-ground experiences of climate harm and suggest strategies for remedy.

However, these efforts would vary significantly because of the uniqueness of each extreme event and its context. This, combined with the nascent stage of attribution science, makes it difficult to provide concrete proposals about how this type of commission ought to operate at this time. For this reason we have focused on our second potential scale for a truth commission process – a global one.

Whereas national truth commissions are established to foster solidarity or at least the ability to cooperate moving forward, an international truth commission would similarly aim to facilitate trust building in the global climate policy context. Two different institutional pathways could be pursued to do this at the global level.

One option would be for the UNFCCC itself to request a commission, or to internalize the work of such a commission within one of its subsidiary bodies like the subsidiary body for implementation (SBI). To the extent that the UNFCCC is the entity across which greater cooperation and solidarity are sought, this would somewhat mimic nationally focused truth commissions in which the goal is to enhance national functionality. However, this would add a burden to the UNFCCC and would represent a major innovation within international environmental agreements. The effort of establishing something like this within the UNFCCC would be monumental and could detract from the suite of issues already being addressed by this institution. In addition, it is likely that some parties would aggressively block this proposal out of fear that establishing such an entity within one of the environmental treaties would set an informal precedent for others. Such fears could make an already difficult political proposition even less feasible than it otherwise might be. Moreover, as has become increasingly recognized in both academic work (Chan et al. 2015; Hale 2016) and through the rapid development of the nonstate actor zone for climate action (NAZCA), states parties are not the only actors to consider (UNFCCC 2015b). Because the UNFCCC is a treaty explicitly among countries, there is limited capacity to include other actors (except informally such as through the NAZCA) in the process. For all of these reasons we suggest that the UNFCCC itself is not the best fit for establishing a truth commission.

A second option would be for a separate existing body, possibly another UN body or even a high-profile civil society organization, to establish a truth commission.[4] This independent commission would be charged with providing commentary on historical emissions and nonbinding recommendations for further action. Keeping the commission separate from the UNFCCC would free it to consider a wider range of issues and to be less constrained by the specific debates happening within the UNFCCC at any given time. In addition, it would not be constrained by the normal bounds of the UNFCCC and could possibly include nonstate actors in its deliberations of responsibilities. The primary benefit of using another UN body instead of civil society to convene this type of independent commission is that it would more likely be seen as neutral by a greater range of countries.

Appointing commissions is perhaps the most important part of creating a truth commission. We argue that whoever convened the commission, commissioners could consist of former COP presidents or other high-profile individuals with the expertise required to meaningfully engage with the diversity of data likely to emerge from a truth commission. Selecting commissioners based on their internationally recognized ability to work constructively in the climate context could contribute to the facilitative power of the commission. Already the UNFCCC regularly integrates speeches, events, and engagement by globally respected individuals (such as current or former senior UN officials, former high-profile UNFCCC secretariat employees, and other individuals internationally recognized for their contributions to global well-being) alongside negotiations, suggesting that there is a subset of people who are informally recognized as having some of these capacities. We will return to this basic idea later once we have also considered what this commission might examine and how it would present its findings.

Truth, data, and documentation

Truth commissions can involve both truth seeking and truth telling. A truth-seeking approach is investigative: in the climate context this would focus on assessing data to clarify historical responsibilities. The central focus of a truth-telling approach would be elucidating experiences of loss. It would seek to elicit testimony about what it means to experience a climate-related harm. To date, both truth seeking and truth telling have been supported by parties to the UNFCCC and civil society, although rarely in concert and never framed using either of these concepts.

Truth-seeking efforts have already been led by civil society groups such as Eco-Equity (2017). Here, emissions data are gathered and explored over time, sometimes in comparison with the actions each country has pledged to take ("Climate Action Tracker" 2015). Reflecting the documentation of harms often undertaken by nongovernmental organizations in transitional justice contexts, the goal of this work has been to track and publicize emissions trends in conjunction with the scope of the global challenge. In a more institutionalized vein, parties have consistently been required to report current – although not past – emissions data through their national communications.

Although these data have focused on emissions as the central component of responsibility, several additional efforts have widened the notion of 'truth' to include a greater variety of metrics. The Climate Access Indicators Tool (CAIT) project run by the World Resources Institute is a case in point. This database collates statistics across a range of indicators, including multiple human development metrics, current and historical emissions data, and several vulnerability indices. These data can be explored with an 'equity explorer,' which facilitates comparison across countries (WRI 2015). The underlying premise of this tool is that developing an understanding of the 'truth' of responsibility requires the integration of a breadth of data about the context of each particular country.

However, truth seeking may not end with the provision of such data. As seen in the South African experience, institutional hearings were designed to help publics think about how diverse institutions supported the apartheid system. These hearings were not only about documenting 'data' but also about opening up a broader sense of responsibility, one that included acknowledgment of the institutionalization of an unjust system and the privileges that went along with it.

Here, the passive beneficiaries of the apartheid regime could be seen to share some responsibility for apartheid's legacies, although this responsibility would be invisible through a strict legal liability frame. This notion of truth seeking would widen the conversation about responsibility in the climate context significantly and facilitate the inclusion of a much wider suite of possible actions both state and nonstate actors could take to address the complexity of responsibility for climate harms.

Simultaneously, several entities have started to support some form of truth telling, although this has not yet become as institutionalized as the truth-seeking efforts listed earlier. For example, the United Nations Educational, Scientific and Cultural Organization (UNESCO) and several other UN agencies are supporting a forum in which indigenous peoples' responses to climate change can be documented and shared (UNESCO 2017). So far, efforts to bring the experiences of suffering into the climate conversation have remained outside of formal processes, although they have often been timed to coincide with UNFCCC negotiations and other politically important moments.

One high-profile example of an attempt to bring the voices of loss into the international discussion was the decision to feature the poet Kathy Jetnil-Kijiner in the opening ceremonies of the 2014 UN Climate Summit, held to garner political support in the lead-up to the Paris Negotiations. In her poem "Dear Matafele Peinam," Jetnil-Kijiner speaks as a mother to her child, promising that she and others are fighting to save its home on the Marshall Islands. She articulates the predictions that the sunny lagoon they are walking around will "gnaw at the shoreline/chew at the roots of your breadfruit trees/gulp down rows of your seawalls/and crunch your island's shattered bones." She then places this potential loss in the context of the suffering of others who have already lived through such losses: "to the carteret islanders of papua new guinea/and to the taro islanders of the solomon islands/i take this moment/to apologize to you/we are drawing the line here" (Jetnil-Kijiner 2014). Climate loss is unfolding, it is not over, and there is loss rooted even in the acknowledgment that places at the center of human identity are being eroded.

Both the collection of stories about responses to climate change and the explicit use of poetry to frame a UN event contain elements of truth telling. The power of these stories is not only in the documentation of loss but also in the emotional and personal telling of these experiences. In this regard they echo some of the intended healing of truth telling within truth commissions. To date the elicitation of these experiences is being conducted in an entirely uncoordinated manner as communities, civil society, and academics start to realize what is at stake with climate change and grapple with notions of loss and grief from these changes (Wapner 2014).

It is entirely possible that a truth commission in the climate context could integrate both truth seeking and truth telling. A truth-seeking component could build on but extend beyond efforts to gather statistical data about climate impacts and their triggers. Importantly, questions about intention and need are central to climate justice debates, and these ought to be part of the suite of evidence brought together. Why are certain emissions being emitted? What are the possibilities for other pathways to be taken, or to have been taken? What knowledge was present for which emissions, and how ought knowledge shape our discussion of the justice of these? What are the broader processes through which these emissions were created, and what would change for these look like? Such questions are not resolvable through data provision alone but also require a space to more broadly reflect on and include accounts of the underlying cultural, economic, and political-institutional underpinnings of emission trajectories.

Simultaneously, efforts to document experiences and to support people recounting their stories of climate harms could also be accommodated in a truth commission–like process. Due to the evolving nature of climate loss, including this aspect of documentation would both serve the emotional aspects of truth telling and feed into longer-term understanding of what – exactly – climate loss entails over time.

Both the truth-telling and truth-seeking approaches could be supported by processes in the UNFCCC, even if the truth commission itself were entirely independent of it. A number of suggestions have been made to expand the range of data included in national reporting. For instance, the Africa Group has suggested that a suite of indicators (including historical emissions but also climate adaptation vulnerabilities) could be used to generate data from all countries and help shape the range of acceptable contributions of countries (Africa Group 2013). Similarly, Switzerland is unique among the developed countries in having already voluntarily included historical emissions in its NDC. Although making such reporting mandatory within the UNFCCC would likely be contentious, possibly to the point of exacerbating justice debates, an independent commission could encourage contributions of such data. Although much of these data reside in the public realm, voluntary involvement in this process could support trust-building efforts as participation from perpetrators has done in other contexts. In addition, including the type of wider 'institutional hearings' described earlier could create spaces for a greater range of actors to acknowledge the ways in which they have been passive beneficiaries of processes creating harm. Similarly, including the documentation of people's accounts of climate loss could be used to inform country-specific experiences of climate impacts. As we will discuss in more detail in Chapter 5, one institutional possibility moving forward would be to formalize loss and damage scoping studies that identify specific harms.

Outcomes and recommendations

Determining the final products of a truth commission and how they would be disseminated is a third necessary design component. Truth commissions typically release a final report on their findings, including a set of recommendations for the way forward. These recommendations often focus on the kinds of measures for accountability, reparations, and institutional reform needed to address past harms and build a platform for the new relationship being nurtured through the process.

As argued earlier, we think that an independent truth commission with truth-telling and truth-seeking elements would be the most useful adaptation of traditional truth commissions for the climate context. The final outcome of this report could contribute to the UNFCCC by being 'taken note of,' and some of the substantive findings and documentation (such as experiences of climate losses or recognition of how broader processes have fed into historical patterns of emissions and impacts) could be selectively brought into the process through country submissions. For example, a particular country could cite information or ideas being developed through the truth commission when explaining its position on a particular agenda item within the UNFCCC.

In light of the influence of nonstate actors in climate governance, it seems important that the recommendations emerging from a truth commission in this context be quite broad. The Canadian TRC, held to create a pathway for understanding and addressing the individual and cultural harms stemming from Canada's imposition of the residential school system on First Nations children, provides a potential model. The commission's recommendations extend far beyond the state. For example, they include provisions for apologies from church groups who facilitated, and in some cases ran, the schools. They include clear requests for changes in how educational institutions teach Canada's history.

What is useful about the Canadian truth commission is that in recognizing that reconciliation is a task "for all Canadians" (TRC of Canada 2015), it empowers all groups within the society to grapple with their own – sometimes amorphous – sense of responsibility. As discussed in Chapter 1, this includes statements and actions even from groups such as Canadian Sikhs who were not directly responsible for harming the school children, but who participated as an expression of their responsibility as Canadians and as a form of solidarity with First Nations communities.

Nonstate actors are undeniably essential for climate action. It has been estimated that only about ninety companies are directly implicated in 63 percent of total cumulative global historical emissions starting in the 1750s (Heede 2014). Meanwhile, as demonstrated by the Clean Development Mechanism (CDM) experience, many private entities are immediately involved in the actual work of reducing emissions (and in a few cases of supporting adaptation). Efforts like the NAZCA can be useful because they bring recognition to the diversity of actions being facilitated by nonstate actors. However, a limitation of this is that to date, such efforts have also not called these entities to account. Instead, the celebration of their voluntary action reinforces a discourse that there is no responsibility for past or current actions: climate action is a form of charity or virtue, not justice or responsibility.

If a truth commission were to help widen and deepen understandings of how responsibility could be included in the climate change action conversation, then directing concrete recommendations to particular nonstate actors would be an obvious way to do so. These recommendations could be targeted at some entities – such as states – very specifically, while issuing invitations for entities with more amorphous responsibility to reflect on how they could best express their accountability.

Proposal: a truth commission on climate change

Based on the discussions earlier, we propose that a truth commission composed of high-profile individuals in the climate context could be created, independently of the UNFCCC. This independent commission could be sponsored by a group of civil society organizations and possibly supported logistically – or at least politically – by the UN General Assembly or another UN entity. The civil society organizations need to be rooted in and led by the global South. This is a process the large organizations from the global North should support, but not lead.

After an open nomination process, commissioners would be selected by a task force created by the civil society organizations. Criteria would include long-term engagement with climate policy issues politically, through applied practice, or in some other form of expertise. This might include individuals such as former COP presidents or senior secretariat staff; former senior negotiators or climate diplomats (such as climate envoys, for those countries that have them); former senior advisors to governments or to the secretariat; NGO representatives; practitioners with long-standing experience in climate-vulnerable communities; and academics specializing in climate policy, the history of industrialization or international affairs, and other relevant fields. Obviously, regional diversity would be an essential component of the final selection of commissioners. Despite this being a civil society–run body, it would be nonsensical to ignore global power dynamics when designing an institution intended to have broad-based legitimacy. The commissioners should be chosen to enable the widest, most independent, and in-depth examination of the case possible.

As mentioned earlier, civil society organizations have already started informally to play some of the roles a truth commission might undertake, such as gathering relevant data and providing fora for victims. This commission would build on these efforts and seek to integrate the statistical data commonly included in civil society assessments with broader accounts of why and how emissions have been contributed to globally and how climate impacts are (or will) shape the lives of diverse people. The latter component might draw on studies of climate impacts, but could also feature opportunities for direct contributions from those immediately affected by climate impacts, including the impacts of climate policies. Opportunities for collecting such testimony could include mobile units that gather testimony from diverse communities or digital submission options.

This commission would be charged with identifying recommendations for all possible actors – state and nonstate. These recommendations would not be binding but would be intended to support the kinds of changes seen as necessary for enabling recognition of the past while building strong forward-oriented climate action. Products created during the commission's work – such as detailed accounts of particular experiences of loss or summaries of emission patterns – could be either noted by the COP or used in party submissions as desired.

Timing is a crucial aspect of any truth commission, and we suggest that this one would be most useful when pursued enough in advance of major moments in the international climate negotiations that any products it generates could be used to inform them. At the time of writing, a commission that concludes its work just before the 2023 stocktake would appear logical. Clearly 'climate harm' will not be over within this period, but enough knowledge of the likely future impacts combined with existing ones would provide sufficient evidence to generate recommendations capable of meaningfully informing global negotiations moving forward.

Responsibility and climate justice

In this chapter we have interrogated several ways that the climate regime could learn from efforts to build accountability into transitional justice processes. We have argued that although some form of amnesty for past emissions is likely to be politically desirable, to the point of being irresistible at least in the short term, amnesties should be developed transparently to include explicit identification of what is being forgiven and why. They should also be designed in conjunction with other mechanisms, such as reparations. Not including some limits to amnesties could simply create a culture of impunity and increase mistrust over time. For this reason we propose a process of acknowledgment that will seek to formalize and make explicit country requests to have portions of their historical emissions publicly forgiven.

Simultaneously, the chances of developing better amnesties are heightened through the ongoing development of legal institutions capable of holding actors to account. Building on our discussion in Chapter 2 of the current state of climate law, we identify several possible pathways for increasing legal accountability of individuals and collective entities such as states and corporations. Specifically, expanding human rights norms to encompass grievous individual contributions to environmental harm could be paired with domestic legislation facilitating legal accountability, or the use of the ICC in light of its recent announcement that it would consider cases based on environmental harm. Strengthening the use of fiduciary duty law would be another strategy that could be directed at either individuals or corporate actors. A second pathway for increasing the accountability for corporate actors could be built on the emerging interest for creating an international treaty focused on corporate accountability. Finally, as has already been discussed in the climate context, exploring the utility of an ICJ opinion on state responsibilities could be useful in this arena.

Overall, transitional justice experiences highlight the reality that calls for justice will not go away, and that engagement with these claims can change what is seen as morally and legally acceptable. Actively pairing legal challenges with pressure for reparations, transparent amnesties, or engagement in a truth commission process would strategically maximize the resources invested in legal actions.

Given the complex and diffuse nature of the relationship between the production of emissions and climate harms, we recognize that the vast majority of harms will likely not be justiciable, even with the development of new legal institutions. For this reason, we propose a truth commission that could help create accountability for harms that elude legal processes and connect this to reparations and long-term institutional reform. This leads us into the discussion in Chapter 4, in which we examine approaches to reparations in transitional justice and insights that might be gleaned for the climate context.

Notes

1 For descriptions of truth commissions around the world, see, United States Institute for Peace, "Publication Type: Truth Commissions," www.usip.org/publications (accessed 7 September 2017).
2 This statement was made by a former oil executive to the lead author during an informal discussion of this book.
3 For instance, Chevron has been involved in a multiyear debate with Ecuador and the United States in the face of its contamination of Amazonian lands. Similarly, Shell Petroleum and the Nigerian National Petroleum Company were charged with violating rights to life under both the constitution of Nigeria and the African Charter on People's and Human Rights (Nwokorie 2005). Exxon-Mobile was the primary target for the Kivalina village's human rights–based tort attempt (United States Court of Appeals for the Ninth Circuit 2012). Extractive-based industries are another common suite of corporate actors various groups are attempting to hold to account, and this sector, too, has a significant carbon footprint.
4 Third-party states have sometimes established truth commissions but in the climate context all countries have a political stake which would almost certainly compromise any claims toward neutrality. The inability to be (and be perceived to be) neutral makes a single state–hosted commission nonviable.

References

Africa Group. 2013. *Submission by Swaziland on behalf of the African Group Under Workstream I of the ADP*. Mbabane: Government of Swaziland. http://unfccc.int/files/documentation/submissions_from_parties/adp/application/pdf/adp_african_group_workstream_1_20131008.pdf.

Amnesty International. 2012. "Universal Jurisdiction: A Preliminary Survey of Legislation Around the World." https://www.amnesty.org/download/Documents/24000/ior530192012en.pdf.

Bosco, David. 2014. *Rough Justice: The International Criminal Court's Battle to Fix the World, One Prosecution at a Time*. Oxford: Oxford University Press.

Bradley, Megan. 2017. "More than Misfortune: Recognizing Natural Disasters as a Concern for Transitional Justice." *International Journal of Transitional Justice* 11(3): 400–20.

Chan, Sander, Harro van Asselt, Thomas Hale, Ken Abbott, Marianne Beisheim, Matthew Hoffmann, and Brendan Guy. 2015. "Reinvigorating International Climate Policy: A Comprehensive Framework for Effective Nonstate Action." *Global Policy* 6(4): 466–73.

Chapman, Audrey R., and Hugo van der Merwe, eds. 2008. *Truth and Reconciliation in South Africa: Did the TRC Deliver?* Philadelphia, PA: University of Pennsylvania Press.

Climate Action Tracker. http://climateactiontracker.org.

Daly, Erin. 2008. "Truth Skepticism: An Inquiry Into the Value of Truth in Times of Transition." *International Journal of Transitional Justice* 2(1): 23–41.

De Schutter, Oliver. 2016. "Towards a New Treaty on Business and Human Rights." *Business and Human Rights Journal* 1(1): 41–67.

Duggan, Colleen. 2010. "Editorial Note." *International Journal of Transitional Justice* 4(3): 315–28.

EcoEquity. 2017. "EcoEquity: Global Climate Justice." www.ecoequity.org.

Ellis, Mark S. 2014. *Sovereignty and Justice: Balancing the Principle of Complementarity Between International and Domestic War Crimes Tribunals.* Newcastle Upon Tyne: Cambridge Scholars Publishing.

Engstrom, Par, and Gabriel Pereira. 2012. "From Amnesty to Accountability: The Ebbs and Flows in the Search for Justice in Argentina." In *Amnesty in the Age of Human Rights Accountability: Comparative and International Perspectives,* edited by Leigh A. Payne and Francesca Lessa. Rochester: Social Science Research Network.

EPRS. 2017. "Towards a Binding International Treaty on Business and Human Rights." www.europarl.europa.eu/RegData/etudes/BRIE/2017/608636/EPRS_BRI(2017) 608636_EN.pdf.

Fletcher, Laurel E. 2015. "A Wolf in Sheep's Clothing? Transitional Justice and the Effacement of State Accountability for International Crimes." *Fordham International Law Journal* 39: 447–532.

Freeman, Mark. 2006. *Truth Commissions and Procedural Fairness.* Cambridge: Cambridge University Press.

Gready, Paul, and Simon Robins. 2014. "From Transitional to Transformative Justice: A New Agenda for Practice." *International Journal of Transitional Justice* 8(3): 339–61.

Hale, Thomas. 2016. "'All Hands on Deck': The Paris Agreement and Nonstate Climate Action." *Global Environmental Politics* 16(3): 12–22.

Hayner, Priscilla B. 2010. *Unspeakable Truths: Transitional Justice and the Challenge of Truth Commissions.* 2nd edition. New York: Routledge.

Heede, Richard. 2014. "Tracing Anthropogenic Carbon Dioxide and Methane Emissions to Fossil Fuel and Cement Producers, 1854–2010." *Climatic Change* 122(1–2): 229–41.

Höhne, Niklas, and Kornelis Blok. 2005. "Calculating Historical Contributions to Climate Change – Discussing the 'Brazilian Proposal.'" *Climatic Change* 71(1–2): 141–73.

Huyse, Luc, and Mark Salter. 2008. *Traditional Justice and Reconciliation After Violent Conflict: Learning From African Experiences.* Stockholm: International Idea.

IBA. 2013. "Presidential Task Force on Climate Change Justice and Human Rights." www.ibanet.org/PresidentialTaskForceCCJHR2014.aspx.

ICTJ. 2008. "Truth Commission II." www.ictj.org/sites/default/files/ICTJ-Global-Truth-Commissions-2008-English2.pdf.

Igreja, Victor. 2015. "Amnesty Law, Political Struggles for Legitimacy and Violence in Mozambique." *International Journal of Transitional Justice* 9(2): 239–58.

Jetnil-Kijiner, Kathy. 2014. "Dear Matafele Peinam." www.kathyjetnilkijiner.com/videos-featuring-kathy/.

Johns, Leslie. 2015. *Strengthening International Courts: The Hidden Costs of Legalization.* Ann Arbor: University of Michigan Press.

Kysar, Douglas. 2013. "Climate Change and the International Court of Justice." *Yale Law School, Public Law Research Paper No. 315.*

Laplante, Lisa J. 2008a. "Outlawing Amnesty: The Return of Criminal Justice in Transitional Justice Schemes." Rochester: Social Science Research Network.

Laplante, Lisa J. 2008b. "Transitional Justice and Peace Building: Diagnosing and Addressing the Socioeconomic Roots of Violence Through a Human Rights Framework." *International Journal of Transitional Justice* 2(3): 331–55.

Lessa, Francesca, and Leigh A. Payne, eds. 2012. *Amnesty in the Age of Human Rights Accountability: Comparative and International Perspectives.* Cambridge: Cambridge University Press.

Mallinder, Louise. 2007. "Can Amnesties and International Justice Be Reconciled?" *International Journal of Transitional Justice* 1(2): 208–30.

Mallinder, Louise. 2008. *Amnesty, Human Rights and Political Transitions: Bridging the Peace and Justice Divide.* Oxford: Hart Publishing.

Michalowski, Sabine, ed. 2013. *Corporate Accountability in the Context of Transitional Justice.* 1st edition. London: Routledge.

Mutua, Makau. 2001. "Savages, Victims, and Saviors: The Metaphor of Human Rights." *Harvard International Law Journal* 42: 201–46.

Nwokorie, C. 2005. "Gbemre v. Shell Petroleum Development Company of Nigeria Ltd. and Others." Federal Court of Nigeria. Docket Number FHG/B/CS/53/05. http://wordpress2.ei.columbia.edu/climate-change-litigation/files/non-us-case-documents/2005/20051130_FHCBCS5305_judgment-1.pdf.

Office of the Prosecutor, International Criminal Court. 2016. "Policy Paper on Case Selection and Prioritisation." www.icc-cpi.int/itemsDocuments/20160915_OTP-Policy_Case-Selection_Eng.pdf.

SEC. 2016a. "Rule 14a-8 No-Action Request to SEC from Chevron Corp. Regarding Shareholder Proposal Submitted by Hermes Equity Ownership Services and UMC Benefit Board, Inc." Securities and Exchange Commission.

SEC. 2016b. "Rule 14a-8 No-Action Request to SEC from Exxon Mobil Corp. Regarding Shareholder Proposal Submitted by As You Sow et al." Securities and Exchange Commission. http://blogs2.law.columbia.edu/climate-change-litigation/wp-content/uploads/sites/16/case-documents/2016/20160323_docket-na_letter-1.pdf.

Stahn, Carsten, and Mohamed M. El Zeidy, eds. 2011. *The International Criminal Court and Complementarity 2 Volume Set: From Theory to Practice.* Cambridge: Cambridge University Press.

Switzerland. 2015. "Switzerland's Intended Nationally Determined Contribution (INDC) and Clarifying Information." UNFCCC http://www4.unfccc.int/ndcregistry/PublishedDocuments/Switzerland%20First/15%2002%2027_INDC%20Contribution%20of%20Switzerland.pdf.

Teitel, Ruti. 2000. *Transitional Justice.* Oxford: Oxford University Press.

TRC of Canada. 2015. "Honoring the Truth, Reconciling for the Future." www.trc.ca/websites/trcinstitution/File/2015/Honouring_the_Truth_Reconciling_for_the_Future_July_23_2015.pdf.

Treaty Alliance. 2016. "Global Movement for a Binding Treaty: Movimento Global por un Tratado Vinculante." www.treatymovement.com/statement.

Trump, Donald. 2017a. "Presidential Executive Order on Promoting Energy Independence and Economic Growth." www.whitehouse.gov/the-press-office/2017/03/28/presidential-executive-order-promoting-energy-independence-and-economi-1.

Trump, Donald. 2017b. "Statement by President Trump on the Paris Climate Accord." www.whitehouse.gov/the-press-office/2017/06/01/statement-president-trump-paris-climate-accord.

UNESCO. 2017. Climate Change Frontlines. http://www.climatefrontlines.org.

UNFCCC. 2015a. "Adoption of the Paris Agreement: Decision 1/CP.21." https://unfccc. int/resource/docs/2015/cop21/eng/l09.pdf.

UNFCCC. 2015b. "Non-State Zone for Climate Action." http://climateaction.unfccc.int.

United Nations. 2011. "Guiding Principles on Business and Human Rights: Implementing the United Nations 'Protect, Respect, and Remedy' Framework." *United Nations Office of the High Commissioner on Human Rights.* www.ohchr.org/Documents/Publications/ GuidingPrinciplesBusinessHR_EN.pdf.

United States Court of Appeals for the Ninth Circuit. 2012. "Native Village of Kivalina, City of Kivalina vs Exxon Mobile." http://cdn.ca9.uscourts.gov/datastore/opinions/ 2012/09/25/09-17490.pdf.

Verein KlimaSeniorinnen Schweiz. 2016. "Request to Stop Emissions in Climate Protection: Petition Submitted to European Commission on Human Rights." http://blogs2.law. columbia.edu/climate-change-litigation/wp-content/uploads/sites/16/non-us-case-documents/2016/20161025_3585_petition-1.pdf.

Wapner, Paul. 2014. "Climate Suffering." *Global Environmental Politics* 14(2): 1–6.

Watt-Cloutier, Sheila. 2005. "Petition for the Inter American Commission on Human Rights Seeking Relief From Violations Resulting From Global Warming Caused by Acts and Omissions of the United States." www.inuitcircumpolar.com/uploads/ 3/0/5/4/30542564/finalpetitionicc.pdf.

Williams, Sarah. 2016. "Hybrid Tribunals: A Time for Reflection." *International Journal of Transitional Justice* 10(3): 538–47.

WRI. 2015. "CAIT Climate Data Explorer." http://cait.wri.org/equity.

4 Addressing climate harms
Strategies for repair

No one in the climate context disagrees that climate change will result in harm, but few topics have been as difficult to discuss in the international climate negotiations as reparations. For some, the concept of reparations, along with liability and compensation, is on the other side of a deep red line they will not cross. For others, some notion of repair is an essential part of a legitimate global agreement due to the uneven nature of harms and benefits associated with climate change. In this chapter we deal with this difficult issue head on and explore possibilities for new ways of approaching it, inspired by the broader perspective on reparations taken by transitional justice.

Reflecting on the concept of reparations, Pablo de Greiff (2008) argues that reparations are an important part of transitions because, unique among all other mechanisms, they place the harms experienced by people at the center of the conversation. In transitional justice, this conversation is not about identifying or punishing perpetrators, but about asking what needs to happen to address harm as part of a transition to a new regime or an improved relationship among actors. By focusing directly on those who are most harmed, reparations fill a gap left by other mechanisms more oriented around deterrence, punishment, or institutional reform.

This harm-centric approach to the question of reparations is orthogonal to the way it is typically discussed in the climate negotiations, particularly by representatives of developed countries, who, as Maxine Burkett (2009) describes, seem to treat it as a 'third rail' capable of killing all other components of a climate agreement. During the workshops on which this book is based, we were repeatedly told not to use "that word" (i.e., reparations) for precisely the reasons Burkett describes. However, we argue that reparation is necessary if we take a transitional justice approach to climate change. Moreover, based on a wider view of reparations, to some extent the international climate regime already has a proto-reparation system. If the global community is going to have a reparations program – which we suggest it has decided to do – then it makes sense to reflect on which, if any, lessons from previous experiences would be applicable.

In this chapter we take de Greiff's commentary to heart and explore what it would look like, within the larger geopolitical tensions of climate justice, to place those most harmed by climate impacts at the center of attention. We first reflect on the theory and practice of reparations in transitional justice contexts. What is the theory behind reparation, and what options are available? What lessons have been learned about the processes of designing and implementing reparations programs in diverse contexts? We then return to the climate context to ask how these ideas have, and could be, applied. Where do current conversations about reparations and compensation for climate impacts stand? How could we reimagine reparations using insights gleaned from other contexts?

Because of the intensity of debates about reparations, compensation, and liability in the climate context, we now lay out a few core definitions that guide this chapter and that are likely to be particularly important to those reading from the climate change perspective. First, by reparations we are referring to any and all actions explicitly designed to address the specific needs of those most affected in the climate context. Although global climate governance prioritizes country-to-country negotiations, we include here both individuals and states widely affected by climate harms. In order to focus squarely on reparations, we are putting other considerations temporarily to the side in order to obtain clarity about what types of repair would best address the identified (and evolving) needs of those most affected by climate impacts.

Second, in our approach compensation emerges as only one possible form of reparation, with its own specific pros and cons. Although related and sometimes used interchangeably in the climate context, the roots of the terms 'reparation' and 'compensation' are different. Reparation comes from the root for repairing or mending, *reparare*, and is sometimes linked to the idea of restoring something so that it can function more or less the way it did before the harm (of course, even the best mending leaves the garment different than it was). Compensation is, at its heart, about trading or comparing one thing with another. Its root, *compensare*, combines the notion of comparing with that of hanging or weighing, invoking images of people in a market trying to determine how much of one thing to trade for another. In this chapter we are primarily interested in the repair or mending elements of reparations. What would help mend the disruption in people's lives stemming from climate change? In some situations this could include compensation, but the two ideas ought not be conflated. We suggest that our approach broadens the conversation, avoids some of the most intractable political disputes, and enables a cleaner focus on efforts to address suffering.

Finally, in this chapter we separate the question of reparations from that of causal responsibility or liability. Separating reparations from moral responsibility is necessary to ensure we are looking squarely at the needs of those affected and not getting this issue caught up with inevitably highly politicized questions of blame. Debates about responsibility are essential in the climate context, but can easily overshadow our ability to think creatively about the notion of repair. The issue of legal liability is different not only because of its punitive focus on the perpetrator, but also because it assumes that the legal system has leverage over the issue. As Eric Posner and Adrian Vermeule argue, one common characteristic of reparations schemes is that they largely take place outside of court and are "precisely cases in which sovereign immunity or some other bar to recovery has cast the issue out of the courts and into legislatures" (Posner and Vermeule 2003: 692). We deal with possible approaches to responsibility, including liability, in Chapter 3. The following section outlines the theory and practice regarding reparations in transitional justice.

Reparations in the transitional justice context

The history of reparations involves both redress between states and – increasingly, with the individualization that has accompanied the rise of human rights – redress by states to affected individuals. Whereas in transitional justice the term 'reparation' refers primarily to the national level and to transitional states' obligation to provide a remedy to those who suffered past harms on their territory, this section takes a broader approach, presenting an overview of both interstate and intrastate reparations and of reparations across as well as within borders.

What unites these forms of reparation are principles of restorative justice, which hold that restoring divided societies requires acknowledging past harms and meeting the ongoing needs of those affected, while recognizing that no effort can completely repair a grievous harm. These measures are deemed necessary to promote social solidarity, increase trust in new regimes, and establish institutions and norms that can help address or prevent future harms. In expanding from the traditional focus on interstate relations to include intrastate relations, reparations in theory and practice have increasingly responded to the concerns of the people most affected by harms as the key to restorative justice (de Greiff 2008).

The restorative aims of reparations are captured by the UN *Basic Principles and Guidelines on the Right to a Remedy and Reparation for Victims of Gross Violations of International Human Rights Law and Serious Violations of International Humanitarian Law*, adopted in 2005 after fifteen years of consultation and negotiation with a range of state actors, international agencies, nongovernmental organizations, and scholars. The Basic Principles refer to five types of reparation, which overlap with each other:

- **Restitution**, for example, of freedom, property, land, employment, and identity. The aim is to restore those harmed to their original situation.
- **Compensation** for economically assessable damage. The aim is to provide monetary compensation for past harms, particularly in cases where restitution is not possible, including, for example, for physical or mental harm, lost opportunities, and costs of services such as healthcare and legal assistance.
- **Rehabilitation**, in the form of health, legal, educational, vocational, and social assistance. The aim is to repair the harm done to the extent possible.
- **Satisfaction** for past harms, for example, through truth seeking, the recovery of remains, public apology, and memorialization. The aim is to acknowledge the moral damage done to those affected and to affirm their dignity.

- **Guarantees of nonrepetition** through policies and institutional reforms. The aim is to put in place barriers to harms being committed in the future.

It is important to note that the Basic Principles go beyond civil and political rights violations to define victims broadly as individuals who suffered physical or mental harm, economic loss, or other impairments of their rights. They include those directly affected and their family members or dependents. They also acknowledge that harms can be individual or collective. The Basic Principles apply both to states' responsibility to other states and to a state's responsibility to individuals. Importantly, they also apply to nonstate actors (van Boven 2010). Although they are not applied fully in most contexts, the Basic Principles provide normative guidelines for the design and implementation of reparation efforts.

The Basic Principles elaborate on the right to reparation put forward in long-standing international human rights and humanitarian law instruments.[1] The right is further strengthened by the institutionalization of reparations by the ICC and its Victims' Fund and the responsibility for reparations – in the form of restitution, compensation, or satisfaction – provided for in the *Draft Articles on the Responsibility of States for Internationally Wrongful Acts* adopted by the UN in 2001. These developments in international law have contributed to establishing reparations as a norm, and they have been used by courts, international agencies, NGOs, and other actors as standards and precedents in efforts to uphold the right to reparations (García-Godos 2008).

Although most people think of reparations as one-off compensation payments, in fact, they take many forms. Reparations can be **material**, which includes monetary compensation, funding for or privileged access to dedicated services (healthcare, psychosocial counseling, education, legal support, vocational training, housing), and the establishment of institutions (commissions, victims' units) or physical infrastructure (clinics, schools, museums, sanitation) aimed at redressing particular harms. They can also be **symbolic**, which includes official apologies, memorials, and commemoration for those most affected, and truth-seeking and truth-telling measures. Reparations are distributed **individually** to people directly affected and their families and dependents, as well as **collectively** to those harmed as a result of being present during mass violations or affected by being members of a specific group.

Reparations may be a mix of material and symbolic measures, delivered individually and collectively, either at one time or in increments. Reparations can occur at the same time as other transitional justice mechanisms, well after political transition, or in fits and starts over time. They may also redress a narrow or broad range of abuses, and thereby a small or large number of those affected. The form reparations take is determined by political will, public awareness, and the extent of social mobilization around redress.

Interstate reparations tend to emerge from litigation or from arbitration. An example of litigation-based interstate reparations is *Cyprus v. Turkey* (2001), in which the European Court of Human Rights ordered Turkey to pay compensation to Cyprus for human rights violations its agents committed during its 1974 invasion of Cyprus. An example of interstate reparations emerging from arbitration is the reparation paid by Germany to several European states and to Israel in the decades following World War II (Buxbaum 2005). A new approach is represented in the 2013 establishment of the Caribbean Community (CARICOM) Reparations Commission, consisting of commissioners from twelve national reparations committees in regional member states and tasked with pursuing reparations for genocide, the slave trade, and chattel slavery from former colonial powers.

In addition to states seeking reparations from other states, since the 1980s victims themselves have increasingly sought reparations across state borders. As outlined in Chapter 3, one avenue for accessing these reparations is criminal cases, with international, regional, hybrid, and foreign domestic courts ordering that individual perpetrators' funds be used for victim reparations. Another avenue is civil litigation. For example, in recent years Kenyan survivors of torture and other abuses during the Mau Mau anti-colonial uprising have filed lawsuits against the British government in UK courts. In the United States, victims of human rights abuses have used that country's Alien Tort Claims Act and Torture Victims Protection Act to file class-action lawsuits against state agents abroad. For instance, Philippine victims filed a lawsuit against former president Ferdinand Marcos for abuses during his rule, which resulted in a proportion of the court's $1 billion award being paid. As the Alien Tort Claims Act also applies to nonstate actors, numerous groups have filed human rights–related lawsuits against multinational corporations in United States courts, including the South African apartheid victims' group Khulumani Support Group, with its litigation against corporations that profited from the apartheid regime (REDRESS 2006).

One case that combines interstate reparations with reparations to individual victims is the UN Compensation Commission, established in the wake of Iraq's 1990 invasion of Kuwait to determine Iraq's liability and administer a claims-based victims' fund. As part of the peace settlement after a military intervention by the United States and other powers, Iraq agreed to provide reparations for losses, injury, and damage (including environmental damage) incurred during the invasion, largely through revenues from its oil exports. Although individual claims have been prioritized, the commission has also paid compensation to states, international organizations, and corporations affected by the conflict. The Compensation Commission is an innovation because it is a large-scale international program run by the UN that addresses a range of civil-political and socioeconomic abuses, but it is also part of a trend of mass claims programs emerging in post-conflict contexts. Other examples include the Housing and Property Claims Commission in Kosovo and the Claims Resolution Tribunal for Dormant Accounts in Switzerland (Van Houtte, Das, and Delmartino 2008).

As noted earlier, however, in the transitional justice context reparations are commonly thought of as **intrastate** reparations, meaning that redress measures are instituted by the state within which harms were committed. In cases where a state is reluctant to meet its obligations to provide an effective remedy, intrastate reparations usually result from decisions by international, regional, hybrid, or domestic courts or commissions, as well as settlements during litigation. For example, regional human rights mechanisms have ordered member states to provide reparations to citizens affected by grave abuses, as have various national courts, both ordinary courts and those mandated with guaranteeing human rights.

It is important to note that court-ordered reparations – intrastate and interstate – often face enforcement issues, as decisions may be nonbinding and implementation may be influenced by global and regional power imbalances or limited by a lack of resources. The IACtHR has attempted to address this issue by monitoring and requiring compliance reports from the relevant states, providing instructions on meeting obligations, establishing trust funds to oversee compensation payments to victims, and reporting on noncompliance to the General Assembly of the Organization of American States (REDRESS 2006).

In cases where policy makers recognize the benefits of providing redress for past harms, intrastate reparations may be **stand-alone measures** instituted by domestic legislation or presidential decree. More commonly they are **administrative programs** established through government policy and legislation as part of a larger transitional justice process, usually informed by truth commission recommendations. At the national level, reparations programs signal a departure from the abusive practices of the past, highlighting the legitimacy of the new regime, its acceptance of international norms, and the trustworthiness of its reformed institutions. They also acknowledge that those who benefitted from past harms, whether directly or as passive beneficiaries, must give back to those most affected. Although reparations acknowledge responsibility, they often are not accompanied by a public admission of guilt or liability, the naming of those most responsible, or any explicit punishment. In this sense, reparations are not as politically or legally threatening as more retributive mechanisms.

Administrative reparations programs have taken various forms. Argentina, for example, offered a series of substantial one-off compensation payments for different harms in response to individual pieces of legislation. Chile offered a diverse package of reparations, including small monthly compensation payments; assistance for medical, educational, and social services; support for erecting memorials and memory sites; and business loans for those most affected. Instead of the state deciding which form all reparations should take, Peru delivered collective reparations in the form of a payment to municipalities so that those most affected could decide on how best to repair their own communities in a participatory manner. In a number of cases, reparations have been offered well after the political transition and in response to sustained advocacy, as with the South African government's tentative offer of educational support to apartheid survivors some fifteen years after disbursing small one-off compensation payments.

In addition to states undergoing political transition, reparations programs have been instituted in countries not transitioning away from dictatorship or war. The important example for the climate context is **reparations in long-standing democracies**, which generally have come from inquiries and truth commissions on historical injustices emerging from settler colonialism, slavery, and institutionalized discrimination. In the United States, the federal government made substantial payments to Japanese American citizens it interned during World War II, and the Oklahoma state government provided educational and memorialization support to victims of the Tulsa Race Riot and their descendants. The Canadian government distributed compensation payments to former students of Indian residential schools as part of a larger institutional reform package. Provincial governments in Australia have provided compensation to indigenous Australians, combined with healthcare and memorialization support packages. These efforts have generally been coupled with individual and collective official apologies.

Although often criticized for being too little, too late and a state exercise in political legitimation, reparations efforts in long-standing democracies have highlighted the continuities between historical injustices and ongoing structural inequality at the global and national levels (Winter 2014). They have also pointed to the unfolding nature of past harms. In Canada and Australia, for example, activism around reparations programs has demonstrated that settler colonialism continues to shape the lives of all citizens, and particularly of the populations most affected by the harms. In these cases broader reforms take on extra significance as an acknowledgment that both the nature of harm and its repair are continuing to evolve.

Financing for reparations programs may come from special funds established by international or regional bodies, or by states at the national level, which usually rely on voluntary domestic and international contributions and at times are funded through perpetrators' illicit gains that have been recovered. Financing may also be allocated from national budgets – an approach that is dependent primarily on political will and has to date proved the most sustainable, even in developing countries with restricted public budgets (Segovia 2008).

In terms of access to reparations, evidentiary thresholds tend to be fairly low. Although this may carry the risk of false or double claims, in the vast majority of cases it is those affected by harms who attempt to access reparations. The evidentiary threshold usually depends on the context, for example, the extent to which official records proving violations or injury exist and victims' ability to access such documents or the institutions that issue them. For example, Argentina's reparations program required corroborating testimony from two persons or proof in the form of civil society or national human rights commission documentation or media articles. Morocco's Equity and Reconciliation Commission accepted testimony as is and required no further evidence (OHCHR 2008).

In addition to demonstrating the diversity of approaches to reparations, the sampling of cases here shows that the practice of reparations is evolving and expanding, much as for other transitional justice mechanisms. It similarly shows the ongoing nature of transitions, which are not completed through one mechanism or in a short period, but rather call for long-term vision and ongoing attention as contexts change. A few significant lessons regarding reparations in transitional justice experiences should be stressed. First, reparations tend to be put on the 'back burner' while other measures, particularly prosecutions and truth commissions, are designed and implemented. This often results in reparations not being implemented when or as envisioned by transitional justice actors and those most affected by harms. As the issue of reparations never goes away and can deepen divisions in divided societies over time, transitional justice actors are increasingly pushing to integrate reparations into peace building and transitional justice plans from the beginning.

Second, effective reparations which meet their restorative justice aims require at least consultations with those most affected by harms, but preferably their full participation in the design and implementation of reparations. This not only contributes to reparations being responsive to the needs of diverse kinds of victims in diverse contexts, it also promotes the kind of oversight that prevents states and other actors from taking services they are ordinarily obligated to provide, such as development programs, and labeling them reparations.

Third, reparations are one of the transitional justice mechanisms best positioned to acknowledge abuses of economic, social, and cultural rights, along with the socioeconomic fallout from civil-political rights violations, such as loss of land and livelihoods through forced displacement. Whether implemented as a result of a settlement, criminal or civil litigation, or an administrative program, reparations call attention to both the roots and effects of past harms. Particularly when viewed holistically as in the UN's Basic Principles, they reconcile the backward- and forward-looking aspects of transitional justice (Saffon and Uprimny 2010).

Reparations in the climate context

In the international climate context the idea of reparations has been almost exclusively linked to liability and compensation. For many years a number of developed countries have made it clear that this is a red line they will not cross due to fears that compensation for climate damages could be substantial. Moreover, they have argued that providing no compensation is legitimate because of the complexities of historical emissions.

The fear of reparations expressed in global negotiations focuses on their punitive potential. Although a reparations conversation could evolve around questions of how to address the needs of people and nations most severely affected by climate harms, this has not been the international focus. From this perspective it is unsurprising that the issue has become so politicized in the international arena. A punitive frame for reparations is radically different than in transitional justice, where the focus is on strategies to repair relationships and lives concretely damaged by harms. Moreover, as indicated earlier, transitional justice practices have pulled on a variety of forms of reparation through the UN Basic Principles, including but not limited to, compensation.

In this section we focus explicitly on reparations from the perspective of those most affected by climate change. Several others have also explored climate reparations in this nonpunitive sense. Most notably Maxine Burkett (2009, 2015) has proposed a 'rough justice' nonliability-based compensation mechanism that would operate as a claims facility aimed at supporting reparations for small island developing states (SIDS). She argues that this system would be driven by countries' desires for and dedication to developing solidarity, attesting to the costs of continuing conflict in the international arena. Edward Page and Claire Hewyard (2017) have also developed a nonliability approach to compensation in which fault is entirely separate from the question of which harms warrant compensation and how to provide it.

Many of those invested in trying to find a politically workable solution in this space similarly separate blame from reparations. For instance, Jonathan Pickering and Christian Barry (2012) argue for 'bridging rhetoric' that can help move toward collective action, rather than away from it, despite arguing that there are defensible climate 'debts' to be paid to many developing countries. These debts emerge from the uneven utilization of atmospheric space, along with other resources. In contrast, Ewan Kingston (2014) comes down on the opposite side on the question of historical debt, claiming that this is not a valid argument, but also sees the political utility in separating reparations from debates about causality.

We build on the separation of responsibility and reparations and use experiences from transitional justice to reimagine how a nonpunitive reparations program aimed at addressing concrete harms and nurturing global solidarity might be built. Specifically, we see three principles that could steer these efforts. Throughout this discussion we focus on communities or subnational regions as the actors who should be receiving reparative resources. Although nations may be involved in administering these programs, the ultimate beneficiaries are those who have most concretely experienced harm.

The first is that reparations mustbe **appropriate to the specific climate harm**. We take as our starting point the idea that reparations must be appropriate to the context. The variation in reparations design across transitional justice experiences stems from this basic requirement. Reparations must respond to the actual experiences of those affected by past harms and make sense within the larger political and institutional context of the harms and the jurisdictions involved. In the climate context reparations will need to make sense both at the local level at which the harm is experienced and in the larger political context.

Importantly, *harms for which reparations are sought ought to be directly linked to climate change*. The goal of climate reparations is to repair harm from climate change. Although climate impacts will intersect with ongoing human development challenges, reparations are not aimed at development per se but at supporting individuals and communities facing climate impacts and at building greater solidarity in the face of climate change generally.

The second principle is that reparations must be **embedded in the political context**. Reparations are an extremely sensitive part of transitional justice processes, and this is particularly acute in the climate context. Reparations cannot be punitive if they are to successfully build solidarity and generate the support of a wide range of actors, including those who have been high emitters. However, they also cannot be entirely blind to the source of harms, or they will not be reparative. Any reparation effort needs to navigate the delicate line between acknowledgment and liability.

In light of this we suggest that *causal responsibility ought not to render claims ineligible*. In many cases those most affected by climate impacts have done comparably little to contribute to climate change, which makes them 'innocent victims.' Others, however, may have contributed more emissions over time, resulting in a 'guilty victim' situation. In our nonpunitive, non–guilt-based approach to reparations we do not distinguish between these two sets of claimants. Other mechanisms – including amnesty, legal accountability, and truth recovery – are designed to deal with responsibility.

Here, reparations are due only for harms resulting from climate change, not climate impacts per se. It is well acknowledged that wealthier countries are better placed to protect their citizens from harm. Because any reparations initiative will be limited in its munificence, we argue that claims ought to be evaluated in light of the degree to which impacts have resulted in harm to individuals despite efforts to protect them, or are likely to do so as a result of limited national capacities.

The third principle is that reparationsaspire to **build social trust and solidarity**. Reparations are a key part of a regime's efforts to rebuild social trust and legitimacy, and thus have a strong psychological role to play. Reparations may look like regular human development or philanthropic endeavors; however, if they are to contribute to solidarity and rebuild social trust, they need to be framed within a context of repair. This repairing function may require explicit acknowledgment of harm, transparency and nonarbitrariness of redress measures, and dependability. Even if reparations cannot fully address the entire scope of harms experienced by individuals, it is hoped that reparations can help build trust and legitimacy for the climate regime.

The challenge is to build a reparations framework around these three principles. As we discuss later, a number of reparative measures are already embedded in the global climate context, but these remain ad hoc and have not been consolidated into a coherent program. Although this is not uncommon in transitional justice contexts – for instance, Argentina's reparations were spread across multiple ministries, departments, and policies – it can impede these measures' potential to meet the concrete needs of those most harmed by climate impacts and to contribute to solidarity across countries. We build on the existing reparations measures, but also seek to integrate them with each other and within a broader approach to repair.

We propose a reparations process for climate harms, which we describe in detail next. The process contains two primary steps: requesting reparations, and contributing to and receiving reparations. The reparation request process we propose begins with expert panels within states conducting scoping studies of actual harms experienced at the local level on their territory. These studies are then submitted to a **Reparations Commission** created by and housed within the UNFCCC. This commission is responsible for determining which harms can be linked to climate change and for helping national governments develop explicit requests for repair based on these harms. Eligible requests, articulating not only the harms incurred but also the most appropriate types of remedy and recipients, are then registered in a database available to both UNFCCC parties and registered nonstate actors. Requests are based on community or regional analyses of harm. Thus, a single state might submit requests for multiple discrete acts of remedy. In addition to its role in identifying and facilitating requests for repair, the Reparations Commission would be responsible for tracking reparations dynamically and connecting progress on them to the global stocktake process. Reparations would be seen as final, but would be conditional on mitigation achievement levels. If insufficient mitigation is achieved globally, countries would be allowed to revise their requests for repair.

The second part of the process focuses on the generation of resources for reparations and the allocation of this. Broadly speaking, we use the UN Guiding Principles to expand the set of reparations, which in turn generates extended opportunities for a greater range of types of contributions. As we discuss in more detail later, we also create multiple pathways by which state and nonstate actors can make financial and nonfinancial contributions to reparations. Simultaneously, although separate from the reparations process itself, any assets recovered through legal accountability mechanisms could be funneled toward reparations.

In the following sections we provide further details about each of these steps: identifying eligible harms; linking harms to reparations; facilitating contributions to repair; and managing the reparations process within the context of climate impacts and mitigation efforts. Many of these elements could use institutions that are already part of the climate regime. A few new institutional investments would be needed, primarily the Reparations Commission. We return to these institutional questions at the end of the chapter.

Identifying eligible harms

In line with the central principle that reparations must be appropriate to the harm, accurate and timely identification of climate harms is an essential building block of a functioning reparations process. This also meets one of the main goals of reparations, which is to address the harms experienced by people on the ground. This requires first that the experience of harm be understood, and second that a link between these harms and climate change be established. We propose that community-based or subnational scoping studies would be a useful starting place for identifying harms. We further propose a process for thinking about how to link these harms to climate change and how to think about 'eligibility' for assistance in this context.

Harm is a subjective experience and may be rooted in particular processes. In transitional justice, other mechanisms, such as truth commissions, have often been used to identify harms. For example, the Canadian TRC gathered testimony from more than 6,000 victims and witnesses over six years. This process yielded reparations recommendations aimed at addressing the core harms articulated by these witnesses (TRC of Canada 2015). For the climate context, we suggest that national governments convene permanent expert panels to coordinate scoping studies at the community or subnational level. These scoping studies could build on the National Adaptation Planning (NAP) and National Adaptation Plan of Action (NAPA) processes by using participatory methods to carefully identify concrete needs.[2] Although these processes focus on adaptation, they could fairly easily be expanded to focus on harms and losses as well.

As others have argued (Ngwadla and El-Bakri 2016), support could be made available to allow all countries to conduct in-depth scoping studies for both adaptation and loss and damage needs.

Importantly, we argue that a harm-based approach to reparations should remain explicitly focused on addressing climate harms. A climate harm is different from a climate impact, as not every impact will result in harm. Those with greater resources will likely experience significantly less harm than those with fewer resources, because thus far countries with greater resources have enjoyed greater adaptive capacity and are likely to be able to better protect their citizens from harm (Yohe and Tol 2002; Brooks, Adger, and Kelly 2005). Accordingly, the scoping studies would take into account the capabilities countries have to manage harms and protect their citizens, along with any actions they have taken or are planning on taking to do so. Only developing countries would be eligible for financial and technical support to undertake the scoping studies. However, all countries would be encouraged to conduct them, particularly in light of the potential for highly vulnerable populations (such as indigenous peoples) to be overlooked otherwise.

The scoping studies would yield documentation of harm, but the crucial part – linking this harm to climate change – would be difficult. It is useful to note that evidence has also been a challenge for reparations efforts in transitional justice processes. The typical solution in that context has been to have a lower evidence threshold than in a legal case. As noted earlier, Morocco accepted victims' testimony and claims as is and required no additional proof to provide reparations. There are several ways we could go about dealing with the question of evidence in the climate context: the use of attribution science, listening to claimants, and categorizing bundles of harm. We propose that the last of these – developing shorthand categorizations of harm – would be the most immediately applicable in the climate context, although all three have potential.

The last few years have seen growing interest in using probabilities to detect the contribution of climate change to extreme events (James et al. 2014; Otto 2015). This form of evidence may become very important in terms of liability (see Chapter 3), but has disadvantages from the perspective of reparations. First, not all climate impacts mean the same thing to all people. Due to our varied capabilities, cultural frameworks, and subjective experiences, not all people experience the same scientifically defined climate impact in the same way. However, effective reparations must respond to the actual experiences of those who have lost something.

Second, attribution science remains expensive and limited. In order to use probabilistic models, very large data sets are required that cover long periods of time. Ironically those locations in which the most vulnerable and least financially able to withstand climate impacts live are the very areas for which we have the weakest data. This means that until broad investments in research and data collection are regionally reallocated, harms in data-poor locations will be underrepresented in attribution studies (James et al. 2014). The first problem is epistemological, and the second is technical, but both limit our ability to depend on attribution science to determine climate harms. However, over time this line of research could be increasingly relied on to indicate the probability that particular impacts in a region are linked to climate change. This could help establish a defensible line of evidence for reparations claims and would bolster the categorizations of harm we suggest later.

Listening deeply to claimants in each particular instance is a second possible approach to designing a comprehensive reparations framework. For instance, Page and Heyward (2017) divide harms into two categories: those in which the means to one's life goals are damaged, and those in which the ends themselves are made impossible. This resonates with Amartya Sen's notions of capability, in which the more serious harm would be a loss of capabilities (Sen 2005). An example of 'means' damage is the destruction of a school, whereas an example of 'ends' damage is loss of the ability to become educated at all. In Page and Heyward's model, ends and means are important for articulating the kind and depth of repair needed. However, the only way to fully tell them apart is "to listen to an individual's account of the importance of the object in question" (Page and Heyward 2017: 6).

In theory, we agree that listening ought to be at the heart of a climate reparations program. A pragmatic step in the right direction would be providing financial and other support for the scoping studies, as described earlier, and helping country governments assess and articulate the losses experienced by their citizens. In order to ensure that local community experiences are included in these accounts, states could be encouraged or required to demonstrate some level of community participation in the articulation of such harms (as is done in both NAPs and NAPAs).

The disadvantages of depending entirely on a 'bottom-up' listening strategy to identify the connection to climate change in each instance of harm are threefold. First, communities have differing abilities to make their case and provide adequate evidence. Although assistance could be provided to communities, securing this assistance would add more barriers to assistance for some of the most vulnerable communities. Second, some kind of uniformity and transparency would be desirable. As seen in transitional justice reparations programs such as in Chile, having some established framework to ensure comparability across reparations is important. A reparations program that appears to be arbitrary is unlikely to productively contribute to broader solidarity or unity. Third, the time delay associated with creating a sufficient institutional process to 'listen' to each claim in detail could itself be a source of harm, as it could deny help for those who need it immediately.

We propose a third pathway for linking the scoping studies with well-established categories of likely climate harm. Although not ideal, it is pragmatic. This pathway uses the evidence base we have about the kinds of harms people are experiencing or will experience from climate change (Popovski and Mundy 2012; SBI 2012; UNFCCC 2013), including work on the intersection of human rights and climate change (see Chapter 2), to create categories of harm. Building on existing discussions of climate harms, we propose a simplified typology (Table 4.1). Each category represents a stylized linkage between climate impacts and actual harms

Table 4.1 Climate harms categorized into 'bundles of harm'

Harm	Examples
Loss of territory (individual, community, national)	This has been a major discussion within the migration community as loss of territory is a profound climate impact. It could result in both internal displacement and cross-territorial migration. Sea-level rise, profound drought, or ice melt and rapid erosion would be example pathways for this type of impact.
Destruction of property (collective, individual)	Destruction of property (less profound than loss of entire territory) is expected particularly as an outcome from extreme events. This could include individual homes and capital investments (e.g., boats, farm equipment, buildings) and collective property (e.g., schools, health centers, wharfs, collective irrigation infrastructure) central to the economic or social life of communities.
Loss of means to supply basic needs (e.g., forests, fishing, fields)	Ecological destruction or lost access to resources is expected across a very wide range of contexts. This would include things like lost productivity of marine resources, water shortages, and loss of forest productivity. These could shape well-being for people whose livelihood and subsistence is immediately tied to ecological resource use, feed into internal or transnational displacement/migration if extreme, or be a drain on other resources if less extreme but persistent harms emerge.
Loss of cultural resources or ability to perpetuate cultural practices	Deep ecological harm or loss of territory could trigger the loss of cultural resources through destruction of specific places and/ or destruction of systems so that cultural practices cannot continue (e.g., loss of culturally important species, changes to migration pathways, or climatic conditions necessary for cultural celebrations).
Loss of life	Loss of life could result from climate impacts in multiple ways. Extreme events, including profound drought, could be a direct cause of loss of life, as could changes in disease distributions (such as malaria) if not accompanied by appropriate responses. There could be some indirect loss of life through secondary interactions with other forms of harm (e.g., farmer suicides after long-term drought).
Economic loss through loss of employment or other means	Some climate impacts may work indirectly on people. For instance, ecological degradation could lower employment in key sectors (agriculture, fishing), or community-wide losses could have broader economic ripple effects, resulting in lost economic capabilities for a much wider range of people.

to individuals. Effectively, fitting specific experiences into this framework facilitates a shortcut in generating site-specific evidence linking harms with climate change.

Each of these 'bundles of harm' represents a pathway by which climate impacts result in concrete forms of harm to individuals. The harms documented by the scoping studies could be juxtaposed with this framework and the best scientific region-specific knowledge about climate impacts in order to create a short-hand evidence base for ensuring that reparations specifically address climate harms (or at least as narrowly as possible in light of the multifaceted factors leading to harm). As noted earlier, in this process we are purposefully softening the evidence demands of linking climate impacts and harms compared to those utilized in a legal liability context. The end goal here is to address climate harm, not to determine causal responsibility or guilt. Much of this process could function by adapting the NAP/NAPA process, but it would require the development of a Reparations Commission. The details of this commission are discussed at the end of this chapter.

Overall eligibility for assistance would emerge from the process of identifying harms. For her proposed climate reparations facility, Burkett limits the recipients of assistance to the small island developing states (Burkett 2015). Some have challenged this approach, noting the extent of harm beyond this region (Abate 2015). We suggest that an explicitly regional focus to determine eligibility would be counterproductive for several reasons. First, it would feed disputes among countries and reduce solidarity. Second, it would fail to meet the objectives of a reparations program focused on addressing harm because by definition it would overlook many likely harms.

We recognize that resources will be limited (see later), which is why our approach provides reparations only for harms emerging from climate change, not for climate impacts per se. Because any reparations program will be limited in its munificence, we argue that claims ought to be evaluated in light of the degree to which impacts have resulted in harm to individuals despite efforts to protect them, or are likely to harm them due to limited state capacities.

Linking harms and reparations

Ideally a reparations program would be consistent in its approach to repair as part of its trust and solidarity building aims. Although the scoping studies would include community-driven suggestions for repair, the program would need a process to ensure comparability and to help communities think broadly about what forms of repair are possible and desirable. We suggest that the Reparations Commission could help systematize the reparations program by using the categorizations of harm in Table 4.1 to organize claims and develop common patterns of repair. Bottom-up suggestions for reparations could be matched with types of repair. As precedents are established for different kinds of harm, this structure would facilitate the development of international norms about climate reparations, which could reduce the burden on those seeking assistance.

As discussed earlier, reparations have often been conflated with compensation in the climate context. The UN Basic Principles provide a useful framework for articulating multiple forms of repair. We briefly discuss how these types of reparation could be integrated into the climate context and how they might interact with the typology of harms presented earlier. Multiple existing mechanisms within the UNFCCC resonate with these categories, highlighting that to some extent the international community is already engaged in providing de facto reparations.

Compensation features efforts to use financial resources to improve the well-being of those most affected by harms. In the climate context direct contributions and insurance are the most obvious forms of monetary compensation. Insurance in particular has become a focus of sustained interest as it softens the immediate costs of direct payments by making them more diffuse.[3] Based on existing practices, financial compensation generally could be applied to several forms of harm – including territorial loss, property damage, loss of means through serious degradation of land or marine-based subsistence systems, and loss of life. Many of these possibilities build directly on current practices. For instance, property damage accrued through extreme events could be managed through insurance systems, as is already done in many places and is being discussed in the loss and damage context. Similarly, forms of compensation – albeit it with mixed successes – have previously been sought for domestic environmental degradation.

Although compensation is important in transitional justice processes, some forms of harm – such as loss of life – cannot be truly compensated. In addition, there has rarely been sufficient political will to generate the monetary resources that full compensation to all victims would require. Both these conditions resonate with the climate context. However, even partial compensation can provide immediate, material benefits to those who have sustained profound loss.

Looking beyond compensation, **restitution** refers to efforts to restore individuals, as much as possible, to their original situation before the harm, which could entail a diversity of actions. For instance, monetary compensation was criticized by rural indigenous communities in Chile who argued that livestock – a form of in-kind restitution – would have been more appropriate in recognizing and addressing the specific harms they experienced (Lira 2008). Property damage in transitional justice is commonly addressed through efforts to rebuild infrastructure and can include in-kind and financial support. When a restitution approach cannot rebuild or repair a situation, it may focus on providing alternatives that replicate or improve on the original, bearing in mind that direct replication may be neither desirable nor possible.

Restitution in the climate context opens the door to in-kind support beyond financial compensation that could help address some harms. For example, territorial loss at the national or community level could be addressed through the provision of alternative lands. In 2014 the government of Kiribati purchased land in Fiji, setting a precedent for thinking about land transfer as a potential long-term mechanism for managing slow-onset impacts. At the domestic level, alternative land provision is being pursued using strategies such as land swaps or provision of alternative public lands, although the logistics of this have already proven complicated (Bronen and Chapin 2013). A form of restitution used in other contexts focuses on efforts to directly address ecological degradation and the loss of means this entails. For instance, situated within broader reconciliation efforts in New Zealand, the Whanganui River itself received reparations in the form of restitutive efforts to restore its ecological integrity (Hsiao 2012).

Rehabilitation, meanwhile, refers to initiatives to help individuals or communities recover economically and socially from climate-related trauma. This could include efforts to recover after a particular extreme event, but may also include efforts to help communities resettle after displacement due to slow-onset events. Rehabilitation has not been a major conversation in the climate context, but may be central in relation to some harms. For instance, territorial loss or loss of means due to ecological harm sufficiently severe to cause internal displacement or transnational migration are situations in which rehabilitation would be an appropriate form of reparation, and has been mentioned by some already (Biermann and Boas 2010). In transitional justice contexts this approach has included guarantees of health coverage and basic social and psychological support to enable individuals or communities to function. Similarly, rehabilitation in the forms of vocational development, mental health support, or assistance with access to resources needed for entrepreneurship could help those suffering from loss of means to the extent that livelihoods are no longer tenable. For example, facing severe drought and a recognition that these events are correlated with an increased male suicide rate (Hanigan et al. 2012), the government of Australia has provided one-on-one mental health and business counseling in drought-affected areas and implemented regulatory provisions (including taxation changes) to reduce burdens on stressed communities and farming families (Australia et al. 2014).

Satisfaction aims to address harms for which financial or material remedies would be deeply insufficient or inappropriate. Satisfaction encompasses actions such as apologies, memorialization, and truth seeking, which are often paired with more tangible reparations, such as compensation, restitution, and rehabilitation. Importantly, in order to be effective, satisfaction must be seen as proportional and genuine by those it is meant to benefit. In the climate context satisfaction would be potentially useful in dealing with several of the more profound forms of loss, such as losses of territory, culture, and life. For example, memorialization is already being explored as a response to territorial and cultural loss at the community and national levels (Pocantico Signatories 2016). Some form of apology could also be used to address aspects of territorial and cultural loss. As others have argued, apologies could be drafted in such a way as to provide satisfaction while avoiding legal liability (Hyvarinen 2014). In addition, truth-seeking mechanisms, such as in Canada and Australia, have resulted in acknowledgment of nonlegally binding and collectively diffuse responsibility for all three forms of profound loss likely to also be seen in the climate context. The climate change truth commission process discussed in Chapter 3 could effectively contribute to these aspects of satisfaction.

Finally, **nonrecurrence**, one of the most crucial forms of reparation, encompasses efforts to prevent further harms. Although this may be seen as impossible in the climate context, given the ongoing nature of climate change, the aim of nonrecurrence is to create an environment in which harms are more difficult to inflict over time. This aspiration, cemented in particular actions, is a form of repair because it signals a long-term intention to change the social, economic, or legal structures that enable harms. Efforts to guarantee nonrecurrence most frequently take the form of institutional reform, which we discuss in detail in Chapter 5.

As we have demonstrated, although compensation is an extremely important form of repair, all five forms of reparation outlined in the UN Basic Principles could be used in the climate context. Moreover, many of them are already being provided or considered to address harms from climate change. For instance, the interest in insurance for covering loss and damage fits squarely within the realm of compensation. Some elements of restitution, including restoration of damaged ecosystems, in-kind assistance, and social service support, are often included in NAPs and NAPAs, although funding has remained a difficult issue. Although rehabilitation is not yet a common aspect of adaptation or loss and damage programs, there is growing recognition that displacement and migration due to climate impacts will require such efforts (e.g., Biermann and Boas 2010). Moreover, the UNFCCC itself, with its objective of avoiding dangerous anthropogenic climate change, is already an attempt at nonrecurrence broadly.

Other forms of repair have been avoided in the climate context. Any notion of apology has been excluded, but there have been some acknowledgments of historical responsibility broadly. For example, Switzerland's NDC explicitly features recognition of its historical contributions to emissions, although it does not link this to specific acts of repair.[4] Similarly, during the workshops that gave rise to this book, multiple participants noted the usefulness of President Obama's framing remarks at COP21, where he stated "the truth that many nations have contributed little to climate change but will be the first to feel its most destructive effects. For some, particularly island nations . . . climate change is a threat to their very existence." Obama went on to discuss America's contribution to the Least Developed Country Fund (LDCF) and to climate insurance systems explicitly targeted at helping those affected by climate disasters (Obama 2015). The speech was not an apology, but the recognition it implies can be seen as a form of satisfaction, albeit a weak one.

One benefit of using the broader suite of reparations in the climate context is that it brings attention to the need to innovate across these forms of repair. For example, although some financial compensation for lost material resources may be appropriate for individuals, it might be most effectively paired with in-kind rehabilitation efforts or community restitution. We are proposing that the Reparations Commission could use this reparations framework to help countries use the scoping studies (which may include community-based requests for assistance) to identify forms of repair most appropriate for addressing their particular harms, recognizing that in many cases more than one reparative approach could be (or is already being) taken. This request for repair would then be lodged, via the state, in a central database available to parties and registered nonstate actors. This database would be similar to the NAPA project database but tailored so that a broader range of actors could access and contribute to it (see Chapter 5). Because each request would be for a particular harm or set of harms (for instance, for an entire region of a country facing permanent inundation), each country could file multiple nonoverlapping requests.

From a transitional justice perspective, it would be ideal for individuals to be able to request repair. However, facilitating individual requests would be difficult to implement in the climate context for two reasons. First, climate change could affect literally billions of people. If even a fraction of these individuals experience some form of harm, the sheer volume and diversity of requests would quickly swamp an international commission. Second, many harms may be diffuse and fully manifested at a regional level. Relying on individual requests could result in many harms not being addressed at all, and focusing on individual remedies may not be the most effective strategy in the face of regionalized impacts. Finally, the UNFCCC is a state-centric entity. Expanding the ability to request reparations to nonstate actors would already stretch this institution significantly. Attempting to incorporate individuals would, at this time, stretch it even further and could end up creating more political animosity toward reparations. However, it should be noted that in our proposal scoping studies and the resulting state requests for repair are tied to particular subnational regions and communities in order to help align reparations with the concrete harms experienced. Although state governments are responsible for submitting these requests, to be eligible they would need to demonstrate regional or local relevance.

Facilitating contributions to reparations

Transitional justice processes commonly face limited financial resources, but reparations initiatives have been implemented even within these constraints. In the climate context, concerns about the ultimate costs of repair have been central drivers of tensions in any discussion of redress. Funding for adaptation and for loss and damage has consistently been a source of consternation.

As noted earlier, we propose expanding notions of reparation in the climate context beyond compensation and separating reparations to some extent from blame or causal responsibility, which may be better addressed through other mechanisms. These conceptual shifts could provide advantages in the face of resource limitations in two ways: a broader notion of redress could facilitate the incorporation of nonfinancial contributions, and focusing on specific harms changes the frame of reference from conflicts about burden sharing to climate assistance. Both pathways could broaden the scope and sources of resources available in the climate context. Realistically these alterations to current practice will not solve the funding gap for addressing climate harms, but they may facilitate a move in the right direction.

Currently, only financial contributions to adaptation or loss and damage are recognized in the international system. Using the broader notion of reparation offers greater leeway to expand the scope of resources made available. Developing international recognition for both financial and nonfinancial contributions could facilitate integration of forms of repair currently overlooked, such as in-kind contributions toward restitution or rehabilitation. These forms of repair could conceivably be connected to a database of reparation needs. We discuss potential shifts to financial mechanisms further in Chapter 5.

In addition, until recently, only parties could contribute to the UNFCCC mechanisms most aligned with reparations, and this remains the norm. The province of Quebec was the first subnational entity to contribute money directly to the LDCF. Expanding sources to include nonstate actors (which includes subnational governments) could both boost the total quantity of resources and help build solidarity. It is notable that Quebec explicitly framed its contributions as "focuse[d] on climate solidarity" (Quebec 2015). Although the UNFCCC system is designed around countries, the role of nonstate actors is growing increasingly prominent and could be integrated in this way. Soft-linking a reparations process with a truth commission–like process could be a parallel strategy for encouraging such contributions (see Chapter 3).

Many developing countries have been, and will increasingly be, required to divert resources toward preventing harms from climate impacts. Recognition of these domestic efforts has been limited – a feature that contributed to the Africa Group's insistence that the Paris Agreement include a Global Goal for Adaptation (Ngwadla and El-Bakri 2016). Making adequate adaptation a global goal – much as there is a global mitigation goal – highlights the obligations of all parties to contribute to protecting humans from harm within and beyond country borders. We suggest that developing country governments' domestic investments in adaptation should be included in a reparations process. Recognizing these efforts as contributions to reparations would continue to direct attention to vulnerable communities and concrete harms, and would help demonstrate solidarity. In addition, recognition would reinforce the positive role many vulnerable countries are already playing in collective climate action, further reducing the image of reparations as punitive or purely responsibility based.

Without significant financial and in-kind contributions from developed countries, however, this arrangement will be unable to increase solidarity or adequately address harm. Separating reparations from admissions of 'guilt' and ensuring that they are nonpunitive does not negate the importance of actors acknowledging their contributions and privileges in relation to the creation and experience of harms from climate change. One of the interesting elements of reparations programs in transitional justice contexts is the norm that new regimes pay for reparations with funds provided by populations who did not directly cause harms but who may have been passive beneficiaries within the society. This aspect of transitional justice practice reinforces a broader understanding of responsibility and draws attention to the potential obligations for those who may not otherwise see themselves as 'causally responsible.'

Managing the reparation process

The indeterminate nature of climate impacts – and accordingly climate harms – is one of the most difficult challenges facing climate reparations. Existing atmospheric emissions concentrations are likely to continue causing climate impacts, and although recent mitigation commitments are to be lauded, it remains unclear to what extent these commitments will be realized. Simultaneously, a political barrier to reparations has been the concern that, once started, compensation demands will be never ending. Finality within a reparation process denotes the degree to which a party's acceptance of reparations is seen as closing the door to other efforts to seek repair or to use other mechanisms (de Greiff 2008).

It is not entirely clear what would be desirable from the perspective of finality in the climate context. On the one hand, finality would be highly desirable because it could generate confidence among states with high emissions that a transitional process would not become punitive through continually deepening demands. It is for this reason that Burkett (2015) argues that the principle of solidarity would suggest that countries receiving assistance may agree to consider such reparations final and not pursue further actions. On the other hand, finality is a difficult concept to apply in a context where deepening harms are almost inevitable.

We suggest a *conditional finality*, which could harness the dynamism of the relationship between climate harms and mitigation achievement. The problem with attaching finality to reparations is that climate harms typically intensify with increasing climate impacts, which in turn stem from insufficient mitigation. Because of the dynamic nature of climate change policy, states often use conditional clauses when communicating their NDCs. Parties have routinely indicated how much effort they can undertake on their own and how much additional effort they could make with assistance or in light of other countries' commitments.

With the conditional finality approach, any reparations received within a certain level of climate impact (measured either as global average temperature increase or atmospheric concentrations) could be considered final, subject to increased climate impacts. So, if in an under-2°C world a community received assistance in relocating due to a certain amount of sea-level rise, this would be considered final until (unless) average global temperature reached 2.5°C and/or there was a significant increase in the severity of the climate impact. This would facilitate trust building, as it would place limits on requests while allowing reparations to be dynamic and strengthening incentives for strong mitigation.

This entire process could be tied to the global stocktake instigated by the Paris Agreement. In addition to providing an overview of global action, these assessments are likely to generate substantial contributions from climate science regarding the state of climate impacts and harms. These discussions could be used by the Reparations Commission to provide an overview of where reparations stand and the extent to which further requests for a given region are warranted by global progress (or lack thereof).

Institutional needs for a reparative approach

The reparations approach we propose would take advantage of a range of existing institutions (Table 4.2), but also require the development of one new institution: the Reparations Commission.

In her climate reparations proposal for SIDS, Burkett (2015) suggests developing a claims facility for each country claimant. This facility would be responsible

Table 4.2 Summary of institutional needs for the proposed climate reparations process

Feature	Existing institutions	New institutional arrangement
Bottom-up scoping studies	Build on NAP/NAPA process for developing countries Encourage developed countries to conduct self-funded scoping studies	Soft link to a truth commission–like process
Identification of eligible harms and link to types of repair		Reparations Commission
Country-driven requests for repair	Adjust NAPA project database	Reparations Commission
Resource provision other than national government	Alter existing finance bodies to accept greater range of contributions from greater range of contributors	Soft link to a truth commission–like process
Resource provision by national government	Include domestic resource provision in NDCs and national communications	Soft link to a truth commission–like process
Tracking and dynamic revision of reparations	Link to global stocktake	Reparations Commission Soft link to broader accountability mechanisms

for gathering and hearing evidence in order to determine damages, allocate payments, and evaluate implementation. As discussed earlier, the reparations process we propose is somewhat broader than Burkett's because it is not limited to the small islands, but it also requires the development of a similar body. The Reparations Commission would need to be composed of highly qualified individuals capable of handling claims about climate harms, assessing the relevant evidence, and providing general cohesion and oversight to the entire process. Unlike in Burkett's proposal, the commission could not be specific to each country but would need to be an internationally based board of experts, appointed with consideration for regional diversity and coverage.

The commissioners' role would require a slightly lighter touch than Burkett's proposal allows for, as well. Their primary role would be to help states turn scoping studies into intelligible requests for remedy across a diversity of harms and forms of reparation and to oversee to the reparations negotiation process. This would include helping to assess evidence about intensifying climate impacts and determining the eligibility of particular harms for reparations based on shifts in the extent of climatic changes.

Other than this new Reparations Commission, our proposal substantially uses existing institutions. We suggest the following: 1) building on and/or slightly adjusting the NAP/NAPA process, including both the scoping studies and the database of projects; 2) altering how resources for repair are dealt with; 3) adding recognition of domestic contributions to avoiding or addressing harm to NDCs; and 4) adding an evaluation of reparations in light of climate science to the global stocktake.

Although these specific suggestions about how reparations could be approached in the climate context may be useful, perhaps just as important moving forward is recognition of the broader set of concepts that taking a transitional justice lens to this challenge provides. The first is simply the recognition that the global climate community is, albeit informally, already embarking on a path of reparation, which highlights the relevance of seeking insights from other fields like transitional justice to guide this work more explicitly. In addition, moving beyond compensation as the only approach to repair opens the door for a much wider range of efforts to address harm, and could be central in facilitating participation in reparations from a greater range of state and nonstate actors. Finally, perhaps the single most important lesson transitional justice has to offer about reparations is the absolute, non-negotiable insistence that acts of repair must resonate with and directly benefit those who have been most harmed. Reparations that remain divorced from the on-the-ground realities of climate harms are unlikely to be productive. Finally, as our proposal for the Reparations Commission suggests, new approaches to addressing climate change are likely to require institutional reforms, which is the focus of our next chapter.

Notes

1 These include the Universal Declaration of Human Rights, the International Convention on the Elimination of All Forms of Racial Discrimination, the Convention against Torture and other Cruel, Inhuman or Degrading Treatment or Punishment, the Convention on the Rights of the Child, and the Hague Convention respecting the Laws and Customs of War on Land and the Protocol Additional to the Geneva Conventions relating to the Protection of Victims of International Armed Conflicts.
2 The NAP process is designed to help identify and prepare for mid- and long-term climate impact adaptations, and the NAPA process is targeted at addressing the most acute short-term impacts in least developed countries only.
3 Designing a functional insurance program for these harms is beyond the scope of this discussion. A large literature on insurance for climate change is emerging. See for instance (Mills 2005; Patt et al. 2009; Thomas and Leichenko 2011; Kousky and Cooke 2015), to name a few.
4 It would be interesting to explore the internal decisions that resulted in Switzerland's acknowledgment of historical responsibility. Switzerland is part of the Environmental Integrity negotiating group, which includes Mexico and the Republic of Korea. It is possible that these relationships gave rise to Switzerland's self-acknowledgment in this context, but this remains conjecture without empirical investigation.

References

Abate, Randall S. 2015. "Comment on Maxine Burkett's Rehabilitation: A Proposal for a Climate Compensation Mechanism for Small Island States Symposium: Environment and Human Rights." *Santa Clara Journal of International Law* 13: 125–32.

Australia, New South Wales, Victoria, Queensland, Western Australia, South Australia, Tasmania, Australian Capital Territory, and Northern Territory of Australia. 2014. "Intergovernmental Agreement on National Drought Program Reform." www.agriculture. gov.au/SiteCollectionDocuments/agriculture-food/drought/drought-program-reform/ iga.pdf.

Biermann, Frank, and Ingrid Boas. 2010. "Preparing for a Warmer World: Towards a Global Governance System to Protect Climate Refugees." *Global Environmental Politics* 10(1): 60–88.

Bronen, Robin, and F. Stuart Chapin. 2013. "Adaptive Governance and Institutional Strategies for Climate-Induced Community Relocations in Alaska." *Proceedings of the National Academy of Sciences* 110(23): 9320–25.

Brooks, Nick, W. Neil Adger, and P. Mick Kelly. 2005. "The Determinants of Vulnerability and Adaptive Capacity at the National Level and the Implications for Adaptation." *Global Environmental Change Part A* 15(2): 151–63.

Burkett, Maxine. 2009. "Climate Reparations." *SSRN Scholarly Paper ID 1539726.* Rochester: Social Science Research Network.

Burkett, Maxine. 2015. "Rehabilitation: A Proposal for a Climate Compensation Mechanism for Small Island States." *Santa Clara Journal of International Law* 13: 81.

Buxbaum, Richard M. 2005. "A Legal History of International Reparations." *Berkeley Journal of International Law* 23(2): 314–46.

De Greiff, Pablo, ed. 2008. *The Handbook of Reparations.* 1st edition. Oxford: Oxford University Press.

García-Godos, Jemima. 2008. "Victim Reparations in Transitional Justice: What Is at Stake and Why." *Nordisk Tidsskrift for Menneskerettigheter* 26: 111.

Hanigan, Ivan C., Colin D. Butler, Philip N. Kokic, and Michael F. Hutchinson. 2012. "Suicide and Drought in New South Wales, Australia, 1970–2007." *Proceedings of the National Academy of Sciences* 109(35): 13950–55.

Hsiao, Elaine. 2012. "Whanganui River Agreement: Indigenous Rights and Rights of Nature." *Environmental Policy & Law* 42(6): 371–75.

Hyvarinen, Joy. 2014. "Respect and Protects Human Rights: Lessons from Transitional Justice." *Mary Robinson Foundation for Climate Justice.* www.mrfcj.org/wp-content/ uploads/2015/09/JoyHyvarinen_Respectandprotecthumanrights_lessonsfromtransitional justice.pdf.

James, Rachel, Friederike Otto, Hannah Parker, Emily Boyd, Rosalind Cornforth, Daniel Mitchell, and Myles Allen. 2014. "Characterizing Loss and Damage From Climate Change." *Nature Climate Change* 4(11): 938–39.

Kingston, Ewan. 2014. "Climate Justice and Temporally Remote Emissions." *Social Theory and Practice* 40(2): 281–303.

Kousky, Carolyn, and Roger Cooke. 2015. "Climate Change and Risk Management: Challenges for Insurance, Adaptation, and Loss Estimation: Working Paper DP 09-03-REV." *Resources for the Future.* http://www.rff.org/research/publications/climate-change-and-risk-management-challenges-insurance-adaptation-and-loss.

Lira, Elizabeth. 2008. "The Reparations Policy for Human Rights Violations in Chile." In *The Handbook of Reparations,* edited by Pablo De Greiff, 55–101. Oxford: Oxford University Press.

Mills, Evan. 2005. "Insurance in a Climate of Change." *Science* 309(5737): 1040–44.

Ngwadla, Xolisa, and Samah El-Bakri. 2016. "The Global Goal for Adaptation under the Paris Agreement: Putting Ideas into Action." *CDKN.* https://cdkn.org/wp-content/ uploads/2016/11/Global-adaptation-goals-paper.pdf.

Obama, Barack. 2015. "Remarks by President Obama at the First Session of COP 21." *The White House Office of the Press Secretary*. https://obamawhitehouse.archives.gov/the-press-office/2015/11/30/remarks-president-obama-first-session-cop21.

Office of the United Nations High Commissioner for Human Rights. 2008. "Rule of Law Tools for Post-Conflict States: Reparations Programmes." http://www.ohchr.org/Documents/Publications/ReparationsProgrammes.pdf.

Otto, Friederike E. L. 2015. "Climate Change: Attribution of Extreme Weather." *Nature Geoscience* 8(8).

Page, Edward A., and Clare Heyward. 2017. "Compensating for Climate Change Loss and Damage." *Political Studies* 65(2): 356–72.

Patt, Anthony, Nicole Peterson, Michael Carter, Maria Velez, Ulrich Hess, and Pablo Suarez. 2009. "Making Index Insurance Attractive to Farmers." *Mitigation and Adaptation Strategies for Global Change* 14(8): 737–53.

Pickering, Jonathan, and Christian Barry. 2012. "On the Concept of Climate Debt: Its Moral and Political Value." *Critical Review of International Social and Political Philosophy* 15(5): 667–85.

Pocantico Signatories. 2016. "Pocantico Call to Action on Climate Impacts and Cultural Heritage." www.ucsusa.org/sites/default/files/attach/2016/04/Pocantico-Call-to-Action-on-Climate-Impacts-Cultural-Heritage-4-11–2016.pdf.

Popovski, Vesselin, and Kieran G. Mundy. 2012. "Defining Climate-Change Victims." *Sustainability Science* 7(1): 5–16.

Posner, Eric A., and Adrian Vermeule. 2003. "Reparations for Slavery and Other Historical Injustices." *Columbia Law Review* 103(3): 689–748.

Quebec. 2015. "Press Release: $25.5 M in Funding for International Climate Cooperation." http://premier.gouv.qc.ca/actualites/communiques/details-en.asp?idCommunique=2838.

REDRESS. 2006. "Enforcement of Awards for Victims of Torture and Other International Crimes." London: REDRESS.

Saffon, Maria Paula, and Rodrigo Uprimny. 2010. "Distributive Justice and the Restitution of Dispossessed Land in Colombia." In *Distributive Justice in Transitions*, edited by Morten Bergsmo, César Rodriguez-Garavito, Pablo Kalmanovitz, and Maria Paula Saffon, 379–420. Oslo: Torkel Opsahl Academic EPublisher.

SBI. 2012. "Approaches to Address Loss and Damage Associated With Climate Change Impacts in Developing Countries that Are Particularly Vulnerable to the Adverse Effects of Climate Change to Enhance Adaptive Capacity FCCC/SBI/2012/INF.14." *Subsidiary Body for Implementation, United Nations Framework Convention on Climate Change*.

Segovia, Alex. 2008. "Financing Reparations Programs: Reflections From International Experience." In *The Reparations Handbook*, edited by Pablo de Greiff, 650–75. Oxford: Oxford University Press.

Sen, Amartya. 2005. "Human Rights and Capabilities." *Journal of Human Development* 6(2): 151–66.

Thomas, Adelle, and Robin Leichenko. 2011. "Adaptation Through Insurance: Lessons From the NFIP." *International Journal of Climate Change Strategies and Management* 3(3): 250–63.

TRC of Canada. 2015. "Honoring the Truth, Reconciling for the Future." *Truth and Reconciliation Commission of Canada*. www.trc.ca/websites/trcinstitution/File/2015/Honouring_the_Truth_Reconciling_for_the_Future_July_23_2015.pdf.

UNFCCC. 2013. "Technical Paper: Non-Economic Losses in the Context of the Work Programme on Loss and Damage." http://unfccc.int/resource/docs/2013/tp/02.pdf.

Van Boven, Theo. 2010. "The United Nations Basic Principles and Guidelines on the Right to a Remedy and Reparation for Victims of Gross Violations of International Human Rights Law and Serious Violations of International Humanitarian Law." *United Nations Audiovisual Library of International Law*. http://vengeancemedia.net/wp-content/uploads/2017/02/ga_60-147_e.pdf.

Van Houtte, Hans, Hans Das, and Bart Delmartino. 2008. "The United Nations Compensation Commission." In *The Handbook of Reparations*, edited by Pablo de Greiff. Oxford: Oxford University Press.

Winter, Stephen. 2014. *Transitional Justice in Established Democracies: A Political Theory*. Basingstoke: Palgrave Macmillan.

Yohe, Gary, and Richard Tol. 2002. "Indicators for Social and Economic Coping Capacity – Moving Toward a Working Definition of Adaptive Capacity." *Global Environmental Change* 12(1): 25–40.

5 Institutional reform for future-oriented climate action

Efforts to restructure the future conditions of society, a key part of transitional justice processes, resonate strongly with the climate context. Although past harms can be recognized in multiple ways, as we discussed in the previous chapters, durable arrangements need a believable vision of an improved future. At the very least, there must be clearly intelligible efforts to avoid any recurrence of the situation that resulted in past harms if a transitional justice process is to have any chance of creating the kind of solidarity to which it aspires. Institutional reform is a pillar of transitional justice processes, explicitly intended to result in long-term changes that will move toward nonrecurrence.

In this chapter we look at the scope of institutional changes common in the transitional justice context and juxtapose it with the international climate context. Institutional design is a timely and important consideration, particularly in light of the Paris Agreement. Although the Agreement set in place a number of broad structures and goals, many of the details about how these will run, including what specific institutional arrangements or processes are needed, remain open for debate. We use transitional justice experiences here to generate ideas for what kinds of institutional reform could support efforts toward nonrecurrence in the post-Paris international climate context. Broadly speaking, we discuss three pathways by which institutional reforms could be used to support the Agreement's objectives: changes to core legal institutions, changes to service systems or implementing institutions, and indirect changes to affiliated institutions.

Institutional reform in transitional justice

As central measures in transitional justice, reforms of existing institutions and the establishment of new institutions – official bodies, laws, and customs – are intended to have a number of effects. First, they are meant to prevent the recurrence of past harms. Although 'guarantees of nonrecurrence' is the phrase used, it is important to understand this as aspirational or normative. Harms may continue, but reformed institutions contribute to an environment where abuses are less accepted, more difficult to commit, and carry real consequences if committed. As such, nonrecurrence is a long-term and incremental goal. Second, institutional reforms are intended to promote accountability for past harms by building institutions that can establish responsibility as well as repair harms. Third, these reforms are linked to democratization, creating transparent, accountable governance structures and other institutions that ensure the rule of law, align with international norms, build civic trust, and help entrench a human rights culture (Super 2015; OHCHR 2008). This section will primarily use the South African process as an example, as it is lauded as a 'model' of transitional justice.

In transitional justice institutional reform typically refers to changes at the national level. Usually, it entails the **establishment of new institutions**. This may include legal frameworks that signal a break with past abuses and promote nonrecurrence, such as a new constitution, a bill of rights, and legislation that domesticates international law. It may also include new public bodies that ensure accountability in governance, such as a national human rights commission and an ombuds office. For example, in addition to having a TRC and establishing a TRC Unit to continue the commission's work after its closing, South Africa adopted a progressive constitution that promotes both civil-political and socio-economic rights. The constitution also established a number of independent institutions mandated to protect constitutional democracy, including the South African Human Rights Commission and the Public Protector (De Vos, Freedman, and Brand 2015).

Institutional change also usually involves **reform of existing institutions**, particularly those implicated in past abuses, such as the security sector (police and military) and the judiciary. These reforms consist of internal restructuring and human rights and democracy training for officials. In South Africa, the state instituted a program to disarm, demobilize, and reintegrate apartheid-era combatants into civilian life or into a reformed and more representative professional defense force, while also overhauling the police, as indicated by its name change from South African Police Force to South African Police Service (Van der Merwe and Lamb 2009). In many cases, other state services, such as education, housing, and healthcare, are also reformed in order to be more accountable and transparent to the public, to redress past harms and inequities, and to raise awareness of a new social order. This takes the form of internal restructuring, staff (re)training, and new public programs. For example, post-apartheid South Africa integrated its multiple and unequal race-based educational systems into one system with a human rights–based curriculum (Jansen and Taylor 2003).

In some cases, institutional reform includes **vetting** – also called 'lustration' or 'administrative justice' – through which individuals accused of complicity in past harms, either through their own actions or as members of a complicit group, are pressured to resign, purged from public sector positions, and/or barred from such positions in the future. In some cases they are required to disclose the details of their participation in abuses in order to remain in office or to avoid prosecution. Although this was common practice in the transitions from communism to democracy in Eastern Europe, many countries, including South Africa, do not practice vetting, at least in the first several years after transition, because of a need for the specialized skills in the old civil service or as part of peace agreements in contexts where the previous regime still holds sway (Mayer-Rieckh and Greiff 2008).

Changes at the national level characterize institutional reform in transitional justice; however, it is important to note that **international and regional institutions** relevant to the field similarly change over time, and new ones emerge, in response to advocacy and policy developments. As argued in Chapter 1, one of the roots of transitional justice is international norms that emerged in the early twentieth century, which were given expression in international treaties and other institutions. Taking human rights norms as an example, the International Covenant on Civil and Political Rights (1966) later gave rise to a number of new international treaties regarding specific rights or affected groups, such as the Convention Against Torture (1984) and the International Convention for the Protection of All Persons from Enforced Disappearance (2006). It also led to new international bodies, such as the International Criminal Court, as well as reforms to existing bodies, as in the case of the UN Commission on Human Rights being replaced by the stronger and more effective Human Rights Council. Similar developments have occurred at the regional level, for example, in the Americas with the American Convention on Human Rights (1969) and the subsequent adoption of regional treaties such as the Inter-American Convention to Prevent and Punish Torture (1987) and the establishment of official bodies like the IACHR and IACtHR. In addition, various international and regional institutions that do not have a mandate to protect human rights – ranging from UN agencies to regional economic communities – have contributed to the elaboration of global human rights norms.

These examples of human rights institutions evolving over time suggest that the UNFCCC and other institutions addressing climate change will experience similar changes. Transitional justice thus may offer lessons for the climate context in two ways here: by its approach to reform at the national level opening new avenues of thinking about climate-related institutional change, and by example in the elaboration of norms through international and regional institutions. Creative thinking has allowed transitional justice actors to pursue their goals using various institutions in various combinations over time, both by advocating for institutional reform and by mobilizing existing institutions at the national, regional, and international levels, including those that are not obviously relevant to addressing past harms (Brankovic and Van der Merwe 2018).

Two caveats, however. First, institutions, much like transitional justice mechanisms, are tools that can be used to pursue disparate goals – they are politicized. As policy makers know well, establishing or reforming an institution does not mean that it will in itself pursue or achieve one's intended goals. For example, although transitional justice is lauded for its role in democratization and facilitating good governance, it is also critiqued for linking political liberalization to economic liberalization and helping create conditions that deepen conflict-exacerbating inequalities in transitional contexts (Kagoro 2012). Second, rapid institutional reform is a primary focus in transitional justice contexts, but it often leads to institutions that hold little relevance for local populations or those they are meant to assist, or that look good on paper but in reality are either not thoroughly implemented or are ineffective (Gready and Robins 2014). Transitional justice experiences indicate that institution building and reform are important – not just at the national level but also at the regional and international levels – but that they are also just one, even small, part of a larger constellation of measures needed to ensure responsibility and repair for harms.

Nonrecurrence and institutional reform in the climate context

Institutional reform in transitional justice focuses on the need to build a credible and desirable future for all those involved. At a minimum, these reforms need to chart a believable pathway toward nonrecurrence. This raises interesting questions. What would nonrecurrence look like in the climate context, and which institutional reforms would be most effective at moving us toward this goal?

In this section we first define how we interpret nonrecurrence in this context. Then, using the diversity of types of institutional reform in transitional justice processes, we identify three sets of reforms we could consider in efforts to achieve nonrecurrence: 1) changes to core legal institutions; 2) changes to service systems or implementing institutions; and 3) indirect changes to affiliated institutions. We briefly lay out some ideas about what a transitional justice approach might add to these discussions in the climate context.

As discussed earlier, nonrecurrence is the central goal for institutional reforms, but this is a highly problematic concept in the climate context. Climate impacts are necessarily intensifying, in part due to emissions already in the atmosphere. Climate harms have not yet stopped, so to some extent nonrecurrence is a premature consideration. To make the situation even more conceptually ambiguous, the actual harms people experience from climate change are never linked only to climate impacts, but emerge from the intersection of a multitude of factors and processes already in play. In light of these complexities we focus our discussion of nonrecurrence on two sets of justice claims that continually appear in this context.

The first set of justice claims features the potential for climate impacts to be distributed unevenly and with increasing intensity. Arguments about the importance of limiting temperature to 1.5°C above preindustrial levels are an illustration of this line of argument. Pursuing nonrecurrence in this context would involve supporting efforts designed to ensure that as few people as possible should face 'dangerous climate change.' Relevant efforts toward this objective could include increased mitigation, investing in adaptation, and addressing loss and damage where the other two forms of action are inadequate.

However, adequate global emission reductions will now necessarily have to include efforts from developing countries (see Chapter 1). A second set of justice concerns central to the climate negotiations from the very beginning revolves around the extent to which mitigation obligations in developing countries could force them to prioritize climate policy effort over investments in human development needs. Moreover, inadequate mitigation efforts will result in developing countries having to use their own funds to deal with climate impacts.

Underneath both of these concerns is a broader claim about structural injustice: climate change or not, there is a global obligation to address the radical inequality that exists across human development achievements. Because climate policy intersects with this inequality at multiple points, this generates a special obligation for any policy design and implementation process not to deepen human needs or add more pressures to those who are already most vulnerable.

Accordingly we propose that nonrecurrence ought to focus on the core injustice in the climate context: those who are most seriously affected are not those who have most benefitted from the creation of the problem, and the depth of these impacts are, for some, existential. In our definition nonrecurrence is a dynamic, aspirational goal that would include all efforts to manage climate change in ways that systematically promote human development achievements preferentially for those who are least well off. We identify options for moving toward nonrecurrence within three categories of institutional reform, including those within 1) core legal frameworks, 2) implementing bodies, and 3) affiliated institutions.

Changes to legal frameworks: the Paris Agreement

Many transitional justice processes include changes to foundational legal institutions such as a country's constitution or bill of rights. These shifts are intended to capture the new social contract negotiated through the transitional justice process and provide a basis for ongoing efforts to make these intentions manifest through society.

We argue that far from being irrelevant to the climate context, such developments have already happened. Although the Paris Agreement is an international treaty and so is a fundamentally different kind of legal institution than a constitution, in many ways the Paris Agreement can be seen to be playing a similar role as a constitution might in a conventional transitional justice process. For instance, the Paris Agreement attempts to formalize a new (or revised) social contract among parties and articulates specific obligations and expectations of all those within its mandate. Both of these elements echo the purpose of including constitutional changes in transitional justice processes. Moreover, as in many transitional justice contexts, these changes emerged through extensive dialogue, and the resulting document is widely seen as imperfect but the best that could be done in the circumstances by those involved in its design and negotiation (Rajamani 2016; Dimitrov 2016). In this respect the political process strongly resembles the 'hurting stalemates' associated with many transitions (Zartman 2001).

In addition, as with changes to constitutions or other foundational legal institutions in transitional justice contexts, the Paris Agreement lays out an aspirational vision of a future that speaks directly to the specific demands of nonrecurrence it faces. It contains both elements of nonrecurrence identified earlier: it tries to establish a pathway for increasing climate action (mitigation and adaptation) and includes recognition of the importance of promoting human well-being.

Importantly, like reforms to core institutions in any transitional justice context, the Paris Agreement may have been an initial formalized signal of intent, but it can be interpreted and used in multiple ways. It could be the basis for the resolution of deep justice conflicts and significant progress toward an adequate response to climate change, or it could be eroded to the point that it not only does not provide a framework, but also adds to justice tensions. Reflecting on the Agreement from the perspective of a negotiator, Radoslav Dimitrov captures the dual-edged nature of this diplomatic feat. On the one hand the Agreement is a dizzying political success because it represents a compromise position across difference, as he notes, "Remarkably, all major protagonists endorsed the deal, and countries with diametrically opposed interests supported it." On the other hand, the depth of compromise, power politics and compromise necessarily resulted in a document with "considerable weaknesses . . . And it is still too early to assess its effectiveness" (Dimitrov 2016: 2).

From this perspective one of the big institutional signals we would expect in a transitional justice process has already been given: a shift in the core legal institution of the social space. The Paris Agreement attempts to formalize basic obligations of different parties and establish a suite of mechanisms for making the vision of a global social contract of cooperation and solidarity materially apparent over time. For this reason we treat the Paris Agreement itself as a newly formalized social contract which provides a baseline for how to proceed. However, as transitional justice experience has amply illustrated, big-picture reforms to core legal institutions are only the beginning. Meeting the aspirational goals of the Paris Agreement will most certainly require engagement with a plethora of more specific mechanisms, clauses, and rounds of interpretation. Transitional justice experience is littered with empty institutional reforms.

Changes to implementing institutions

A second major category of reform in transitional justice processes has featured changes to the institutions people engage with directly that manifest the promises of the new social contract. This might include reforms to military or police in contexts where these sectors contributed to violence or oppression. It might also include changes to education, housing programs, or other social services if systemic discrimination in service provision fed into the conditions that facilitated human rights abuses (or constituted human rights abuses by the state in themselves).

Thinking about what reforms would be required to bring life to the aspirations of the new social contract regarding climate change is timely due to the focus on climate action implementation post-Paris. Because many of the subsections of the Paris Agreement have been discussed in depth elsewhere, here we focus only on a few elements for which ideas from transitional justice may be most relevant or offer new perspectives. Specifically we consider, in brief, financial mechanisms, institutions for due process and redress associated with market mechanisms, and mechanisms for adaptation and loss and damage. Our goal is simply to illustrate new ideas that emerge from using experiences from transitional justice, as a book could be written on each one of these mechanisms and its role in facilitating adequate global climate action.

Financial mechanisms

Finance has been one of the central discussions in the international climate context for many years and has resulted in a substantial literature (e.g. Ciplet, Roberts, and Khan 2013; Grasso 2010b; Buchner et al. 2014; Haites 2013). Taking a transitional justice approach to the challenge of developing financial mechanisms capable of meeting the aspirations of nonrecurrence formalized in the Paris Agreement draws attention to three core aspects of the finance conversation: adequacy and accessibility, transparency, and recognition and attitude. We discuss each briefly and end with a proposal about how finance could be approached that would integrate these concepts.

Adequate and accessible finance appear as essential requirements in order to achieve the ultimate goals of nonrecurrence and solidarity. Adequate funding is necessity for facilitating emissions reductions in developing countries without imposing additional burdens on them. Similarly, failing to ensure adequate support for adaptation and loss and damage would simply erode any basis for long-term trust. In both cases financing must be easily accessible to those who need it. A key message from transitional justice is that failures in accessibility can also erode the perceived legitimacy of the regime. To date, accessing funding has been an ongoing struggle for developing countries.

Although the bulk of attention in the climate space has been on adequacy, ongoing problems with a number of mechanisms – including the distribution of CDM projects – have highlighted the importance of taking accessibility seriously. Not only did the CDM tend to privilege relatively large developing country emitters, it preferentially funded mitigation and largely overlooked adaptation despite its importance to vulnerable communities. Other funds, such as the LDCF, have at times had excess funds available due to the complexities of funding rules and requirements for cofinancing from other sources (Ciplet, Roberts, and Khan 2013). Combined with accessibility difficulties, the LCDF's dependence on voluntary contributions has made it unpredictable (Tenzig et al. 2016) and less able to respond to country needs than it otherwise should be (GEF IEO 2016).[1]

In order for international funds to reach the people who need them, significant effort must be invested in creating and maintaining social and bureaucratic infrastructure. Accessibility is particularly essential for resources intended to be a form of reparations: difficulty accessing resources intended to benefit those harmed can function as an additional harm and insult (de Greiff 2007).

Transitional justice adds little new insight here but strongly highlights the need for adequate and accessible funding, which has been repeatedly called for in the climate context. The importance of ensuring adequate adaptation (and loss and damage as this intensifies) is also highlighted here: funding for mitigation is needed for nonrecurrence of climate impacts, but funding for adaptation is required for nonrecurrence from the perspective of human development concerns. Prioritizing one at the expense of the other will erode the capacity to build trust and solidarity.

Transparency discussions have typically focused on mitigation efforts more than other elements of climate policy (Gupta and van Asselt 2017), but during the lead-up to the Paris Agreement developing countries made clear demands for transparency of support. These demands are driven by concerns that developed countries simply relabel money already intended for development assistance; the lack of clarity about where the $100 billion annually in climate finance promised during the Copenhagen negotiations and reiterated as a 'floor' in the Paris Agreement will come from; and the sheer diversity of pathways climate finance can take, making it difficult to track (PACJA 2015a). Many parties and civil society organizations have been critical that developed countries have not been more forthcoming about providing the promised $100 billion in support, or been clear about where it is supposed to come from. Meanwhile, the multiplicity of funds and the potential for money to become mixed with regular overseas development assistance make it particularly difficult to track (Ciplet, Roberts, and Khan 2013).

From a transitional justice perspective, transparency in the provision of support ought to be seen as a core element of accountability, in the sense of holding those who have made promises about financial provision responsible for fulfilling these promises. Failing to do so will erode the potential for financial transfers to contribute to long-term legitimacy and trust building. This takes us to our last point: finance is about more than money.

Recognition and attitude are not demands regularly voiced in the climate finance context, but we argue that they are central to this issue. For example, arguments that finance is owed as part of a 'climate debt' (Bolivia 2009) and insistence that climate finance is not and must not be seen as a form of charity but is a rightful settlement (Africa Group and Sudan 2014) speak directly to the symbolic elements of finance. If financial transfers are not done in a way that recognizes the justice claims being made and that expresses an attitude of repair and interdependence among parties, their ability to help build social trust and solidarity may be limited.

One of the clearest examples of the extent to which discussions about finance have these broader elements is demonstrated in the tensions about the proportion of public versus private money included in global climate finance funds. As PACJA argues, "the obsession with Private financing by industrialized countries as opposed to public finance supported by developing countries is the current area of contestation" (2015a: 18). Although it is widely recognized that the sheer volume of finance needed to address mitigation and adaptation likely requires private and public money, this does not mean that public and private money are or should be treated in the same way. A number of developing countries and civil society organizations have argued that public money must play a central role for two reasons.

First, private finance requires significant rates of return, which may incentivize allocations that prioritize return over human needs. As demonstrated thus far, despite the centrality of adaptation finance in justice demands from vulnerable communities, it has been far harder to find private money for adaptation (Haites 2013).[2] Similarly, as seen through experiences with the CDM, it can be difficult to design market mechanisms to meet human development goals while also attempting to maximize financial returns (Banuri and Spanger-Siegfried 2002; Olsen 2007). For those for whom an adequate response to human development is part of the justice claims at the heart of climate change policy tensions, public money is likely to appear preferable as it may be more easily directed to recognize and address these needs.

Second, reliance on private money may be seen as an abdication of responsibility by developed countries. For instance, the PACJA argues that public money "can be regarded as compensation to poorer countries for losses incurred as a result of Greenhouse Gas emissions by richer countries" (2015b: 15). This framing suggests that financial contributions are being expected to function as a form of repair. But to do this, they must be accompanied by some measure of acknowledgment or remorse. The reallocation of public money suggests intention and possibly some pain: presumably there is a fixed sum of public money, which means its reallocation has some consequences domestically. In contrast, encouraging private investment – which does not affect the availability of financial resources in donor countries and can actually increase revenue in them through returns on investment – may achieve the same financial goals but fails to communicate remorse because it does not suggest that any trade-offs had to be navigated.

Both tensions underline the importance of recognizing that climate finance is not 'just money' but rather a tangible representation of relationships. Not tying finance to recognition of justice claims or using it to express remorse or a commitment to building trust may reduce its ability to support the development of solidarity.

A PROPOSAL FOR AUGMENTING EXISTING FINANCE MECHANISMS

We suggest that financial mechanisms ought to be designed around these three sets of considerations if they are to play the most productive role possible in building social trust and enabling nonrecurrence of the core harms expressed in the climate context. The existing funding mechanisms already have the potential to this, but they need to be fully funded, accessible, and approached transparently if they are to function as they ought. This is not a new insight (see, e.g., Ciplet, Roberts, and Khan 2013) but would be central to a transitional justice approach. Moreover, building on the notion of a truth commission–like process (Chapter 3), we propose an extension of the existing finance mechanisms.

In the truth commission process articulated earlier, multiple actors, including nonstate actors, at any scale could be explicitly identified as sharing partial responsibility. One way that actors could discharge their responsibility would be to contribute to mechanisms in the climate context most clearly tied to notions of repair: to date these would include the LDCF and the Adaptation Fund. These two funds would be the most appropriate because they are explicitly focused on addressing issues of most concern to those who are most vulnerable and who have the deepest human development needs. The Adaptation Fund has the added advantage of being governed by a mix of developed and developing country representatives[3] and being seen as a 'model' for the development of new funding mechanisms (PACJA 2015a). In contrast, the LDCF is governed by the Global Environment Facility and is administered through eight different international entities, such as the UN Development Programme and the UN Industrial Development Organization. This means there is very little direct engagement by least developed countries in the administration of the fund, which has led to sustained criticisms of its lack of transparency and accountability to recipients of the funds. Despite pressure to reform this fund post-Paris (Tenzig et al. 2016), such changes have not yet been made.

Encouraging nonstate actor contributions to these funds is not a new idea. In 2015 the province of Quebec was the first nonparty to contribute to the LDCF, and the state of Massachusetts in the United States is considering a bill that would allow individual citizens to direct their tax refunds to the LDCF (Barrett 2017). Expanding this pattern of engagement so that all types of nonstate actors are encouraged to contribute to central funding bodies would both allow actors to demonstrate remorse and signal their interest in solidarity, along with possibly generating additional financial resources.

Routing nonstate actor contributions through these two particular funds (particularly if the LDCF is reformed to be more responsive to demands for shared governance) would ensure that decision-making authority is shared in a transparent multilateral structure. If this is tied directly to a truth commission–like process, the intent for repair and solidarity would be cleanly communicated. A key element is that the countries in which contributing entities reside would not be able to take credit for these contributions: this finance must stay separate from country-level contributions. For example, if individual citizens in the state of Massachusetts contribute directly to the LDCF, the United States government ought not to be able to get credit or use it as part of its financial commitments. This clarity would be essential in order to maintain the level of recognition and attitude of these contributions. Their power lies in their ability to communicate the desire for solidarity from a much wider swath of global society. Moreover, these contributions should remain distinct from the back-and-forth tensions of negotiations. They are not in exchange for anything, but are offered as open invitations to move toward repair and solidarity.

Due process for human development safeguards

A common institutional reform in the transitional justice space is the development of mechanisms for due process and redress. This might include improving access to and the fairness of the legal system, or creating new institutions such as a human rights commission capable of hearing complaints and administering remedies. Such institutional reforms could be used for inspiration in the climate context in two ways: the development and integration of safeguards and through the creation of a process for redress associated with market-based 'cooperative' mechanisms facilitated by the UNFCCC.

Safeguards designed to integrate human development into climate action have emerged in the context of the CDM and REDD programs due to concerns that they could erode human development for vulnerable communities. Although the CDM was supposed to have human development benefits, these remained informally recognized in comparison to the protocols developed to ensure emission reductions were real and additional (Sutter and Parreño 2007. Eventually, the CDM executive board developed a tool designed to identify 'co-benefits' from mitigation action (UNFCCC 2014). This tool focuses largely on particular projects instead of on country-wide governance investments, and is strictly voluntary, but it demonstrates an interest in tying human development concerns more strongly to climate action.

Almost simultaneously, concerns emerged about the potential for REDD and the search for quantified forest offset credits to result in decreased access to and control over forest resources for indigenous and forest communities who may, or may not, have formal title or land ownership, and who may be excluded from decision-making processes (Blom, Sunderland, and Murdiyarso 2010; Mustalahti et al. 2012; Larson 2011). Decreased access to subsistence-based systems clearly has the potential to erode a number of human development components, including those connected to identity and cultural dignity.

In REDD and now REDD+,[4] concern about the potential implications for vulnerable communities led to substantial efforts to create 'safeguards' against potentially negative consequences. These safeguards encourage (not require) REDD+ host countries to ensure transparent forest governance, respect the rights and knowledge of indigenous populations, establish broad stakeholder participation, and use REDD+ in ways that protect entire forests, rather than allow for the establishment of industrial plantations. Whereas some civil society groups have critiqued these safeguards for not going far enough (e.g., REDD Monitor 2015), others have pointed out that explicit attention to them within specific countries has helped create ways of sharing the benefits from REDD+ appropriately (Brockhaus et al. 2014). These safeguards remain specific to REDD+ and depend on each host country to operationalize and report on them.

In both the CDM and REDD+ contexts, frameworks designed to protect human development represent attempts to integrate human development concerns into mitigation action. However, in both cases the creation of these frameworks emerged after considerable experience with each mechanism: human development was tacked on to climate action, not integrated from the start.

The Paris Agreement includes REDD+ and a skeleton framework for the creation of the SDM, which is expected to function largely in the same way that the CDM did under the Kyoto Protocol. Although these cooperative mechanisms are welcome components of the Agreement for many, as they may facilitate mitigation, concerns abound that they will also prioritize the development of markets without accompanying provisions for sustainable development and human rights. As the Like-Minded Developing Country submission on the creation of the SDM notes,

> [W]e need to be cognizant of the lessons learnt from the implementation of these types of approaches/mechanisms that left to their own devices will invariably introduce negative social and economic impacts through perverse incentives (e.g., speculation) causing harmful spillover effects and undue welfare burdens to vulnerable, often uninvolved, stakeholders.
>
> (Ecuador 2017)

From a transitional justice perspective, the SDM, or any cooperative measure, should deviate from the established pattern of adding human development to climate action after the fact: human development concerns must be fully integrated from the beginning. Without integrating human development concerns and human rights protections into their design, it will become increasingly difficult for countries to argue that mechanisms such as REDD+ or SDM are able to proactively contribute to a better future or avoid deepening gaps in levels of human development in a warming world.

The first due process mechanism we suggest is a set of mandatory **human rights–based safeguards** to ensure that no activities emerging from cooperative mechanisms will infringe on the human rights of communities hosting them. Each project financed through one of the cooperative mechanisms would have to include a summary assessment of how it will intersect with human rights and how actions are being taken to safeguard these. Financing the preparation of these reports would be the responsibility of the investing entity. Because each project and each country is different, these reports would vary in terms of which human rights are of greatest concern and what amelioration would look like.

The UNFCCC has long acknowledged that adaptation must be undertaken in ways that proactively promote local human development priorities. For instance, the 2010 Cancun Adaptation Framework explicitly states that enhanced adaptation efforts are needed and that they

> should follow a country-driven, gender-sensitive, participatory and fully transparent approach, taking into consideration vulnerable groups, communities and ecosystems, and should be based on and guided by the best available science and, as appropriate, traditional and indigenous knowledge, with a view to integrating adaptation into relevant social, economic and environmental policies and actions, where appropriate.
>
> (UNFCCC 2010)

This stated intention demonstrates a broad interest in connecting adaptation to local needs and vulnerabilities, which resonates with concerns about human rights. Despite these general guidelines, however, there is no framework mandated to evaluate any climate action efforts (mitigation, adaptation, or loss and damage) from a human development or human rights perspective.

The underlying principles of transparent governance, stakeholder participation, and awareness of potentially highly vulnerable populations used in the REDD+ safeguards would be transferrable to this human rights–oriented approach. A basic template for assisting in the assessment could be generated and made available through the UNFCCC – similar to the CDM development tool that already exists – but countries would have to tailor it to meet the specific challenges of each context. Any project approved through the UNFCCC market mechanism window would need to demonstrate that it has assessed its potential implication for human rights and has either already established or is proposing a suite of institutional supports to protect the human rights of those communities affected by any projects. This assessment should include an evaluation of the contextual factors shaping vulnerabilities, from gender norms to legal, social, or political structures that increase the vulnerability of specific groups. Possible supports could include everything from institutional investments designed to enable participation in decision making, to community-based designs sensitive to the gendered ramifications of methods for allocating revenues from such projects (Brockhaus et al. 2014). As others have pointed out (Hall and Weiss 2012), one benefit of using a human rights framework to assess adaptation in particular is that it forces engagement with the lived experiences of people at the community level. In addition, because human rights are necessarily multifaceted, they provide a means for climate policy implications to be evaluated in the context of other ongoing policy interventions.

The concern with safeguards generally is that they could add onerous reporting obligations to developing countries struggling with capacity limitations. However, countries already have international human rights obligations and are expected to run projects in their territories in ways that augment the lives of their citizens. Expecting countries to report on this is not therefore unreasonable, especially as substantial flexibility could be included in implementation, and perceived capacity gaps could be subject to requests for support. For instance, a country that was unable to provide gender-sensitive documentation of project implications due to insufficient monitoring systems could apply for additional funding to establish such a system. Moreover, the costs of such investments could be included in the initial agreement between the cooperating entities: the protection of human rights ought to be the responsibility of both parties, not only the host, although the appropriate roles of the two are clearly different. Requests for assistance with setting up monitoring systems could also be funneled through other funding mechanisms, such as the Green Climate Fund, or other means of support for adaptation and loss and damage, such as the Adaptation Fund or the LDCF.[5]

The second mechanism we propose would provide a **means for seeking redress in market-based mechanisms**. If the UNFCCC itself is going to be directly involved in the creation and regulation of projects, a further step of creating a complaint process – akin to a human rights commission or a legal means for redress – would be productive. This is not a new idea. For instance, some have suggested that means of redress ought to be seen as part of the REDD+ safeguards regarding transparent and effective forest governance (Brockhaus et al. 2014).

In this version, redress would function at the domestic level as part of the host country's commitment to implementing the human rights–oriented safeguards described earlier. Another related suggestion has been made by Jouni Paavola (2005). Recognizing the cross-scalar challenges of dealing with justice claims emerging from harms caused by internationally funded projects, Paavola proposes an international commission housed within the UNFCCC with the mandate to hear and adjudicate claims. His proposal builds on the North American Agreement on Environmental Cooperation, which contains a mechanism in which individual citizens or civil society organizations that feel their government has failed to sufficiently follow its own environmental laws can request that the council established under this agreement examine the case and, if the council agrees with the complainants, request that the state respond. He has suggested that establishing a similar process would allow "controversies regarding national adaptation planning and measures undertaken on the basis of international agreements to international scrutiny" (Paavola 2005: 318).

We argue that a version of this model could be implemented, not only for adaptation efforts but also for any market-based cooperative mechanisms in which a disjuncture between communities and national economic interests could result in harms at the local level. A rotating board consisting of country representatives (with regional representation in mind) could receive complaints from individuals or civil society. These complaints could be directed toward either states or the nonstate actors involved in project finance or implementation. The board would investigate the claims, prepare a report, and present it to the COP or the SBI. The entity in question could be offered an opportunity to propose redress at this point, and the board would be responsible for facilitating these negotiations. In order to make the mechanism effective, a database of reports could be maintained and linked to future funding and project approvals. The benefit of this approach is that it could be designed to incorporate both state and nonstate actors involved in project implementation.

Although such mechanisms could be beneficial to communities, the benefit of a due process mechanism is that it is directly implementable by the UNFCCC. Even if individual countries choose not to use a human rights framework domestically, this mechanism provides a resource for communities globally to use when advocating for greater protections for their well-being. From this perspective the creation of such a mechanism could provide both immediate and long-term benefits, as it changes the dynamics of activism for local-level human development and human rights protections.

Adaptation and loss and damage

Like finance, adaptation and loss and damage discussions are deeply rooted in the global debates about climate policy. To some extent a transitional justice approach has limited added value in this realm. At its most basic level substantial support for both adaptation and loss and damage is necessarily central to this approach. An implementation pathway for the Paris Agreement that did not feature concrete efforts to minimize the negative implications of climate change for those who are most vulnerable could not be said to be demonstrating a genuine effort at building solidarity or creating the basis for deepening trust.

However, using a transitional justice lens does highlight several dimensions of this issue that may have received less attention in other discussions and are thus worth mentioning. Specifically, in addition to reiterating calls for adequate and accessible financial support, experiences from the implementation of reparations highlight the need to create adequate knowledge about local experiences of climate harms, and then to develop institutional means that connect these experiences with appropriate support. Finally, a transitional justice approach reiterates the symbolic importance of clear and consistent commitments to address the concerns of those who are most affected or most vulnerable. We briefly discuss each of these next.

KNOWLEDGE ABOUT CLIMATE HARMS

Adequate and accessible financing for efforts at repairing harms is clearly an essential element of a transitional justice approach. However, transitional justice experiences also suggest that effectively addressing harms and re-establishing social trust requires that strategies for repair resonate with the site-specific losses and experiences they intend to address. However, before such planning can be conducted, **adequate knowledge about site-specific losses** must be generated. The international climate community has already started to invest in organizing knowledge about the effects of climate change. Specifically, to date both the NAP and the NAPA processes have been widely applied, resulting in a database articulating NAPA priorities (UNFCCC 2017) and a wide range of country NAPs.

These programs provide a strong foundation for developing a knowledge base about climate impacts but have several limitations, particularly in the face of loss and damage. For instance, because they focus explicitly on adaptation, they may not be capturing losses that are accruing despite adaptation efforts. Several civil society organizations have attempted to fill this gap. For instance, ActionAid conducted a four-country scoping study of loss and damage across Bangladesh, India, Nepal, and Sir Lanka at the community level. By focusing explicitly on loss and damage and taking a regional perspective, this study identifies risks of migration, floods, and drought management both within and across borders (ActionAid 2016). Although the NAPAs have proven to be a useful exercise for least developed countries, they focus only on immediate adaptation needs, consider only existing data, and are country specific. Similarly, the NAPs are also country specific and may or may not have the capacity to do additional data gathering. Moreover, after the first wave of NAPAs has been completed, it is unclear if the exercise will be repeated, even though climate impacts have continued to advance. Some of the earliest NAPAs were conducted in 2004 and 2005 but already knowledge of climate impacts has shifted.

We propose that countries should be supported in conducting **scoping studies** focused explicitly on loss and damage. These scoping studies would be useful because climate impacts will be diverse and highly localized. Effective responses need to be designed around these specificities. These studies could essentially be an extension of the NAPA process and would be designed to identify concrete, specific losses being experienced or that are at a high risk of occurring at the community to regional levels. As with the NAPAs, these studies would be designed to be participatory. Unlike the NAPAs, they would not have to be country-wide, but could focus on documentation of particular areas of concern within a country. Effectively a country could submit multiple scoping studies, each specific to the experiences of people in particular regions. The UNFCCC secretariat would be requested to facilitate the integration of these studies into biannual reports that would bundle evidence about losses across country borders, taking into account that some local losses could have regional implications if experienced at scale, as has been suggested is already happening in South Asia (ActionAid 2016). These studies should be regularly recurring in light of the evolving nature of climate impacts.

CONNECTING DOCUMENTATION AND SUPPORT

Adequate knowledge generation is essential if impacts are to be dealt with in ways that respond to the needs of local communities. However, there need to be ways of connecting experiences and documentation to broader processes and means of support. We see two concrete pathways that have not been broadly explored but that might help integrate knowledge of loss and damage with the institutional mechanisms needed to facilitate implementation of support.

First, the scoping studies suggested earlier could be used in several nonfinancially oriented components of a transitional justice approach fairly easily. For instance, this documentation could contribute directly to the truth-seeking portion of a truth commission–like process (see Chapter 3), be fed into the global stocktake, and be used in educational materials to facilitate broader social engagement (see the education section later). In addition, as with the NAPA process, specific needs identified within these studies should be eligible for financial or in-kind support and connected to the financial mechanisms in the Paris Agreement. Moreover, a system for documenting concrete needs of particular communities could be linked with the reconciliation aspects of a truth commission process. There is no reason why nonstate actors could not also be asked to contribute to efforts addressing specific harms.

Of course, many specific requests identified in the NAPA process have yet to be funded, even without adding more requests from loss and damage scoping studies. This serves as a reminder: documentation and resource provision both have to be addressed. We should not be interpreted as merely calling for 'more research' or suggesting that documentation alone is adequate. We are, however, arguing that more systematic documentation is an important and potentially powerful component of efforts to generate stronger collective action that has received less attention than the need for adequate financial and nonfinancial resourcing.

A second institutional means of better supporting knowledge of climate impacts would be to **maintain country-specific teams** focused on identifying and addressing climate impacts. One of the strengths of the NAPA process was the creation of national teams of experts who explicitly worked to identify the most important short-term needs in the face of climate change. Unfortunately, support for these teams was available only until the reports were filed. This resulted in a lost opportunity for building long-term capacity for assessing the need for adaptation and understanding loss and damage. Best practices from the NAPA process indicate that implementation was much smoother when some or all of the experts were involved than when it was handed over to entirely new agencies (LEG 2011). Declaring the funds needed to maintain small country teams eligible for climate finance – either through existing pathways or as a form of capacity building – could possibly be a powerful investment in the long-term effectiveness and legitimacy of the climate regime.

CONSISTENT COMMITMENT TO MANAGING CLIMATE IMPACTS

A central part of a transitional justice arrangement is the creation of a believable and credible narrative that a more cooperative and mutually beneficial future is being built. Generating this narrative in the climate context requires consistent demonstrations of goodwill and effort by all parties. Sustained and substantial mitigation effort is clearly a component of this. However, as has been repeatedly called for by developing countries, climate change efforts must also include a strong adaptation and loss and damage focus.

As negotiated in the lead-up to Paris, NDCs all include information about mitigation, but other aspects of climate action are included only voluntarily. As others have described, this has resulted in uneven coverage of mitigation, adaptation, and loss and damage (Mbeva and Pauw 2016). One relatively simple but potentially powerful way to increase the trust-building nature of the NDCs would be to **include adaptation in all NDCs**. For developed countries this could include commitments to adaptation finance, in-kind supports, or cooperative bilateral efforts. Including such efforts in the NDC process makes them more transparent and more likely to be able to contribute to trust building over time.

Indirect changes through affiliated institutions

A common component of transitional justice institutional reforms has been the domestication of international norms regarding human rights. One change often pushed for as part of transitional justice has been the formalization of international human rights norms in domestic laws. In a parallel with international human rights law, international climate law depends in part on domestic legislation and policy frameworks.

The domestication of climate change norms is particularly relevant post-Paris due to the centrality of NDCs to the Paris Agreement. If NDCs were designed explicitly to maximize their utility from a transitional justice perspective, what might they look like? We suggest two components that would signal a country's intention to recognize historically rooted harms and support forward-oriented climate action in a spirit of solidarity.

Strengthening domestic climate law

To the best of our knowledge no NDCs currently contain pledges to develop climate laws aimed at augmenting domestic accountability mechanisms. Integrating such intentions with the international arena through NDCs would be a way of signaling genuine attempts to create a future more likely to be just (at least from the perspective of climate change).

Developing national climate legislation that sets clear legal parameters for climate action is not a new idea. Former UNFCCC Executive Secretary Christiana Figueres has long championed this concept, arguing that it is "the absolutely critical, essential linchpin between action at the national level and international agreements" (Figueres 2013). Domestic legislation could take a range of forms depending on the jurisdiction. In some situations this could include legislating new emission reduction goals. Several countries have done this. In 2012, Mexico passed a General Law on Climate Change that includes an emission reduction target for 2020, as long as there is international support (IDLO 2012). Similarly Ethiopia and South Korea have domestic laws that address mitigation as part of a broader framework of green growth or green economic development (CDKN and GLOBE 2013). In several cases such actions might be accompanied by the development of new regulatory institutions or coordinating bodies. For example, in order to achieve its legislated emission reduction targets, the UK created the Climate Change Committee and, until 2016, a Department for Energy and Climate Change.[6] Empirical evidence suggests that countries are increasingly creating domestic legislation to address climate change. By 2016 a global legislation study database reported 850 laws and policies at the national level (GRI 2016).

Typically proponents of domestic climate legislation have focused on augmenting mitigation capabilities, but such efforts could fit nicely with a transitional justice approach. Depending on how national legislation is designed, it could include mitigation-enhancing efforts and demonstrate country commitments to accountability broadly. As seen in the *Urgenda v. the Kingdom of the Netherlands* case (Hofhuis, Bockwinkel, and Brand 2015), domestic accountability laws can have direct implications for actors not fully covered by international climate law. Strengthening the domestic capabilities of the judicial system to hold nonstate actors accountable sends a clear signal of intent to all parties. This is a particular subset of domestic legislation that could have dynamic implications for the ability of other transitional justice–inspired mechanisms to function.

We propose that including explicit efforts to strengthen domestic legal frameworks for climate action could be made by each country and included as part of its NDCs. Prioritizing domestic legislation would maintain the momentum already generated for this idea. In addition, having a stronger legal framework helps to solidify burgeoning norms about climate harms, and would increase the effective-ness of other efforts, such as partial amnesties, a global truth commission process, and other forward-oriented actions.

Educational programs and investments

Education has featured in a number of transitional justice contexts as an essential element of cultural change. This has included revisiting textbooks to ensure that histories include periods of violence and oppression, and developing broad cur-ricula designed to reposition society in relation to this part of its past. For example, the Canadian TRC made recommendations for the educational sector, including guidelines for education on the history and contemporary relationship between Canada and its First Nations peoples for all students from kindergarten to the end of secondary school (TRC of Canada 2015). In addition, it made specific recom-mendations for culturally appropriate training for people in a number of important professions, including medicine, law, and policing. In the Canadian case such broad cultural change was seen as the necessary basis on which to build a new social contract between Canada's First Nations and settler communities.

Article 6 of the UNFCCC has a provision for education, but it has been used only very lightly (UNFCCC 1992). During COP18 parties adopted the Doha Work Programme on Article 6, which resulted in several workshops and dialogues (UNFCCC 2012). The vast majority of this activity has focused on 'best practices' for public education about climate science generally. To the best of our knowledge very few countries have actively referred to this in their climate action planning domestically or in their international communications.[7] Moreover, although encouraging public understanding of climate science is clearly part of the chal-lenge, it does not necessarily contribute to cultural awareness of the justice dimen-sions of the global climate context. We suggest two ways in which Article 6 could be more effectively used.

First, we propose that parties could **explicitly engage Article 6** to support the development of domestic cultures more in tune with the transitional justice chal-lenge faced by the international community. Countries could commit to providing education not only about climate science but also about the international and transboundary nature of the problem. Educational materials could integrate stories of those directly affected by climate impacts, emissions data across space and time (including cumulative emissions), and information about forward-oriented solu-tions. Such investments could be included in NDCs, which would also provide an easy way for the international community to observe progress on these com-mitments. Although such an effort could be facilitated by a truth commission process, it could also emerge through individual actions of particular countries. Overall, these investments in education would be one concrete way of supporting long-term cultural changes that could facilitate more ambitious mitigation and greater support for adaptation (and, where necessary, loss and damage).

Second, **capacity building** is emerging as a distinct area needed for successful climate action. Investments in higher education and training could be an important component of these efforts. Commitments to capacity building could include scholarships for educational attainment both within and outside countries; direct financial contributions to universities, country-specific research institutes, and training facilities in developing countries; and funded exchanges of students and practitioners between countries to facilitate South–South and South–North learning.

One of the concerns that has emerged in capacity-building conversations is that developed country consulting companies could primarily benefit from capacity building funds if they were hired to do assessments and trainings (Huq 2016). If commitments to capacity building are to be part of a deeper effort toward a more equal world, these investments must be designed to benefit developing countries through the systematic accumulation of capacity in-country. This would preclude hiring developed country consulting companies to conduct work that could be undertaken (possibly with more support) within developing countries by domestic institutions.

As with our proposed expansion of the financial mechanism to include contributions from nonstate actors, support for capacity building could also be satisfied by proactive commitments from a wide range of actors. The Canadian TRC, for example, called upon many nonstate actors to participate in changing Canadian society through their expertise in education and training. Calls for explicit engagement with Article 6 and capacity building could easily be extended to universities and educational institutions, think tanks, philanthropic organizations, and sector-specific practitioner associations (such as urban planners, social workers, and accountants). Each of these entities could be called upon to clearly articulate how it will contribute to capacity building. For instance, think tanks in the global North might commit to not competing for funds against those in the global South, but rather partnering with them when specific expertise is required. Similarly, universities could articulate how their policies support capacity building in the global South by co-developing courses other institutions may not have the capacity to cover, by providing low-cost student exchange and knowledge development opportunities, or by encouraging fully integrated research efforts through which researchers in the global South are at least equal holders of any resulting intellectual property.

Developing a platform by which such nonstate actors could declare their intentions and document their commitments would broaden participation in solidarity efforts. This would have dual benefits. It would increase the total amount of resources and attention dedicated to capacity building. It would also provide increased avenues for society-wide education and cultural engagement with climate change. Without support for public finance for climate action in developed countries, the entire transitional justice–inspired effort will struggle: countries are typically more sensitive to domestic politics than international pressures, and without domestic pressure for action international tensions may have limited impact. Solidarity efforts that engage people in capacity-building work across borders could directly feed into political shifts. For instance, a range of professional associations could commit to engaging with the capacity-building efforts of their members across countries. Such efforts could have dynamic implications for capacity building itself, and for the potential for solidarity to emerge across country borders.

Building on existing institutions and norms

Forward-oriented institutional reform is an absolutely essential part of any transitional process, and it plays a particularly important role in a transitional justice approach to climate change because it is so essential for avoiding future harms. To some extent institutional reform has already been the primary focus of the global community in the lead-up to and following the Paris Agreement.

As summarized in Table 5.1, we have focused on a subset of the possible universe of institutional reforms. A vast amount of energy has already been invested in thinking about how the Paris Agreement will work to create the kind of future it aspires to, and the possibilities are almost endless. In this chapter we looked only at those contributions that become unusually visible when using a transitional justice lens. With these glasses on, the Paris Agreement itself appears as a large institutional signal that a new relationship is desired by all parties, which

Table 5.1 Overview of proposed future-oriented institutional reforms

Area	Proposal	Relationship with existing institutions
Financial mechanisms	Facilitate financial contributions from nonstate actors to Adaptation Fund and LDCF	Build on early-adopter nonstate contributions
	Increased transparency of support	Already called for, not implemented
Due process	Create and use human rights–based safeguards	Build on REDD+ safeguards, plus CDM voluntary tool
	Create a mechanism for redress	New mechanism
Adaptation and loss and damage	Conduct region/community-specific scoping studies of climate harm	Build on NAPA process
	Establish and maintain national expert panels	Build on NAPA process
Domestic climate law	Strengthen domestic climate law, report this in NDCs	Already called for, unevenly implemented
Education and capacity	Engage in and report on Article 6 achievements	Article 6 exists, but rarely used or reported on
	Engage in and report on capacity-building commitments by state and nonstate actors	Some efforts exist, no systematic reporting

leaves the question of how successful it will be. We have identified modest alterations inspired by transitional justice experiences that could be built into existing
efforts.

As with institutional reform in the transitional justice context, the focus here
has been to identify central processes that shape the lived experiences of people
looking forward. Accordingly, we have not included the Reparations Commission
we proposed in Chapter 4 in this suite of reforms. However, we recognize states'
commitments to strengthen domestic climate law as a symbolic contribution to
solidarity and an investment in long-term accountability. In many of these cases,
new mechanisms could be directly connected to other parts of the existing, and
potential, suite of institutions. For example, loss and damage scoping studies could
feed into a truth commission and be used as a foundation for requests for reparations (and the design of these). The national panels of experts we suggest would
also build domestic capacity in the long term.

Several of these reforms are designed to spur wider changes. For instance,
capacity-building commitments for state and nonstate actors, and the public declaration of these commitments, are institutional reforms whose weight resides in
the ability to produce a range of indeterminate ends. For this reason, we revisit
capacity building in the next chapter, which focuses more squarely on transformation, rather than reform.

Notes

1 It should be noted that a 2016 independent review of the LDCF discovered that problems with the accessibility and adequacy of funds inhibited some countries from trying
to access them at all, highlighting the depth of insecurity currently experienced in climate finance (GEF IEO 2016).
2 It should be acknowledged that some private money for adaptation is likely not counted
because it is entirely private. For instance, companies' investments in their own infrastructure to enable them to continue operations are unlikely to be picked up in climate
finance accounting. This being said, the benefits are also largely private, although they
may have some public spillover. The key issue here is that if private finance is fundamentally aimed at providing selective, private benefits, it is less likely to work as a mode
of public repair.
3 The Adaptation Fund emerged as part of the Kyoto Protocol and is funded in part
through the CDM. It is governed by a combination of developed and developing country
representatives. See (Grasso 2010a).
4 REDD eventually changed into REDD-plus (REDD+), as it expanded to include efforts
toward conservation and sustainable management of existing forest stocks to 'enhance'
forest carbon stocks. Because these details are not the focus of our discussion and the
safeguards developed apply to both, we simply refer to them as REDD+ as this is the
more expansive category and is now what is typically included in discussions.
5 Investments in monitoring could be included in the 'enabling activity' category of eligible LDCF funds.
6 In 2016 the Conservative government folded the Department of Energy and Climate
Change into the Department of Business, Energy, and Industrial Strategy.
7 One exception is the government of Canada, which, in a period of very weak climate
action, listed public education as one of its accomplishments without providing any
particulars beyond a few trainings and its social media feed (Canada 2014). We would

see this as an example of how *not* to include education as part of an NDC from a transitional justice perspective, as it appeared insincere and was seemingly designed to avoid, rather than confront, the depth of the problem.

References

ActionAid. 2016. "Climate Change Knows No Borders."www.actionaid.org/publications/climate-change-knows-no-borders.

Africa Group, and Sudan. 2014. "Proposal From the African Group on Draft Elements on Finance Under the ADP Lima Elements on Climate Finance." www4.unfccc.int/submissions/Lists/OSPSubmissionUpload/106_99_130621901867637690-AGN%20ADP%20 Paper.pdf.

Banuri, Tariq, and Erika Spanger-Siegfried. 2002. "Equity and the Clean Development Mechanism." In *Ethics, Equity and International Negotiations on Climate Change*, edited by Luis Pinguelli-Rosa and Mohan Munasinghe. Cheltenham: Edward Elgar Publishing.

Barrett, Michael. 2017. "An Act Enabling Taxpayer Donations to the Least Developed Countries Fund, an Initiative of the UN Framework Convention on Climate Change." Senate Bill 2056. Commonwealth of Massachusetts. https://malegislature.gov/Bills/190/SD2138.html.

Blom, Benjamin, Terry Sunderland, and Daniel Murdiyarso. 2010. "Getting REDD to Work Locally: Lessons Learned From Integrated Conservation and Development Projects." *Environmental Science & Policy* 13(2): 164–72.

Bolivia. 2009. "Climate Debt: The Basis of a Fair and Effective Solution to Climate Change." *UNFCCC (Ad-Hoc Working Group on Log-Term Co-operative Action)*. https://unfccc.int/files/meetings/ad_hoc_working_groups/lca/application/pdf/4_bolivia.pdf.

Brankovic, Jasmina, and Hugo van der Merwe, eds. 2018. *Advocating Transitional Justice in Africa: The Role of Civil Society*. New York: Springer Press.

Brockhaus, Maria, Grace Wong, Cecilia Luttrell, Lasse Loft, Thuy Thu Pham, Amy Duchelle, and Samuel Assembe-Mvondo. 2014. "Operationalizing Safeguards in National REDD+ Benefit-Sharing Systems: Lessons on Effectiveness, Efficiency and Equity." *Center for International Forestry Research*. http://www.cifor.org/publications/pdf_files/SafeguardBrief/5187-brief.pdf.

Buchner, Barbara, Martin Stadelmann, Jane Wilkinson, Federico Mazza, Anja Rosenberg, and Dario Abramskiehn. 2014. "The Global Landscape of Climate Finance 2014." *Climate Policy Initiative*. http://bibliotecavirtual.minam.gob.pe/biam/bitstream/handle/minam/1534/BIV01315.pdf?sequence=1&isAllowed=y.

Canada. 2014. "Canada's Sixth National Report on Climate Change: Actions to Meet Commitments under the United Nations Framework Convention on Climate Change." https://unfccc.int/files/national_reports/annex_i_natcom/submitted_natcom/application/pdf/nc6_can_resubmission_english.pdf.

CDKN and GLOBE. 2013. "National Climate Change Legislation: The Key to More Ambitious International Agreements." https://cdkn.org/wp-content/uploads/2013/08/CDKN_Globe_International_final_web.pdf.

Ciplet, David, J. Timmons Roberts, and Mizan Khan. 2013. "The Politics of International Climate Adaptation Funding: Justice and Divisions in the Greenhouse." *Global Environmental Politics* 13(1): 49–68.

De Greiff, Pablo. 2007. "Justice and Reparations." In *Reparations: Interdisciplinary Inquiries*, edited by Jon Miller and Rahul Kumar, 1st edition. Oxford: Oxford University Press.

De Vos, Pierre, Warren Freedman, and Danie Brand. 2015. *South African Constitutional Law in Context*. Cape Town: Oxford University Press Southern Africa.

Dimitrov, Radoslav S. 2016. "The Paris Agreement on Climate Change: Behind Closed Doors." *Global Environmental Politics* 16(3): 1–11.

Ecuador. 2017. "Submission of the Like Minded Developing Countries on the Article 6.2 & 6.4 & 6.8, 6.9 of the Paris Agreement." *UNFCCC (SBSTA 46)*. www4.unfccc.int/ Submissions/Lists/OSPSubmissionUpload/713_317_131364934648087255-LMDC%20 Submission%20on%20the%20Article%206%20of%20the%20Paris%20Agreement%20 -%20SBSTA%2046.pdf.

Figueres, Christina. 2013. "Statements at the 1st GLOBE Climate Legislation Summit in London, UK." *GLOBE International*. www.globelegislators.org/initiatives/programmes/ climate-change.

GEF IEO. 2016. "Program Evaluation of the Least Developed Countries Fund." *Evaluation Report No. 106*. Washington, DC: Independent Evaluation Office of the Global Environment Facility.

Grasso, Marco. 2010a. "An Ethical Approach to Climate Adaptation Finance." *Global Environmental Change* 20(1): 74–81.

Grasso, Marco. 2010b. *Justice in Funding Adaptation under the International Climate Change Regime*. New York: Springer Press.

Gready, Paul, and Simon Robins. 2014. "From Transitional to Transformative Justice: A New Agenda for Practice." *International Journal of Transitional Justice* 8(3): 339–61.

GRI. 2016. "The Global Climate Legislation Study: Summary of Key Trends 2016." *Grantham Research Institute on Climate Change and the Environment, London School of Economics*. www.lse.ac.uk/GranthamInstitute/wp-content/uploads/2016/11/The-Global-Climate-Legislation-Study_2016-update.pdf.

Gupta, Aarti, and Harro van Asselt. 2017. "Transparency in Multilateral Climate Politics: Furthering (or Distracting from) Accountability? Transparency in Climate Politics." *Regulation & Governance*, July.

Haites, Erik. 2013. "International Climate Finance." In *International Climate Finance*, edited by Erik Haites. New York: Routledge.

Hall, Margaux J., and David C. Weiss. 2012. "Avoiding Adaptation Apartheid: Climate Change Adaptation and Human Rights Law." *Yale Journal of International Law* 37: 309.

Hofhuis, H. F. M., J. W. Bockwinkel, and I. Brand. 2015. "Urgenda Foundation vs Kingdom of the Netherlands." Docket number C/09/456689/HA ZA 13-1396. Hague District Court. http://www.urgenda.nl/documents/VerdictDistrictCourt-UrgendavStaat-24.06.2015.pdf.

Huq, Salemuul. 2016. "Why Universities, Not Consultants, Should Benefit From Climate Funds." *Climate Home – Climate Change News* (blog). www.climatechangenews. com/2016/05/17/why-universities-not-consultants-should-benefit-from-climate-funds.

IDLO. 2012. "A Legal Working Brief on the General Law of Climate Change in Mexico." www.idlo.org/Publications/MexicoClimateChangeLWB.pdf.

Jansen, Jonathan, and Nick Taylor. 2003. "Educational Change in South Africa 1994–2003: Case Studies in Large-Scale Education Reform." *Education Reform and Management Publication Series*.

Kagoro, Brian. 2012. "The Paradox of Alien Knowledge, Narrative and Praxis: Transitional Justice and the Politics of Agenda Setting in Africa." In *Where Law Meets Reality: Forging African Transitional Justice*, edited by Moses Chrispus Okello, Chris Dolan, Undine Whande, Nokukhanya Mncwabe, and Stephen Oola. Cape Town: Pambazuka Press.

Larson, Anne M. 2011. "Forest Tenure Reform in the Age of Climate Change: Lessons for REDD+." *Global Environmental Change* 21(2): 540–49.

LEG. 2011. "Best Practices and Lessons Learned in Addressing Adaptation in the Least Developed Countries Through the National Adaptation Programme of Action Process, Volume 1." *Least Developed Countries Expert Group, UNFCCC.* http://unfccc.int/resource/docs/publications/ldc_publication_bbll_2011.pdf.

Mayer-Rieckh, Alexander, and Pablo de Greiff, eds. 2008. *Justice as Prevention: Vetting Public Employees in Transitional Societies.* New York: Social Science Research Council.

Mbeva, Kennedy, and Pieter Pauw. 2016. "Self-Differentiation of Countries' Responsibilities: Addressing Climate Change Through Intended Nationally Determined Contributions." *German Development Institute/Deutsches Institut für Entwicklungspolitik (DIE).* www.die-gdi.de/discussion-paper/article/self-differentiation-of-countries-responsibilities-addressing-climate-change-through-intended-nationally-determined-contributions/.

Mustalahti, Irmeli, Anna Bolin, Emily Boyd, and Jouni Paavola. 2012. "Can REDD+ Reconcile Local Priorities and Needs With Global Mitigation Benefits? Lessons From Angai Forest, Tanzania." *Ecology and Society* 17(1).

Office of High Commissioner for Human Rights. 2008. "Guidance Note on National Human Rights Institutions and Transitional Justice." Geneva: OHCHR.

Olsen, Karen Holm. 2007. "The Clean Development Mechanism's Contribution to Sustainable Development: A Review of the Literature." *Climatic Change* 84(1): 59–73.

Paavola, Jouni. 2005. "Seeking Justice: International Environmental Governance and Climate Change." *Globalizations* 2(3): 309–22.

PACJA. 2015a. "Climate Finance: An Opportunity or Competitor for Money in the Post-2015 Development Agenda?" www.pacja.org/index.php/resources/presentations.

PACJA. 2015b. "Paying for the Future Today: Climate Finance and the Green Climate Fund." www.pacja.org/index.php/resources/presentations.

Rajamani, Lavanya. 2016. "Ambition and Differentiation in the 2015 Paris Agreement: Interpretative Possibilities and Underlying Politics." *International & Comparative Law Quarterly* 65(2): 493–514.

REDD Monitor. 2015. "REDD Safeguards: What Are They?" www.redd-monitor.org/2015/03/20/redd-safeguards-what-are-they/.

Super, Elizabeth. 2015. "Reform or Transform? Understanding Institutional Change in Transitional Justice." Ph.D., Ulster University.

Sutter, Christoph, and Juan Carlos Parreño. 2007. "Does the Current Clean Development Mechanism (CDM) Deliver Its Sustainable Development Claim? An Analysis of Officially Registered CDM Projects." *Climatic Change* 84(1): 75–90.

Tenzig, Janna, Stephanie Andrei, Giza Gaspar-Martins, Bubu Pateh Jallow, and Evans Njewa. 2016. "A Vision for the Least Developed Countries Fund in a Post-Paris Climate Regime." *International Institute for Environment and Development.* http://pubs.iied.org/pdfs/17372IIED.pdf.

TRC of Canada. 2015. "Honoring the Truth, Reconciling for the Future." *Truth and Reconciliation Commission of Canada.* www.trc.ca/websites/trcinstitution/File/2015/Honouring_the_Truth_Reconciling_for_the_Future_July_23_2015.pdf.

UNFCCC. 1992. "United Nations Framework Convention on Climate Change." http://unfccc.int/resource/docs/convkp/conveng.pdf.UNFCCC. 2010. "Report of the Conference of the Parties on Its Sixteenth Session, Held in Cancun from 29 November to 0 December 2010: FCCC/CP/2010/7/Add.1." http://unfccc.int/resource/docs/2010/cop16/eng/07a01.pdf#page=4.

UNFCCC. 2012. "Report of the Conference of the Parties on Its Eighteenth Session, Held in Doha from 26 November to 8 December 2012 (Decisions 1/CP.18–10/CP.18)." http:// unfccc.int/resource/docs/2012/cop18/eng/08a01.pdf#page=3.

UNFCCC. 2014. "Voluntary Tool for Describing Sustainable Development Co-Benefits (SDC) of CDM Project Activities or Programmes of Activities." https://cdm.unfccc.int/ Reference/tools/index.html.

UNFCCC. 2017. "NAPA Priorities Database." http://unfccc.int/adaptation/workstreams/ national_adaptation_programmes_of_action/items/4583.php.

Van der Merwe, Hugo, and Guy Lamb. 2009. *Transitional Justice and DDR: The Case of South Africa.* New York: International Center for Transitional Justice.

Zartman, I William. 2001. "The Timing of Peace Initiatives: Hurting Stalemates and Ripe Moments." *Global Review of Ethnopolitics* 1(1): 8–18.

6 Transformative approaches to climate justice

Transitional justice largely relies on institutional responses to harms, particularly in practice. This book has drawn on thirty years of experience in the field and outlined how institutional responses have been used in diverse transitional contexts, describing various accountability mechanisms, reparations measures, and institutional reforms that might also help facilitate collective action in the climate context. The focus on institutions in transitional justice is essentially reformist, asking how the backward- and forward-looking aspects of addressing past harms and promoting solidarity can be done without overly 'rocking the boat' in terms of international and national power dynamics and resource distribution. A number of transitional justice scholars and practitioners have increasingly engaged with more transformative approaches, asking what role the field can play in effecting deeper social change, particularly by engaging with long-standing historical injustices and the ongoing structural inequalities that lie at the root of cycles of violence and oppression.

The question of transformation is also central in the climate context. Would altering a few key institutional arrangements within the UNFCCC address concerns about past, current, and future injustices adequately to provide the basis for future-oriented cooperation? Or does the scale of cooperation and engagement needed to minimize future climate impacts – even for the most vulnerable – require more transformative efforts? In this chapter we explore the limitations of transitions in the face of injustice. What would transformational justice look like and require? How would we get there?

In this chapter we grapple directly with the limitations of liberal approaches and purely institutional responses to justice needs, exploring calls for transformation that go well beyond the immediate bounds of the UNFCCC or states themselves. We suggest that there have been two dominant narratives of transformation in the climate justice context – one emerging from grassroots mobilization and the other from efforts to drive rapid mitigation through green growth and technological developments. This then leads us to propose three strategies that emerge out of the creative tension between these narratives: supporting inclusive low-carbon development pathways that go beyond technicist emission pathways to include political realities, cultural perspectives, and lived experiences; developing and using justice-oriented tools for policy analysis; and envisioning an expanded approach to capacity building. Each of these strategies could be pursued independently or integrated into the responsibility, reparations, and institutional reform measures described in previous chapters.

Critiques of reformism in transitional justice

As noted in Chapter 1, transitional justice is marked by the historical context in which it emerged as a discrete field – namely, the transitions from authoritarianism in Latin America and Eastern Europe in the 1980s and 1990s. As such, it is part and parcel of the post–Cold War rise of liberal democracy and human rights, which gained global currency amid the decline of left-wing political movements and thought. This shift was accompanied by a focus on rapid legal-institutional reform and an increasing emphasis on individual agency (Arthur 2009).

The extent to which transitional justice is rooted in liberal democracy theory and human rights discourse is reflected in the field's support for democratization approaches that include both political and economic liberalization; the positioning of institutional reform as a central mechanism; the prioritization of civil and political rights over social, economic, and cultural rights; and the individualization of both victims' suffering and perpetrators' abuses. As transitional justice became a go-to solution in diverse contexts attempting to address legacies of past harms – including not only countries transitioning out of authoritarianism, but also contexts that are emerging from civil war, that have not experienced regime change or that have a long-standing democracy – the formative characteristics of the field attracted critique.

A major critique is the role of transitional justice in legitimizing and entrenching liberal democracy. Although often lauded for contributing to democratic electoral systems and the rule of law, transitional justice is criticized for also contributing to the spread of free-market ideology, with its mix of privatization, deregulation, and structural adjustment and austerity measures. One argument is that economic liberalization can exacerbate existing inequalities, divisions, and social conflict, thereby countering core transitional justice aims (Sriram 2007). Another is that, even in cases where conflict is not exacerbated, the technicist approach to transitional justice – which, in line with dominant thinking on democratization, views transition as a short-term process that primarily requires legal and institutional interventions with narrow mandates – serves to obscure and thereby perpetuate the structural inequalities and historical injustices that tend to underpin social divisions (Sharp 2015). In addition, it often builds 'empty' institutions that have little connection or relevance to realities on the ground, may be mistrusted by those they are meant to serve, and/or make gestures toward meeting international norms while facing serious implementation barriers (Gready and Robins 2014).

These issues are aggravated by the traditional human rights biases within transitional justice. Transitional justice mechanisms tend to focus on civil-political rights abuses, particularly violations of bodily integrity, which prevents due consideration of the socioeconomic rights abuses that often drive civil-political rights violations and affect a larger proportion of the population, demonstrating the wide reach of harms in a given context (Laplante 2008). Although addressing socioeconomic abuses through transitional justice would bring attention to socio-economic drivers of harms, the individualizing approach of human rights serves to cloak the collective nature of harms and the extent to which they affect groups and societies, including across generations. It also often places the onus on individuals to pursue or respond to legal-institutional forms of justice. In this framework, the many passive beneficiaries of past harms, who often glean privileges that pass on to their children and grandchildren, avoid notice and responsibility (Mamdani 2000).

All these arguments contribute to an umbrella critique, which is that transitional justice as it is commonly theorized and practiced represents a 'one-size-fits-all' template prescribed by international elites and their domestic allies in a top-down manner (McEvoy and McGregor 2008; Shaw, Waldorf, and Hazan 2010). In the global South, commentators have extended this argument to note the Eurocentrism of transitional justice, given the historical roots of liberal democracy and human rights in the rise of anti-absolutist liberal capitalism in seventeenth-century Europe. They argue not only that transitional justice solutions are often an ill fit with the historical, political, and social realities in 'developing' countries, but also that they reproduce geopolitical power imbalances in a way that borders on neocolonialism, given the global South's role as the main laboratory for transitional justice ideas (Okello 2010; Brankovic and van der Merwe 2018). Some argue, in addition, that they do little to address the disproportionate burden of past harms and ongoing structural injustices on women (Brown and Ní Aoláin 2015).

The critiques of transitional justice that have emerged over the past thirty years, particularly as it grew into an internationally accepted field, relate to its essentially reformist approach. The field is touted for transforming individual and collective relations in contexts of massive past harms, but it seeks to do this without changing prevalent power relations at the global and national levels. The focus on the 'transitional' in transitional justice suggests that harms can be left behind, obscuring the ongoing nature of harms and the systems that perpetuate them (Miller 2013). To address these issues, a number of theorists and practitioners have put forward more transformative approaches to transitional justice.

Transformative approaches in transitional justice

Transformative approaches to transitional justice are diverse. They range from specific solutions that elaborate on existing transitional justice practice, such as including socioeconomic rights in the purview of transitional justice, to wide-ranging programs, such as distributive and transformative justice. Many of these approaches argue that addressing the shortcomings in the dominant practice of transitional justice requires more inclusive, participatory measures, informed and driven by those most affected by past harms and tailored to the contexts in which they take place.

As noted earlier, transitional justice actors have called for the inclusion of social, economic, and cultural rights (ESCR) by the field (Laplante 2008). Although these rights were for a long time considered 'injusticiable' because the violations are so widespread and a single perpetrator difficult to identify (Arbour 2007), this call is now being heeded to the extent that the UN secretariat included socioeconomic rights in its 2010 *Guidance Note of the Secretary-General on the United Nations Approach to Transitional Justice*. Truth commissions in particular have addressed socioeconomic harms in the findings and/or recommendations of their final reports, as was the case in Peru, Sierra Leone, Kenya, and Timor-Leste. Schmid and Nolan (2014) have warned, however, against the conflation of ESCR with economic marginalization or socioeconomic inequality, arguing that recent developments in ESCR law provide new opportunities for transitional justice actors willing to engage with the intricacies of this legal approach.

Some have argued for expanding beyond the human rights focus of transitional justice to address historical and structural inequality, highlighting the field's forward-looking aims in addition to its backward-looking ones. One suggestion has been to promote 'distributive justice' (Bergsmo et al. 2010). This approach pushes transitional justice mechanisms to address the roots of conflict and promote nonrecurrence through investigations into historically rooted structural inequality and measures that ensure progressive redistribution of resources, particularly land. Again, truth commissions have applied some of this thinking, with, for example, the Kenyan Truth, Justice, and Reconciliation Commission investigating and making recommendations for the restitution of land taken in 'land grabs,' although there have been political obstacles to the commission making the recommendations and their subsequent implementation.

An approach that explicitly highlights transformation is 'transformative justice' (Gready and Robins 2014). This approach critiques the Eurocentrism, legal-institutional focus, and short-term nature of dominant transitional justice practice, instead emphasizing long-term processes, broad participation, rootedness in local practices, and acknowledgment of global and national power dynamics. It promotes local knowledge and voices, particularly, but not limited to, those of victims, as the source of appropriate responses to the contextual specificities of transitional spaces. Looking at reparations from this perspective, Saffon and Uprimny (2010) argue that reparations measures tend to be backward-looking and to focus on restitution and compensation, which does not address ongoing inequalities and associated harms. They propose implementing 'transformative reparations,' which are based on resource redistribution and victim participation in transitional and democratic decision making. Rama Mani (2005) similarly emphasizes the centrality of victims' voices and their right to legal and moral remedies for historical injustices, with her idea of 'reparative justice.'

It is evident from these examples that although the transformative agenda in transitional justice has diverse branches, it generally valorizes 'bottom-up' approaches, local and context-responsive solutions, measures that acknowledge and counter epistemic violence by foregrounding local (and often indigenous) knowledge, community-based initiatives guided by the demands and needs of those most affected by past harms, and efforts to go beyond just consultation and to promote broad-based participation, particularly of marginalized groups, including women. In practice, transitional justice mechanisms have attempted to acknowledge this agenda by pursuing wider consultations with relevant stakeholders and particularly those most affected by past harms, and in the case of the ICC and some state-run truth commissions (and the civil society–run Recovery of Historical Memory project in Guatemala), for example, have attempted to increase victim participation in developing and carrying out processes. To date, however, these are largely top-down efforts where the participation framework is designed by policy makers and experts (McAuliffe 2017; Madlingozi 2010).

Whereas civil society has adopted a range of approaches to transitional justice, with many assisting in the design and implementation of more reformist processes (van der Merwe and Brankovic 2016; Brankovic 2018), community-based organizations and victims' groups have engaged in their own forms of transitional justice thinking and practice, at times with support or participation from human rights and other mainstream NGOs. These have a range of transformative characteristics. For example, victims and victims' groups have engaged in participatory research and activism on continuing socioeconomic marginalization and how long-term transitional processes can address them in the form of improved access to quality education, healthcare, and other entitlements (Robins and Wilson 2015; Sishuba et al. 2017). Members of communities affected by past harms have adapted indigenous or local conflict resolution practices into mechanisms that contain elements of accountability seeking, truth recovery, and reconciliation through restitution. They have designed their own memory and memorialization processes as reparative measures (Arriaza and Roht-Arriaza 2008; Shaw, Waldorf, and Hazan 2010).

Transformative approaches face a number of challenges, including lack of political will, resource constraints, the potentially conservative rather than transformative aims of locally rooted practices themselves, and limitations on the extent to which local practices can be scaled up to the national and international levels – all of which have led transitional justice actors, particularly those working at the policy level, to encourage 'modesty' regarding the field's capacities and reach (McAuliffe 2017). As has become a refrain in previous chapters, however, the norms that underpin transitional justice are continually evolving. Mechanisms are increasingly addressing socioeconomic issues, and even mainstream actors are now promoting the need for participatory approaches (e.g., US Agency for International Development 2014). Social transformation through transitional justice remains an aspiration; however, the transformative agenda and the ways people have implemented it are useful for thinking through the role of local dynamics in global issues and for learning from innovative approaches to dealing with seemingly intractable problems.

Transformational justice in the climate context?

Writing about the Anthropocene, Rob Nixon (2014) identifies a tension between two narratives playing out simultaneously. One narrative focuses on the global ecological threat posed to all of humanity by climate change and a range of other planetary boundaries that are rapidly being approached (Rockström et al. 2009; Steffen et al. 2015). The other narrative centers on the global disparities in wealth and access to human development. Despite efforts to reduce dire poverty, we still exist in a world in which roughly a billion people live on less than two dollars a day. Nixon argues that "a crucial imaginative challenge facing us is this: how do we tell two large stories that seem in tension with each other, a convergent story and a divergent one?" (Nixon 2014: 4).

This imaginative tension is palpable in the climate context, and is particularly important for questions of justice and transformation. We can tell a convergent climate change story that focuses on the potential for climate change to threaten all humanity and on the resulting need for universal collective action. Because greenhouse gas emissions are so intimately embedded in every aspect of our lives, any sufficient response to this story would necessarily be transformational to core social, economic, and technological systems.

We can also tell a divergent climate change story that takes as its starting point profound inequalities in human well-being and then interrogates where these inequalities came from and how climate change will intersect with them. This story points us in a different direction, but one that is no less transformational. This story suggests a rethinking of the underlying norms and economic arrangements that have resulted in patterned and profound inequalities within and among countries.

Both of these storylines have been and continue to be central to efforts to navigate climate change. In Chapter 2 we introduced four key strategies for addressing climate change justice tensions. Two of these – fair burden sharing and legal approaches – have been most closely tied to the kinds of institutional responses we have discussed in the book thus far. The other two – green growth and grassroots mobilization – have influenced global climate negotiations, but have also aimed more widely than policy change by the UN or nation-states. Of the four key strategies these are the two most directly at odds with one another, at least in terms of their relationship to economic and technological issues, and yet they share the recognition that managing climate change is likely to require far more than institutional tinkering within the UNFCCC. Taken altogether the climate justice mobilization and green growth strategies echo Nixon's recognition of the tension between convergent and divergent narratives. One strongly emphasizes the global technological and economic changes necessary for planetary-level sustenance. The other equally strongly emphasizes the voices of individuals and communities affected by climate change and forms of inequality that permeate their lived experience. From this angle, climate change is only one danger and may be symptomatic of deeper ills.

Here we return to the two intentionally transformational approaches to the climate justice tensions – green growth and grassroots mobilization – and then explore the tensions and overlaps between them. Can they be reconciled productively, or are their ideological roots too disparate to integrate? Even if they cannot be truly reconciled, can we think about transformational justice in the climate context without recognition of the concerns of each body of thought?

Transformation through green growth: the convergent climate change story

The convergent climate change story starts with recognizing the depth of the planetary challenges posed by climate change. The Intergovernmental Panel on Climate Change (IPCC) Fifth Assessment report suggests that staying at or below a 2°C temperature increase compared to preindustrial levels would require global emission reductions of 70 to 114 percent by 2100 (Edenhofer et al. 2014). Achieving a temperature increase of only 1.5°C – a goal many civil society groups and SIDS pushed for during the Paris negotiations – would be even more ambitious.

We can get a glimpse of what efforts to achieve these targets might entail by looking at the integrated assessment models (IAMs) and scenarios being developed to explore high-ambition worlds of 2°C or below. It is important to note that many IAMs have not produced scenarios of climate change that stay at or below this threshold because the speed of change and perceived economic costs of doing so are seen as too high to be 'feasible.' The lack of good data about the implications of attempting a 1.5°C temperature increase is one of the reasons the UNFCCC asked the IPCC to do a special report explicitly focused on high-ambition pathways. The depth of the mitigation challenge – and the associated adaptation challenge and potential for human harm – is not to be underestimated.

An examination of the existing high-ambition scenarios reveals several patterns. For instance, many of these pathways include negative emissions in the suite of strategies relied on for the depth of mitigation required (Anderson and Peters 2016). **Negative emissions technologies** include all possible ways of taking greenhouse gas emissions out of the atmosphere permanently (or at least long enough for atmospheric concentrations to stabilize). These technologies include everything from air capture of emissions linked to carbon capture and storage (CCS) in subterranean depositories to mineralization of carbon dioxide and biological sequestration through afforestation or land-use alterations (Lackner 2003). One of the most common features of high-ambition scenarios in IAMs is the use of biomass energy and carbon capture and storage (BECCS) (Rogelj et al. 2015). BECCS includes technologies that sequester (using CCS strategies) the emissions created when energy is generated through the use of biomass, such as wood or liquid fuels from plant matter. Because the biomass is using carbon dioxide during its growth phase, sequestering these emissions after energy production essentially withdraws them from the atmosphere. Most negative emissions technologies are currently in the experimental or prototype phase.[1] Full-scale development of any negative emission technology would entail society-wide funding and experimentation; these efforts require large-scale scientific cooperation and intensive investment.

A second common feature of these scenarios is the sheer **speed of mitigation** that they suggest is necessary. In order to reach high-ambition targets, large-scale mitigation has to happen as soon as possible. Because cumulative emissions drive temperature increases, every delay at this point decreases the likelihood that low-ambition worlds are possible (Millar et al. 2017). The immediacy of these actions stems from the path dependencies created by many infrastructure investments. For instance, every coal power plant built now essentially creates a fifty-year lag in reducing the emissions associated with it. The suite of efforts that would be needed to achieve low emissions pathways includes the mass deployment of renewables (which in turn requires substantial technological development of all forms of renewable energy), electrification of the transportation sector (again involving significant technological and infrastructural developments), rapid and sustained never-before-seen increases in energy efficiency (Grubb 2014), and usually increased reliance on nuclear power (Hong, Bradshaw, and Brook 2015; Pacala and Socolow 2004). Across all of these components technological development is absolutely key, and this is one element of this discussion that has moved into the UNFCCC through the creation of the Technology Mechanism.

Stemming from this foundational recognition of planetary challenges, the convergent story has typically focused on **global-level efforts and requirements** when thinking about solutions. Although many IAMs now include regional specifications (and high-emission countries are often treated as regions of their own), their primary focus remains global pathways. Identifying global targets is one thing, but it is useless if actors cannot be encouraged to take the actions necessary to achieve them. One of the limitations of global pathways analyses is that actual countries, corporations, and individuals do not make decisions at a global level. Global analyses may provide some insights into the depth of change required in core systems, but they provide scant guidance about how to get there. Accordingly, scholars and policy practitioners have started to more closely engage with the political question of how to achieve these targets (Geels et al. 2017; Klinsky and Grubb 2015). Focusing on how to get there has led to more thorough engagement with interests and the mobilization of capital (Victor 2015).

The mobilization of capital emerges as one of the central challenges for the depth of change suggested by global models. Currently over $500 billion annually is spent on subsidies for the fossil fuel industry (IEA, OECD, and World Bank 2010). The global economic system is not only not green but is also actively supporting 'brown' industries. As Kevin Anderson and Glen Peters (2016) point out, despite years of climate negotiations, global emissions trends are pointing in the opposite direction from where they need to be to achieve atmospheric stabilization at the levels aimed for by the UNFCCC. The reality is that current economic and technological systems are not substantially contributing to the reduction of greenhouse gas emissions.

The depth of change being proposed here is not only technological. The importance of engaging with a range of actors becomes immediately apparent when we look at the origins of emissions. Richard Heede and his team demonstrated that only ninety companies – referred to as 'carbon majors' – were responsible for 63 percent of total cumulative emissions from 1854 to 2010 (Heede 2014). Mitigation without **cooperation from the private sector** is impossible: most goods and services are provided by the private sector, and industrial players have significant political power. As seen globally, efforts to regulate emissions have immediately run into challenges when faced with corporate interests.[2]

Entirely new business models will need to be – and are being – developed, which will have long-lasting implications for how capital moves through society and how decisions about the public good are made (Jolly, Raven, and Romijn 2012). For instance, utilities that flourished during efforts at the turn of the twentieth century to electrify North America and Europe are facing profound challenges as distributed renewable electrification threatens to undermine their monopoly on power production and delivery. In some states in the United States, these utilities are as old as or older than the state itself.[3]

Meanwhile, the finance needs of adaptation alone would swamp public coffers, triggering interest in and interrogation of the options for private finance to play a role (World Economic Forum 2013; Pauw 2015; Agrawala et al. 2013). Regulating entities to provide these resources would be politically expensive (and potentially impossible), which highlights once again the need for such entities to do this through their own evaluations of strategic self-interest. Indeed, it does seem that much private adaptation finance is tied to corporate concerns for their own business vitality (Agrawala et al. 2013).

The green growth narrative has been the chief strategy for mobilizing capital and interests across the diversity of actors that must be engaged in these changes. The key characteristics of the green growth narrative have revolved around the necessity of developing and demonstrating the possibilities for climate action to align with the interests of core players. As discussed in Chapter 2, the central premise is that we can solve the ecological crisis by changing the financial incentive structure within our economy. We need not give up growth, but can develop an economy in which efforts that address the core climate challenge also provide economic benefits. There are many possible parts to a green growth economy – in fact the diffuse nature of it is what allows it to be transformative. Individuals, corporations, and even states could all play a role, motivated not by regulations from above but by their emergent realization that there are new opportunities for them to advance their own interests.

Recognition of the potential for and importance of much wider economic mobilization toward green growth has led to the massive engagement of nonstate actors in the lead-up to the Paris Agreement. Climate change cannot be readily addressed if the vast majority of relevant actors – individuals, corporations, local-level governments – are not actively engaged. The Momentum for Change campaign regularly reported on leadership from a wide range of nonstate actors (this includes governments of jurisdictions other than the national level). The NAZCA was initiated ahead of Paris and provides a platform for all nonstate actors to publicly declare their actions (UNFCCC 2015). The broad-based Coalition for

Carbon Pricing Initiative was initiated by the World Bank during the same period and now features a global network of subnational and national governments, along with hundreds of private-sector entities, committed to carbon pricing (CPLC 2017).

The green growth narrative tends to prioritize technological solutions, or at least solutions that can be rolled out at scale. It is impossible to include a million small and possibly idiosyncratic actions in a climate model. Although individual-level decisions about consumption or energy reduction are essential, until recently the psychological aspects of encouraging people to reduce their planetary demands were largely excluded from these forms of aggregate, high-level analysis. Although such 'demand management' has started to be taken more seriously in this arena, it remains somewhat thin (see Shove 2010) and focused on economic incentives.

What makes the green growth approach transformational is that it recognizes that the changes needed, and the forces at play, demand engagement far beyond the boundaries of states. Change here is not something that lies within the full regulatory power of the state. States may help direct the transformation, and could be essential in protecting certain populations from harm during the process, but states themselves are not the prime generators of change. Instead, the central strategy for change involves finding ways in which climate action is aligned with the core interests of diverse players. The momentum here must be self-generating and emergent.

However, although powerful and quite possibly essential in the face of the depth of emissions reduction required to avoid intense climate impacts for the most vulnerable, this convergent narrative of climate action also raises a number of concerns and paradoxes from a justice perspective. One line of concern stems from the potential for the actual policies enacted through this type of 'there is no alternative' approach to have negative repercussions for the most vulnerable members of society. For instance, if we reflect on the scope of BECCS built into transformative pathways for low-emissions worlds, we immediately are faced with risks of large land grabs and fuel–food trade-offs. If huge swaths of land must be transformed for biomass production, whose land will this be? If agricultural production for fuel becomes more lucrative than that for food, what is to prevent food prices from rising to the point at which low-income communities are harmed?

Another line of concern stems from the transfer of decision-making authority from the state to nonstate actors. Although we recognize that states often do not live up to their potential as democratic bodies, they do have obligations to protect the well-being of their citizens and can be pressured to do so. Private-sector actors, however, do not have these obligations as clearly marked out and are unlikely to use explicitly democratic or inclusive decision-making processes. Consider, for example, the potential for the insurance industry to play a major role in shaping responses to climate impacts (Kousky and Cooke 2015). If left entirely unregulated, industry decisions could force changes toward a low-emissions trajectory, but could also result in sharp costs to particular populations. Changing the extent to which homes or businesses are eligible for flood insurance may encourage development away from vulnerable coasts, but could also result in low-income populations being unable or unwilling to migrate until they face life-threatening situations because the move would trigger a sharp financial penalty.

A further justice concern involves the potential for opportunities created through green growth approaches to systematically accrue to those with the capital to invest. Tensions about systemically uneven flows of benefits from market-driven renewable energy investments have already emerged in jurisdictions such as Ontario, Germany, and Australia, in which tools such as feed-in tariffs have been used to spur private-sector investment. If not regulated, rapid changes in opportunities could lead to dynamics that reinforce pre-existing social inequalities. It must not be forgotten that justice per se is not a top priority in the convergent climate change story. Although avoiding climate impacts for the most vulnerable may be a motivating factor, and although this depth of emission reductions is likely necessary to avoid such impacts, a broader set of justice concerns are largely rendered irrelevant in the convergent narrative. From this perspective a desirable future is characterized predominantly as a future without significant climate change – regardless of whatever other characteristics such a world might entail. As seen next, grassroots mobilizing has a very different vision of transformation.

Transformation from the grassroots: the divergent climate change story

As we discussed in Chapter 2, grassroots mobilization around climate justice started to coalesce in the early 2000s and has grown to become a substantial and internationally recognized movement. Through its development this movement has engaged with pre-existing and divergent sets of claims about justice from indigenous peoples' liberation efforts to articulations of the injustices connected to capitalism. Across these divergent strands of mobilization, a core theme has been the argument that a different way is possible.

When faced with claims that "there is no alternative" (TINA), grassroots organizers during the first World Social Forum in Porto Alegre (in 2001) responded that "there are thousands of alternatives" (TATA), a slogan that has continued to resonate (Matthaei 2012). This tradition of recognizing that there are, in fact, alternatives to hegemonic economic structures and that these alternatives would fundamentally change the way that social and economic systems function is a central component of grassroots organizing for climate justice. As one would expect in a divergent story, this narrative argues that there is not one alternative, but many. As one long-time organizer summarized in a discussion with the first author, "when they say TINA, we say TATA."

Across the diversity of civil society mobilization and grassroots activism on climate justice, four central themes have continually emerged: justice is process, place, and identity based; justice claims are interconnected across multiple dimensions of human experience; generating a just system requires fundamental system change; and power and legitimacy ultimately come from people, not states. These themes are important to identify because they help us see the contours of this strategy, what justice is from this perspective, and what might be required to achieve it.

First, many grassroots calls for climate justice are highly **process-, place-, and identity-based demands,** rooted in affirmations of the importance of the daily lived experiences of people and their relationships with land and nonhuman entities. For example, in this discourse forests are not carbon credits, nor are they biodiversity hotpots. Forests are part of entire peoples' identities, which themselves are entwined with nonhuman living and inanimate entities. Although mostly strongly articulated by indigenous and forest people's groups, both inside and beyond the UNFCCC (Indigenous Environmental Network n.d.; Claeys and Pugley 2017), such claims have also been put forward by other grassroots entities. In another example, when members of the Global Alliance of Waste Pickers started attending COPs to object to large landfill and incineration CDM projects, they demanded that their livelihoods be rendered visible. For them, landfills are not just landfills or an opportunity for emissions reductions, but a core resource for employment and human dignity (GAWP 2011).

One of the implications of this focus on engagement and human dignity for actual people in actual places has been the articulation of democratic and participatory processes for the engagement of people and communities in climate policy decision making. Indigenous peoples' climate justice organizing has focused on this very intensively (Claeys and Pugley 2017). These efforts have contributed to recognition of participatory processes for certain policies within the UNFCCC, such as REDD+ and NAPAs, which explicitly identify the importance of participatory processes.

Overall, grassroots claims bring much stronger attention to recognition and procedural dimensions of justice compared to fair burden sharing, green growth, or legal action (Fraser 2001). Here justice is not only about the distribution of burdens or benefits, it is about the dignity of people's lives to be recognized and made visible in planning decisions, and for all people to have a voice in decisions that affect them.

A second strong theme in this form of mobilizing is the **interconnected nature of justice claims**. Likely because climate justice mobilization is focused on the lives of real people, calls for justice emerging from this paradigm are almost always multifaceted. Justice, in this approach, is not only about greenhouse gas emissions, but is also entwined with the pre-existing experiences of those likely to be affected by climate change. Accordingly, as seen in the various declarations that have been released, calls for climate justice quite often combine ecological claims with advocacy around gender justice, rights for indigenous peoples, economic inequalities, race-based discrimination, and large-scale structural injustices (see later).

This profusion of claims can be befuddling for those who have come to think of climate as essentially about emissions or about 'saving the planet,' both dominant strands of thought in the convergent climate change narrative. In this interconnected form of thinking about transformation or justice, the issues are much wider than climate per se because people's lives are multidimensional, and climate

intersects with many other forces. The interconnected and diverse nature of justice claims within this grassroots mobilizing is a feature of its ability to generate
solidarity across communities facing a wide range of particularized challenges.

The ultimate focus of these claims is on finding ways of reasserting the dignity
of human beings. Climate change is one threat among many to social justice, and
the solutions may or may not revolve narrowly around emission reductions or
direct adaptation. The diversity and interconnectedness of claims in this type of
divergent storyline also mean that the possible solution space is much more diffuse. Issues such as food and cultural identity, gender-sensitive development, and
integration of waste pickers into urban waste management planning are not seen
as disparate or isolated from climate change. Similarly, many efforts refer to concepts built on indigenous traditions – such as *Buen Vivir* (good living) – which
propose a fundamental transformation in how well-being is conceived of or pursued through development efforts (Monni and Pallottino 2015; Merino 2016).
Interpretations of *Buen Vivir* assert collectivity, stress the interconnections among
humans and nonhumans, and tend to stand in opposition to capitalism.[4] Even
outside Latin America calls for self-transformation akin to the spirit of *Buen Vivir*
abound. In 2014 the organizers of the People's Climate March chose to use the
Jemez Principles for Democratic Organizing[5] to guide their work, one of which
urges that "we must be the values that we say we're struggling for and we must be
justice, be peace, be community" (SNEEJ 1996). If genuinely used to guide human
development and responses to climate change, this paradigm could result in fundamental social, economic, and ecological changes.

The third, and connected, theme running throughout this approach to justice
is the most explicitly transformational: an insistence on going beyond addressing
climate change to **effecting system change**. The main rallying cry during the 2009
KlimaForum ended up being "system change, not climate change." Note that this
slogan does not identify particular systems but insists that some system – presumably the dominant or hegemonic one – must change. This slogan was chosen not
only because it would leave sufficient space for multiple groups' distinct claims to
be heard, but also because it encompasses the depth of specific critiques aimed at
capitalism and the need for decolonization and re-engagement with other ways of
knowing and living (Eriksen et al. 2009).

As part of this critique of dominant systems, and in direct contrast to the green
growth strategy, much of the grassroots climate justice discourse sees green capitalist efforts as equally – if not more – problematic as climate change itself. This line
of argumentation is ultimately used in order to change the power dynamics in the
global (and many national) systems that were instituted through colonization and
have continued to support spatial and cultural domination. This line of critique
sees climate change as a symptom, not as the ultimate problem.

Because system change is broader than climate change, the solutions space
suggested by this strategy similarly reflects a much broader set of options
than emissions reductions and support for those affected by climate change.
Re-establishing indigenous food and land use practices, imagining some form of
ecosocialism (Ware 2014), and massive reorganization of energy production and

consumption would all fit within this category. These suggestions are also often significantly deeper than those that emerge from a more bounded understanding of the problem. Reducing emissions is one thing; countering capitalism is another.

Finally, climate justice mobilization has focused on claims about people, not states. Consider the World People's Conference on Climate Change and the Rights of Mother Earth (PWCCC 2010); a Call for People's Action against Climate Change (CJN! 2004); the KlimaForum People's Climate Summit; or the People's Climate March.[6] In the rhetoric of grassroots organizing, legitimacy lies not in the power of the state, but in the power of the people.

Focusing on people and peoples rather than states changes the nature of justice claims and the scope of arguments of relevance. For example, although domestic inequality has occasionally emerged as an issue in fair burden sharing work (Muller and Mahadeva 2013; Chakravarty et al. 2009), it is rare. Lack of attention to domestic inequalities and sources of injustice has not been accidental in the fair burden sharing discussions. Concerns about perceived infractions of sovereignty or criticisms of internal affairs have kept UNFCCC-centric justice analyses firmly focused on state-to-state comparisons.

Claiming **justice for people/peoples** immediately calls into question states' legitimacy in terms of adequately protecting, providing for, and representing their citizens. This could, to some extent, cause some complications for civil society organizations that work to defend national interests within the UNFCCC but also recognize that certain structures deepen inequalities domestically. As Jolene Lin (2014) has noted with regard to legal approaches, it is possible that some forms of pressure – such as public litigation – have been avoided by civil society in the global South out of a desire not to erode the negotiating positions of their governments at the international level.

Similarly, the people-focused approach to climate justice mobilizing is in tension with the green growth form of transformation, which, in its espousal of technological solutions within the framework of capitalism, reinforces discourses that downplay the importance of individual rights holders. Indeed, one of the roots of mobilization emerges from anti-corporate organizing insisting on 'people before profits.'

Overall, the vision of justice and transformation in this divergent narrative stresses critiques that go far deeper than simply addressing climate change. They point to spiritual re-engagement with what it means to live well, a multitude of localized engagements and restored connections among humans as well as with nonhuman entities, and a deep commitment to the voices and participation of actual people. In addition, they recognize that injustices are interconnected and that justice demands more than radical emission reductions. These kinds of claims resonate strongly with those promoting a more transformative approach to transitional justice.

Just as in other contexts, this kind of mobilization faces challenges in the climate context, particularly in light of the urgency of extremely deep mitigation action in the near term. Although changes in life values toward *Buen Vivir* or re-engagement with indigenous knowledge would likely lead to sustained mitigation reductions, these may also be quite slow. Similarly, although a more participatory and democratic decision-making process rooted in local specificities may support justice in most contexts, this may not benefit those facing the most intense climate impacts now. To the extent that the climate problem also involves technological innovation, it is unclear how this movement would support the scale-up of the clean energy technologies needed, even if only to address basic energy needs associated with sustainable development.

Integrating narratives in tension

At first glance these two views of what is needed beyond the UNFCCC seem directly at odds with one another. The convergent climate story focuses almost entirely on planetary-level threats and accordingly centers on rapid emission reductions and large-scale (or scalable) technological innovations as solutions. Over time attention to the need to generate momentum in these efforts and reduce resistance from powerful actors has also led to awareness of the need for economic incentives to be aligned with the kinds of emission reductions needed. In this narrative distributive or procedural justice for individuals per se is not a goal, but it is mobilized out of a recognition that deep mitigation is a basic requirement of protection for the most vulnerable. However, this notion of justice is thin: it acknowledges obligations to not cause existential threats, but has nothing to say about the positive demands for justice in people's lives or their ability to have a voice, nor about how we ought to live together generally.

On the flip side, the divergent narrative of climate justice organizing is built around a rich set of justice principles and practices, from commitments to inclusivity, to those insisting on genuine participation and voice for those most affected by climate change and broader pressures. This pathway offers a vision for internal and external transformation: the change is measured not only by the amount of emissions reduced or avoided but also by how we relate to ourselves and to each other. Notably this story is directly antagonistic toward the use of capitalist logics and incentives to address climate change, and although climate change is part of the goal, in reality its aims are much broader. A world of adequate emissions reductions would not, from this perspective, necessarily be just.

The convergent and divergent climate change narratives do, however, contain some overlaps. More to the point, they could be placed in tension in productive ways. The first major overlap is the sheer extent of change both see as desirable or necessary. As seen in critiques of incremental reformism in transitional justice, these two stories suggest that a desirable future will diverge in fundamental ways from the current way of doing things. Both insist that a very different world must become possible.

The second overlap lies in their mutual recognition that power to transform does not reside in the state but in the actions and internal value propositions of ordinary people and their collective representations. Although states may be called upon to guide these transformations – whether by helping to set an agenda, protecting specific people, or enforcing particular standards – the state itself is not the central actor. If nothing else, this recognition of the limited agency of states highlights the importance of engaging outside the UNFCCC and beyond the norms of state responsibility.

If we are to address climate change, both these narratives declare, we need to find ways of mobilizing all kinds of actors in a self-generating and emergent way. For the convergent story, green growth provides the internal engine for momentum because each actor could take climate action in alignment with its own self-interest (defined roughly economically). For the divergent story, transformation is manifested through internal reflection processes and actions taken in solidarity toward ensuring the dignity of human life within and beyond the climate context.

In addition, holding the two narratives in tension draws attention to several possible strategies for addressing climate change. The ability of the green growth narrative to harness self-interest as a driver of climate action has strong appeal when juxtaposed with the depth of climate action required to avoid serious climate impacts. However, the justice concerns that emerge from this approach are significant and cannot be overlooked. This is ultimately the central tension for transformation in this context: How do we achieve the depth of emissions reductions needed while also moving toward a more just world?

Here, we consider three possible ways forward: inclusive low-carbon development pathways, justice-focused policy analysis, and capacity building. These pathways are all currently being used in some capacity by some actors, but they could be significantly augmented.

One potentially transformative narrative that has been emerging from efforts both to acknowledge strong justice claims and to engage with the sheer mitigation pressure imposed by planetary boundaries has centered on **inclusive low-carbon development** pathways. Rhetoric concerning the importance of such pathways has been around for many years, but several innovative projects have attempted to make them a reality. One of these, the Mitigation Action Plans and Scenarios (MAPS)[7] program, worked with academics, state and subnational jurisdictions, communities, and corporate stakeholders across four countries to explore what low-emissions pathways that address the scope of human development needs on the ground entail. The pathways generated by this project echo global calls for mitigation action, but are designed also to resonate with the bottom-up justice concerns emerging from wider mobilization. The book that documents lessons from the program starts by posing this central question (in text so large it takes up an entire page): "Can the world prevent catastrophic climate change while building the energy systems needed to sustain growth, create jobs and lift millions of people out of poverty?" (Raubenheimer et al. 2015).

Other initiatives, such as the Deep Decarbonisation Pathways Project,[8] have also sought to square the circle of low-carbon development, largely through the examination of technological option sets. However, the MAPS program sets an example of how the low-carbon development challenge could be addressed through participatory methods – another effort to include the basic claims of justice emerging from grassroots organizing. The project included substantial facilitation and stakeholder engagement throughout, resulting in the identification of potential technical pathways that resonated with the actual lived experiences and political limitations of the countries in question. Efforts to place human development needs at the heart of any climate mitigation strategy are one way to at least partially combine the insistence on justice emerging from climate justice organizing with the recognition that mitigation must be steeper and more systematic than might be achieved without some coordinated effort.

What seems remarkable about the MAPS program was its awareness not only of the end goals, but also of the importance of attempting to build in bottom-up and participatory processes. This is exactly the transformation question we must address – although, as climate justice organizers would remind us, these changes need to extend beyond energy systems alone. Here we reflect back on the term 'inclusive' to advocate for discussions of low-carbon development that are not only participatory but also inclusive of broader considerations of what it means to live well. One of the powerful contributions of climate justice mobilization around concepts such as *Buen Vivir* is that it highlights the importance of laying the foundations for (or returning to already existing but marginalized foundations for) genuinely different development pathways.[9]

In the face of unimaginably steep mitigation targets and substantial global inequality, efforts to address human development needs must look deeper than technological approaches to low-carbon development. We need to find ways to live fully that are built on fundamentally different relationships with each other and the planet if long-term mitigation goals are to be achieved. This entails engagement with people's central value propositions about what it really does mean to live well. China has articulated a vision for itself as an 'eco-civilization' (Chun 2015), Bolivia and Ecuador have at least rhetorically embraced *Buen Vivir* in their approaches to climate policy, and statements from a number of religious leaders (Pope Francis 2015; IFEES 2015) have started to fuel a wider and deeper conversation about what an inclusive low-carbon development approach could entail. The inclusive low-carbon development processes we propose would feature not only integration of the technological and political resources available and needed for implementation, but also engagement with culturally rooted notions of what kinds of societies we would like to have in the context of human development needs and global pressures manifested by climate change. It is important to note that these processes could apply equally to developed and developing countries: indeed, the cultural challenges posed by inclusive low-carbon development pathways are equally, if not more, profound for developed countries than developing ones.

A second and highly related approach to leveraging the momentum of green growth without losing substantive attention to justice could be the development and use of **justice-based policy analysis**. Although states are not the core actors in these models of transformation, they necessarily retain an important role as facilitators and enablers of action. Encouraging states to use a justice lens to evaluate and guide regulatory efforts would be one way of shaping decision-making processes over time toward a more just future.

Justice-based policy analyses are already conducted by many groups – usually academics, although sometimes also progressive think tanks – and can take multiple forms. For instance, a wide variety of economic analyses examining common mitigation policies have sought to identify heterogeneous implications across sub-populations and demographic groups (Gordon, Burtraw, and Roberton 2015; Gough 2013; Nelson, Simshauser, and Kelley 2011; Neuhoff et al. 2013; Hallegatte and Rozenberg 2017). This work has taken a distinctly distributive justice focus and tends to limit analysis to economic implications only. In addition, this work to date has focused primarily on the issue of who loses from specific policies. One of the central concerns with reliance on green growth for climate action is the possibility that it could drive inequality if new opportunities systematically flow to those who are already advantaged. More dynamic engagement with the possible directionality of (in)equalities in a green growth context would be an important area for greater analytic investment.

Partially in contrast to the economics-oriented approach to analysis, a number of scholars have been advocating multicriteria analysis frameworks more capable of integrating a diversity of concerns into the advising process (Bell, Hobbs, and Ellis 2003; Munda 2004; Gamboa and Munda 2007). The benefit of these approaches is that a variety of different kinds of justice concerns, relating to the scope of potential implications faced by diverse populations, can be brought into the policy-making process. To some extent this approach has been applied to help mediate the justice concerns emerging from the CDM. After many years of debate about the potential for CDM projects to have negative ramifications for local human development, the CDM board developed a voluntary screening tool focused on identifying social impacts (UNFCCC 2014). Although voluntary for the CDM, this type of approach could be made mandatory within the UNFCCC – for instance, in conjunction with the SDM – or used by national or subnational jurisdictions.

Another suite of justice-sensitive policy analysis work has concentrated on developing vulnerability assessments. Recognition that climate change will have deeply uneven implications for populations both because of the variability of climate impacts and because of pre-existing inequalities and systemic processes of discrimination led to early recognition that climate policy analysis (regarding both mitigation and adaptation) needed to address variable vulnerability (Eakin 2005; Dow, Kasperson, and Bohn 2006; Adger 2006). Although the methodologies vary (Brouwer et al. 2007; Tschakert 2007; O'Brien et al. 2007), vulnerability as a framework has become increasingly central in both local and global conversations and is one way of building a greater suite of considerations into analyses of policy options.

For some, justice-oriented policy analysis tools are too labile and too close to incrementalism to warrant inclusion as a transformative approach to the climate justice conundrum. However, in light of the importance that climate justice mobilizing places on the development of norms, practices, and cultural shifts, justice-focused tools should be seen as potentially transformative. Even though these tools would likely be used by institutions within the UNFCCC and states, and so could be said to have limited scope, the decisions they would guide and the kinds of awareness they would build are potentially very wide reaching. Cultural world-views and norms are manifest in the technologies we employ, and this includes the technologies we use to guide our decisions. From this angle, insisting on the creation and use of tools explicitly designed to integrate justice concerns in climate policy design is a potentially transformative contribution. Importantly, because policy analysis tools are cultural artifacts tied to particular places and paradigms, a transformative approach to their design and implementation would insist on increased attention to the development of tools by and for those in the global South.

Finally, **capacity building in both the global North and the global South** could be another pathway for supporting transformative change that addresses the scale of the climate change problem and engages with bottom-up justice demands. Capacity building is not a new concept. It dates back to at least the 1980s, when development agencies began exploring different models of aid (Sagar 2000), and can refer to the capacity to implement particular policies or regulatory visions, as well as the capacity to envision and strategically create the conditions in which this implementation can occur. Within this diversity the central concerns have revolved around the establishment and support for institutions or practices that will facilitate human development. For some, capacity building is ultimately about buoying state capacities to effectively regulate and guide policy action in a context of rapid global change (Eakin and Lemos 2006). Others have centered their attention on the institutional and human resource capacities required to operationalize certain kinds of policy action (Okubo and Michaelowa 2010). Others yet, particularly in the adaptation context, have stressed multidimensional notions of capacity, tied to an even broader set of norms, practices, and resources (including 'soft' resources such as leadership), in addition to institutions (Gupta et al. 2010).

Capacity building in the climate context has long been an issue of concern for developing countries and gained significant momentum in the lead-up to the Paris Agreement. In 2001 the UNFCCC set up a capacity-building framework (UNFCCC 2001) and has conducted quasi-regular reviews of the issue ever since. In 2011 capacity building was slightly more formalized, and the Durban Forum on Capacity Building was established. These workshops are held annually as an open, facilitative event designed to encourage participants to share best practices. Although these workshops have been fairly low profile, they have also experienced less acrimony compared to most justice-related issues.[10] Capacity building turns out to be something of a motherhood and apple pie issue.

The Paris Agreement supports capacity building explicitly in two ways: the Paris Committee on Capacity Building (PCCB) and the Capacity Building Initiative for Transparency (CBIT). The PCCB is a fluid body whose terms are yet to be finalized, although it is expected to focus on coordinating the many areas of the UNFCCC already working on capacity-building components. In contrast, the CBIT is already monetized (by the Global Environment Facility) and ready to start working on efforts to help developing countries better track and understand their emissions portfolios. As Mizan Khan and his co-authors wryly note, "it would appear overall that developed country Parties are more interested in capacity building for transparency, than plugging any overall capacity gaps" (Khan et al. 2016: 10).

The difference in focus between the two forms of capacity building in the Paris Agreement is worth noting. The already-monetized CBIT targets the suite of institutional and human resources capacities essential for the development of a global carbon market, or any market-based mechanisms particular countries might wish to create. These are, essentially, the capacities needed to enable the green growth engine to drive emission reductions globally. However, the CBIT may not help address capacity building designed to facilitate public policy and human development more broadly. Here the PCCB might be of use, but it remains unclear how robust this institution will be. Neither the CBIT nor the PCCB resonates strongly with the calls for justice and transformation emerging from bottom-up climate justice organizing.

Based in a view that capacity building must be an endogenous process and accountable to the people it is supposed to benefit, Khan and his colleagues (2016) make several suggestions for a more transformative approach to capacity building. First, they suggest national capacity centers. These permanent centers would be responsible for assessing specific needs, exploring how best to address them, and strategically guiding the development of capacity-building programs capable of both envisioning and implementing policies and programs. This proposal stresses the need to move away from external consultants and toward national programs with self-identified and directed climate change capacities. They then propose a capacity mechanism at the international level that would help 'marshal resources' for capacity building and serve as a hub for knowledge exchange about capacity-building efforts globally.

Of all the suggestions out there to date, this model appears to respond best to the dual demands posed by the need to respond rapidly to climate change from both a mitigation and adaptation perspective, and to do so in ways that are rooted in the experiences of local communities. Although the model centers on institutional developments at the state and international levels, it recognizes that a range of other actors – including universities, donors, and civil society organizations – are instrumental to envisioning and achieving sustained improvements in the ability to appropriately guide policy. Working further with this proposal to support linkages between communities and national capacity centers, donors, universities, and NGOs would be one pathway forward. However, this model of capacity building remains exclusively targeted at the global South. A second line of thinking has focused on capacity building in the global North.

Although capacity building has traditionally been tied to addressing perceived lack of capacity in the global South, recent work has highlighted the limitations and incapacities linked to climate action experienced in the global North. Ambuj Sagar and Stacey VanDerveer challenge us to "turn the lens around" and highlight the "lack of attention (beyond a few environmental activists and academics) to the role of Northern behavioural patterns and policies as causal variables driving unsustainable development patterns and undermining Southern public-sector capacity" (Sagar and VanDeveer 2005: 18). They argue that capacity building must include work in the global North, designed to help key entities (they focus on donors and aid institutions) understand their own incapacities in managing to address core challenges of sustainable development, particularly in terms of the impacts these failures have on the global South.

Similarly, in their work Karen O'Brien and her co-authors argue for a view of capacity building centered on facilitating transformative changes in light of the depth of global sustainability challenges (O'Brien et al. 2013). In their proposal, universities – as central bodies responsible for capacity building – need to approach education for sustainability in a much more integrative way. Capacity building here revolves around enabling people to see and approach problems in different ways, including in self-critical and reflective modes capable of shifting paradigms and behaviors.

This line of thought resonates with some of the critiques emerging from transitional justice, in which mainstream institutional responses have failed to engage with broader issues associated with passive beneficiaries. One of the transformative shifts needed in these cases – and attempted in some – has been to generate cultural recognition of complex patterns of power and privilege. This is, essentially, the creation of a type of capacity, one that could be transformational, particularly as individuals and communities attempt to build solidarity across diverse experiences of climate change. When the organizers of the 2014 People's Climate March in New York City were faced with the challenge of building solidarity across diverse communities, they turned to the Jemez Principles to guide their work. Principle 6 is entitled "Commitment to Self-Transformation" (SNEEJ 1996). Within this paradigm, capacity building goes far beyond single institutions or mechanisms. Moreover, if solidarity is ultimately what is required for enabling an adequate global response to climate change, then this broader and more self-reflexive approach to capacity building may be absolutely essential.

If building solidarity is one of the most important aspects of the post-Paris era, then both these forms of capacity building are essential. Working to support those trying to develop strategic capacities that are attuned to the development and climate challenges specific to each developing country is one part of this. However, so, too, is the development of people's capacity in the global North to rethink their social, economic, and ecological lives. If the goal is to build a more just world in which far more people have access to human development, and far fewer people are likely to be harmed by climate change, then these two forms of capacity building need to be pursued in tandem.

Emergent transformative practices

By its nature transformation requires the mobilization of actors far beyond the immediate scope of control of governments or institutions. Transformation may reside as much, or more, in the ways in which individuals, private-sector entities, or governmental bodies at all scales understand the problem of climate change in an unequal world and its attendant solutions. Asserting the need for transformation is one thing, but developing strategies for purposefully initiating emergent and indeterminate processes is another. We argue here that the convergent narrative of climate change is essential – we really do have only one planet and we do all share it. But the divergent narrative of climate change, which forces us to look the depth of inequality at all scales of human experience squarely in the eye, is equally essential. How can we move toward a more just world without systematically engaging with what are currently peripheral voices, especially as many of them will be the most affected by the actions of those distant from them?

There are, as the saying goes, thousands of alternatives to the strategies we propose here. It is partly in recognition of this fact that we have focused on the ones we did: the three strategies we identify would, hopefully, be useful in making space for many more such strategies to be created and pursued by many more people and collective entities. For instance, our insistence that inclusive low-carbon development pathways be inclusive – not only of people but also of non-technicist perspectives – aims to articulate a space in which often sidelined voices and insights could be actively integrated into the climate and development discussions. There might be many different options that would only emerge when integration was supported in situ. Similarly, the development of justice-focused modes of analysis and support for strategic capacity building from a perspective of solidarity are strategies purposefully designed to have long-lasting and not entirely foreseeable results.

Pursuing these three strategies together could strengthen each of them. For example, being able to create and apply new tools for integrating justice concerns into climate policy design and implementation is a capacity that needs to be built. Without access to such tools and ways of thinking, low-carbon development plans could all too easily be rolled out without being inclusive. And yet without support for the creation of inclusive low-carbon development pathways in the first place, it may be difficult to mobilize institutions to actively invest in capacity building, or for individuals to gain the knowledge that comes only from experience in trying to create the kinds of shifts that these pathways would require. Transformation may be emergent by necessity, but this does not mean that we cannot, or should not, be focused on identifying ways to nurture it.

Notes

1 Solar radiation management technologies – such as the use of sulfate particles in the upper atmosphere – are another transformational option that some have argued may be essential for the achievement of high-ambition targets. These are more controversial and more experimental than carbon removal technologies, and so are not currently included in IAMs or other modeling efforts. As with carbon removal technologies, proponents have argued strongly for research and development investments in these technologies in order to more fully understand the risks, implications, and potential benefits they may create (Keith, Parson, and Morgan 2010; Parson and Keith 2013).

2 The number of studies documenting the politics of corporate engagement in mitigation policy are far too numerous to list. For discussions of corporate engagement with climate policy see (Victor 2009; Hoffmann 2007; Li et al. 2014; Harrison 2010; Bailey 2007; Colby 2000; Klinsky and Grubb 2015; Meckling 2011).

3 For instance, one of the most powerful utilities in the United States that is actively resisting the disruption distributed solar would entail is Arizona Public Service. The progenitor of the current utility was formed in 1884. The state of Arizona was created in 1912.

4 It should be noted that *Buen Vivir* has also been used by states, particularly Bolivia and Ecuador, in UNFCCC negotiations. Some would argue that geopolitically (internationally and domestically) states have co-opted this term and its tradition to pursue conventional development projects (Merino 2016).

5 The Jemez Principles for Democratic Organizing emerged from a multiday workshop held by the Southwest Network for Environmental and Economic Justice in New Mexico in 1996. The purpose of the workshop was to develop some guidelines for generating solidarity within activism focused on trade, globalization, and the environment.

6 There have been multiple People's Climate Marches. The largest to date were those in Copenhagen in 2009, New York in 2014 (http://2014.peoplesclimate.org/wrap-up/), and Washington, DC, in 2017.

7 The MAPS program resulted in a broad suite of products, from facilitation guides to country-specific energy guides and policy briefs with a domestic and international focus. These materials can be explored at http://mapsprogramme.org/.

8 This project featured sixteen country teams, each of which was charged with assessing which rapid mitigation pathways might work (technically) in that particular country (Bataille et al. 2016).

9 We have to acknowledge the intellectual contribution of José Alberto Garibaldi here. It was ongoing conversations he and Sonja Klinsky had about this topic for an unrelated project that provided the impetus for the articulation of these ideas here.

10 Sonja Klinsky has attended and participated in several of the Durban Forum on Capacity Building workshops, which is where the observation of their collegial, noncontentious tone comes from.

References

Adger, W. Neil. 2006. "Vulnerability." *Global Environmental Change* 16(3): 268–81.

Agrawala, Shardul, Maelis Carraro, Nicholas Kingsmill, Elisa Lanzi, Michael Mullan, and Guillaume Prudent-Richard. 2013. "Private Sector Engagement in Adaptation to Climate Change: Approaches to Managing Climate Risks." *OECD Environment Working Papers, No. 39*, OECD Publishing.

Anderson, Kevin, and Glen Peters. 2016. "The Trouble With Negative Emissions." *Science* 354(6309): 182–83.

Arbour, Louise. 2007. "Economic and Social Justice for Societies in Transition Essay." *New York University Journal of International Law and Politics* 40: 1–28.

Arriaza, Laura, and Naomi Roht-Arriaza. 2008. "Social Reconstruction as a Local Process." *International Journal of Transitional Justice* 2(2): 152–72.

Arthur, Paige. 2009. "How 'Transitions' Reshaped Human Rights: A Conceptual History of Transitional Justice." *Human Rights Quarterly* 31: 321–67.

Bailey, Ian. 2007. "Neoliberalism, Climate Governance and the Scalar Politics of EU Emissions Trading." *Area* 39(4): 431–42.

Bataille, Chris, Henri Waisman, Michel Colombier, Laura Segafredo, and Jim Williams. 2016. "The Deep Decarbonization Pathways Project (DDPP): Insights and Emerging Issues." *Climate Policy* 16(suppl.1): S1–6.

Bell, Michelle L., Benjamin F. Hobbs, and Hugh Ellis. 2003. "The Use of Multi-Criteria Decision-Making Methods in the Integrated Assessment of Climate Change: Implications for IA Practitioners." *Socio-Economic Planning Sciences* 37(4): 289–316.

Bergsmo, Morten, César Rodriguez-Garavito, Pablo Kalmanovitz, and Maria Paula Saffon, eds. 2010. *Distributive Justice in Transitions*. 1st edition. Oslo: Torkel Opsahl Academic EPublisher.

Brankovic, Jasmina. 2018. "Civil Society in African Transitional Justice: Comparing Theory and Practice." In *Advocating Transitional Justice in Africa: The Role of Civil Society*, edited by Jasmina Brankovic and Hugo van der Merwe, 1–16. New York: Springer Press.

Brankovic, Jasmina, and Hugo van der Merwe, eds. 2018. *Advocating Transitional Justice in Africa: The Role of Civil Society*. New York: Springer Press.

Brouwer, Roy, Sonia Akter, Luke Brander, and Enamul Haque. 2007. "Socioeconomic Vulnerability and Adaptation to Environmental Risk: A Case Study of Climate Change and Flooding in Bangladesh." *Risk Analysis* 27(2): 313–26.

Brown, Kris, and Fionnuala Ní Aoláin. 2015. "Through the Looking Glass: Transitional Justice Futures through the Lens of Nationalism, Feminism and Transformative Change." *International Journal of Transitional Justice* 9(1): 127–49.

Chakravarty, Shoibal, Ananth Chikkatur, Heleen de Coninck, Stephen Pacala, Robert Socolow, and Massimo Tavoni. 2009. "Sharing Global CO2 Emission Reductions Among One Billion High Emitters." *Proceedings of the National Academy of Sciences* 106(29): 11884–8.

Chun, Zhang. 2015. "China's New Blueprint for an 'Ecological Civilization.'" *The Diplomat*, September. https://thediplomat.com/2015/09/chinas-new-blueprint-for-an-ecological-civilization/.

CJN! 2004. "Climate Justice Now! A Call for People's Action Against Climate Change." *Climate Justice Now!* http://climatejustice.blogspot.com/2004_11_23_archive.html.

Claeys, Priscilla, and Deborah Delgado Pugley. 2017. "Peasant and Indigenous Transnational Social Movements Engaging With Climate Justice." *Canadian Journal of Development Studies/Revue Canadienne d'Etudes Du Développement* 38(3): 325–40.

Colby, Bonnie. 2000. "Cap-and-Trade Policy Challenges: A Tale of Three Markets." *Land Economics* 76(4): 638–58.

CPLC. 2017. "Carbon Pricing Leadership Report 2016–2017." *Carbon Pricing Leadership Report, World Bank*. http://pubdocs.worldbank.org/en/183521492529539277/WBG-CPLC-2017-Leadership-Report-DIGITAL-Single-Pages.pdf.

Dow, Kristin, Roger Kasperson, and Maria Bohn. 2006. "Exploring the Social Justice Implications of Adaptation and Vulnerability." In *Fairness in Adaptation to Climate Change*, edited by W. N. Adger, Jouni Paavola, S. Huq, and M. J. Mace, 79–96. Cambridge, MA: MIT Press.

Eakin, Hallie. 2005. "Institutional Change, Climate Risk, and Rural Vulnerability: Cases from Central Mexico." *World Development* 33(11): 1923–38.

Eakin, Hallie, and Maria Carmen Lemos. 2006. "Adaptation and the State: Latin America and the Challenge of Capacity-Building Under Globalization." *Global Environmental Change* 16(1): 7–18.

Edenhofer, Ottmar, Ramon Pichs-Madruga, Youba Sokona, Ellie Farahani, Susanne Kadner, Kristin Seyboth, and Anna Adler. 2014. "Summary for Policy Makers: Climate Change 2014: Mitigation of Climate Change." *Contribution of Working Group III to the Fifth Assessment Report of the Intergovernmental Panel in Climate Change*. Cambridge: Cambridge University Press.

Eriksen, Safania, Hans Henrik Samuelson, Ronacke Monabay, and Malte Timpte. 2009. "Klimaforum09 People's Climate Summit: Evaluation Report." *Klimaforum09*. http://klimaforum.org/Evaluation_Report_Klimaforum09_090310.pdf.

Fraser, Nancy. 2001. "Recognition Without Ethics?" *Theory, Culture & Society* 18(2–3): 21–42.

Gamboa, Gonzalo, and Giuseppe Munda. 2007. "The Problem of Windfarm Location: A Social Multi-Criteria Evaluation Framework." *Energy Policy* 35(3): 1564–83.

GAWP. 2011. "Waste Pickers and Allies Demand that the CDM Executive Board Stop Ducking Its Responsibilities." *Global Alliance of Waste Pickers.* http://globalrec. org/2011/12/01/press-release-waste-pickers-and-allies-demand-that-the-cdm-executive-board-stop-ducking-its-responsibilities/.

Geels, Frank W., Benjamin K. Sovacool, Tim Schwanen, and Steve Sorrell. 2017. "The Socio-Technical Dynamics of Low-Carbon Transitions." *Joule* 1(3): 463–79.

Gordon, Hal, Dallas Burtraw, and Williams Roberton. 2015. "A Microsimulation Model of the Distributional Impacts of Climate Policies." *Resources for the Future.* www.rff.org/research/publications/microsimulation-model-distributional-impacts-climate-policies.

Gough, Ian. 2013. "Carbon Mitigation Policies, Distributional Dilemmas and Social Policies." *Journal of Social Policy* 42(2): 191–213.

Gready, Paul, and Simon Robins. 2014. "From Transitional to Transformative Justice: A New Agenda for Practice." *International Journal of Transitional Justice* 8(3): 339–61.

Grubb, Michael. 2014. *Planetary Economics: Energy, Climate Change and the Three Domains of Sustainable Development.* 1st edition. New York: Routledge.

Gupta, Joyeeta, Catrien Termeer, Judith Klostermann, Sander Meijerink, Margo van den Brink, Pieter Jong, and Sibout Nooteboom. 2010. "The Adaptive Capacity Wheel: A Method to Assess the Inherent Characteristics of Institutions to Enable the Adaptive Capacity of Society." *Environmental Science & Policy* 13(6): 459–71.

Hallegatte, Stephane, and Julie Rozenberg. 2017. "Climate Change Through a Poverty Lens." *Nature Climate Change* 7(4): 250–6.

Harrison, Kathryn. 2010. "The Comparative Politics of Carbon Taxation." *Annual Review of Law and Social Science* 6(1): 507–29.

Heede, Richard. 2014. "Tracing Anthropogenic Carbon Dioxide and Methane Emissions to Fossil Fuel and Cement Producers, 1854–2010." *Climatic Change* 122(1–2): 229–41.

Hoffmann, Volker H. 2007. "EU ETS and Investment Decisions: The Case of the German Electricity Industry." *European Management Journal* 25(6): 464–74.

Hong, Sanghyun, Corey J. A. Bradshaw, and Barry W. Brook. 2015. "Global Zero-Carbon Energy Pathways Using Viable Mixes of Nuclear and Renewables." *Applied Energy* 143(April): 451–9.

IEA, OECD, and World Bank. 2010. "The Scope of Fossil-Fuel Subsidies in 2009 and a Roadmap for Phasing Out Fossil-Fuel Subsidies." www.oecd.org/env/cc/46575783.pdf.

IFEES. 2015. "Islamic Declaration on Global Climate Change." www.ifees.org.uk/declaration.

Indigenous Environmental Network. n.d. "REDD – Reaping Profits from Evictions, Land-grabs, Deforestation and Destruction of Biodiversity." www.ienearth.org/REDD.

Jolly, Suyash, Rob Raven, and Henny Romijn. 2012. "Upscaling of Business Model Experiments in Off-Grid PV Solar Energy in India." *Sustainability Science* 7(2): 199–212.

Keith, David W, Edward Parson, and M. Granger Morgan. 2010. "Research on Global Sun Block Needed Now." *Nature* 463(7280): 426–27.

Khan, Mizan, Ambuj Sagar, Saleemul Huq, and Penda Thiam. 2016. "Capacity Building Under the Paris Agreement." European Capacity Building Initiative.

Klinsky, Sonja, and Michael Grubb. 2015. "From Theory to Practice: Climate Policy and Political Feasibility." In *Decarbonizing the World Economy*, edited by Terry Barker and Douglas Crawford-Brown, 259–308. London: Imperial College Press.

Kousky, Carolyn, and Roger Cooke. 2015. "Climate Change and Risk Management: Challenges for Insurance, Adaptation, and Loss Estimation." *Working Paper DP 09-03-REV,*

Resources for the Future. www.rff.org/research/publications/climate-change-and-risk-management-challenges-insurance-adaptation-and-loss.

Lackner, Klaus S. 2003. "A Guide to CO2 Sequestration." *Science* 300(5626): 1677–78.

Laplante, Lisa J. 2008. "Transitional Justice and Peace Building: Diagnosing and Addressing the Socioeconomic Roots of Violence Through a Human Rights Framework." *International Journal of Transitional Justice* 2(3): 331–55.

Li, Jizhen, Si Zhang, Poh Kam Wong, and Xiaolan Fu. 2014. "Harnessing Internal and External Resources for Innovation in Emerging Economies." *Journal of Chinese Economic and Business Studies* 12(2): 99–101.

Lin, Jolene. 2014. "Litigating Climate Change in Asia." *Climate Law* 4(1–2): 140–49.

Madlingozi, Tshepo. 2010. "On Transitional Justice Entrepreneurs and the Production of Victims." *Journal of Human Rights Practice* 2(2): 208–28.

Mamdani, Mahmood. 2000. "The Truth According to the Truth and Reconciliation Commission." In *The Politics of Memory: Truth, Healing and Social Justice*, edited by Ifi Amadiume and Abdullahi An-Na'im, 176–83. London: Zed Books.

Mani, Rama. 2005. "Reparations as a Component of Transitional Justice: Pursuing 'Reparative Justice' in the Aftermath of Violent Conflict." In *Out of the Ashes: Reparation for Victims of Gross and Systematic Human Rights Violations*, edited by Koen De Feyter, Stephan Parmentier, Marc Bossuyt, and Paul Lemmens, 53–82. Antwerp: Intersentia.

Matthaei, Julie. 2012. "Tina, Tata, the Solidarity Economy and Women." *InGenere* (blog). www.ingenere.it/en/articles/tina-tata-solidarity-economy-and-women.

McAuliffe, Padraig. 2017. *Transformative Transitional Justice and the Malleability of Post-Conflict States*. Cheltenham: Edward Elgar Publishing.

McEvoy, Kieran, and Lorna McGregor, eds. 2008. *Transitional Justice from Below: Grassroots Activism and the Struggle for Change*. Oxford: Hart Publishing.

Meckling, Jonas. 2011. *Carbon Coalitions Business, Climate Politics, and the Rise of Emissions Trading*. Cambridge, MA: MIT Press.

Merino, Roger. 2016. "An Alternative to 'Alternative Development'? Buen Vivir and Human Development in Andean Countries." *Oxford Development Studies* 44(3): 271–86.

Millar, Richard J., Jan S. Fuglestvedt, Pierre Friedlingstein, Joeri Rogelj, Michael J. Grubb, H. Damon Matthews, and Ragnhild B. Skeie. 2017. "Emission Budgets and Pathways Consistent With Limiting Warming to 1.5 °C." *Nature Geoscience* 10(10).

Miller, Zinaida. 2013. "(Re)Distributing Transition." *International Journal of Transitional Justice* 7(2): 370–80.

Monni, Salvatore, and Massimo Pallottino. 2015. "A New Agenda for International Development Cooperation: Lessons Learnt From the Buen Vivir Experience." *Development* 58(1): 49–57.

Muller, Benito, and Lavan Mahadeva. 2013. "The Oxford Approach: Operationalizing the UNFCCC Principle of 'Respective Capabilities.'" *Oxford Institute for Energy Studies*.

Munda, Giuseppe. 2004. "Social Multi-Criteria Evaluation: Methodological Foundations and Operational Consequences." *European Journal of Operational Research* 158(3): 662–77.

Nelson, Tim, Paul Simshauser, and Simon Kelley. 2011. "Australian Residential Solar Feed-in Tariffs: Industry Stimulus or Regressive Form of Taxation?" September. http://search.informit.com.au/documentSummary;dn=507147507129574;res=IELBUS.

Neuhoff, Karsten, Stefan Bach, Jochen Diekmann, Martin Beznoska, and Tarik El-Laboudy. 2013. "Distributional Effects of Energy Transition: Impacts of Renewable Electricity Support in Germany." *Economics of Energy & Environmental Policy* 2(1).

Nixon, Rob. 2014. "The Great Acceleration and the Great Divergence: Vulnerability in the Anthropocene." *Profession*. https://profession.mla.hcommons.org/2014/03/19/the-great-acceleration-and-the-great-divergence-vulnerability-in-the-anthropocene.

O'Brien, Karen, Siri Eriksen, Lynn P. Nygaard, and Ane Schjolden. 2007. "Why Different Interpretations of Vulnerability Matter in Climate Change Discourses." *Climate Policy* 7(1): 73–88.

O'Brien, Karen, Jonathan Reams, Anne Caspari, Andrew Dugmore, Maryam Faghihimani, Ioan Fazey, and Heide Hackmann. 2013. "You Say You Want a Revolution? Transforming Education and Capacity Building in Response to Global Change." *Environmental Science & Policy*, Special Issue: Responding to the Challenges of Our Unstable Earth (RESCUE), 28(Supplement C): 48–59.

Okello, Moses Chrispus. 2010. "Afterword: Elevating Transitional Local Justice or Crystallizing Global Governance?" In *Localizing Transitional Justice: Interventions and Priorities After Mass Violence*, edited by Rosalind Shaw, Lars Waldorf, and Pierre Hazan, 275–84. Stanford, CA: Stanford University Press.

Okubo, Yuri, and Axel Michaelowa. 2010. "Effectiveness of Subsidies for the Clean Development Mechanism: Past Experiences with Capacity Building in Africa and LDCs." *Climate and Development* 2(1): 30–49.

Pacala, Stephen, and Robert Socolow. 2004. "Stabilization Wedges: Solving the Climate Problem for the Next 50 Years with Current Technologies." *Science* 305(5686): 968–72.

Parson, Edward A., and David W. Keith. 2013. "End the Deadlock on Governance of Geoengineering Research." *Science* 339(6125): 1278–79.

Pauw, Peter 2015. "Not a Panacea: Private-Sector Engagement in Adaptation and Adaptation Finance in Developing Countries." *Climate Policy* 15(5): 583–603.

Pope Francis. 2015. "Encyclical Letter Laudato Si' of the Holy Father Francis on Care for Our Common Home." The Holy See. http://w2.vatican.va/content/francesco/en/encyclicals/documents/papa-francesco_20150524_enciclica-laudato-si.html.

PWCCC. 2010. "People's Agreement on Climate Change and the Rights of Mother Earth: Final Declaration of the World People's Conference on Climate Change and the Rights of Mother Earth." *World People's Conference on Climate Change and the Rights of Mother Earth*. Cochabamba, Bolivia. https://pwccc.wordpress.com/support.

Raubenheimer, Stefan, Marta Torres, Andrea Rudnick, Michelle Toit, Harald Winkler, Jose Manuel Sandoval, and Emilio La Rovere. 2015. "Stories from the South: Exploring Low Carbon Development Pathways." *SouthSouthNorth*. www.mapsprogramme.org/wp-content/uploads/Stories-from-the-South-Online-Edition-7.1MB.pdf.

Robins, Simon, and Erik Wilson. 2015. "Participatory Methodologies with Victims: An Emancipatory Approach to Transitional Justice Research." *Canadian Journal of Law & Society/La Revue Canadienne Droit et Société* 30(2): 219–36.

Rockström, Johan, Will Steffen, Kevin Noone, Åsa Persson, F. Stuart III Chapin, Eric Lambin, and Timothy Lenton. 2009. "Planetary Boundaries: Exploring the Safe Operating Space for Humanity." *Ecology and Society* 14(2).

Rogelj, Joeri, Gunnar Luderer, Robert C. Pietzcker, Elmar Kriegler, Michiel Schaeffer, Volker Krey, and Keywan Riahi. 2015. "Energy System Transformations for Limiting End-of-Century Warming to Below 1.5 °C." *Nature Climate Change* 5(6): 519–27.

Saffon, Maria Paula, and Rodrigo Uprimny. 2010. "Distributive Justice and the Restitution of Dispossessed Land in Colombia." In *Distributive Justice in Transitions*, edited by Morten

Bergsmo, César Rodriguez-Garavito, Pablo Kalmanovitz, and Maria Paula Saffon, 379–420. Oslo: Torkel Opsahl Academic EPublisher.

Sagar, Ambuj. 2000. "Capacity Development for the Environment: A View for the South, a View for the North." *Annual Review of Energy and the Environment* 25(1): 377–439.

Sagar, Ambuj, and Stacy D. VanDeveer. 2005. "Capacity Development for the Environment: Broadening the Scope." *Global Environmental Politics* 5(3): 14–22.

Schmid, Evelyne, and Aoife Nolan. 2014. "'Do No Harm'? Exploring the Scope of Economic and Social Rights in Transitional Justice." *International Journal of Transitional Justice* 8(3): 362–82.

Sharp, Dustin N. 2015. "Emancipating Transitional Justice from the Bonds of the Paradigmatic Transition." *International Journal of Transitional Justice* 9(1): 150–69.

Shaw, Rosalind, Lars Waldorf, and Pierre Hazan, eds. 2010. *Localizing Transitional Justice: Interventions and Priorities After Mass Violence.* 1st edition. Stanford, CA: Stanford University Press.

Shove, Elizabeth. 2010. "Beyond the ABC: Climate Change Policy and Theories of Social Change." *Environment and Planning A* 42(6): 1273–85.

Sishuba, Yanelisa, Sindiswa Nunu, Nompumelelo Njana, Agnes Ngxuma, Brian Mphahlele, and Jasmina Brankovic. 2017. "Conducting Participatory Action Research With Apartheid Survivors: Lessons From 'Addressing Socioeconomic Drivers of Violence in Khulumani Communities.'" Cape Town: Khulumani Support Group Western Cape and Centre for the Study of Violence and Reconciliation.

SNEEJ. 1996. "Jemez Principles for Democratic Organizing." *Southwest Network for Environmental and Economic Justice.* www.ejnet.org/ej/jemez.pdf.

Steffen, Will, Katherine Richardson, Johan Rockström, Sarah E. Cornell, Ingo Fetzer, Elena M. Bennett, and Reinette Biggs. 2015. "Planetary Boundaries: Guiding Human Development on a Changing Planet." *Science* 347(6223).

Sriram, Chandra Lekha. 2007. "Justice as Peace? Liberal Peacebuilding and Strategies of Transitional Justice." *Global Society* 21(4): 579–91.

Tschakert, Petra. 2007. "Views from the Vulnerable: Understanding Climatic and Other Stressors in the Sahel." *Global Environmental Change* 17(3–4): 381–96.

UNFCCC. 2001. "Report from the Seventh Session of the Conference of Parties (COP7)." *Fifteenth Sessions of the Subsidiary Bodies, 29 October–9 November 2001, Marrakech, Morocco.*

UNFCCC. 2014. "Voluntary Tool for Describing Sustainable Development Co-Benefits (SDC) of CDM Project Activities or Programmes of Activities." https://cdm.unfccc.int/Reference/tools/index.html.

UNFCCC. 2015. "Non-State Zone for Climate Action." http://climateaction.unfccc.int.

United States Agency for International Development. 2014. "Community Participation in Transitional Justice: A Role for Participatory Research." https://www.usaid.gov/sites/default/files/documents/1866/CPTJUSAID.pdf.

Van der Merwe, Hugo, and Jasmina Brankovic. 2016. "The Role of African Civil Society in Shaping National Transitional Justice Agendas and Policies." *Acta Juridica:* 225–46.

Victor, David. 2009. "The Politics of Fossil-Fuel Subsidies." *IISD Global Subsidy Initiative.*

Victor, David. 2015. "Embed the Social Sciences in Climate Policy." *Nature.* www.nature.com.ezproxy1.lib.asu.edu/polopoly_fs/1.17206!/menu/main/topColumns/topLeftColumn/pdf/520027a.pdf.

Ware, Michael. 2014. "Toward an Anticapitalist Climate Justice Movement." *International Socialist Review* 94. https://isreview.org/issue/94/toward-anticapitalist-climate-justice-movement.

World Economic Forum. 2013. "The Green Investment Report: The Ways and Means to Unlock Private Finance for Green Growth." www3.weforum.org/docs/WEF_GreenInvestment_Report_2013.pdf.

Conclusion
Building solidarity across divides

The social psychologist of justice Melvin Lerner once described justice as frustrating because of its "chameleon-like quality" (Lerner 1975: 2). Justice can be ambiguous: what is seemingly just from one vantage point may be unjust from another. This ambiguity can reside within individuals but also across them. What seems just to you based on your position may be seen as unjust to me when viewed from mine. Justice claims can be transformational. Their moral clarity can cause us to reconsider practices and viewpoints previously assumed to be just, but shown to be the opposite. But justice – more accurately a sense of injustice – can also be visceral. The depth of moral outrage when faced with injustice has fueled more than one revolution. Debates about justice are too powerful to isolate in a corner or slip under a rug.

The issue of justice in the climate context is no less troublesome. Opposing claims abound. Actors use justice claims communicatively to articulate passionately felt experiences of injustice, and persuasively to shape contexts around their own interests. It is precisely because justice is an ambiguous and powerful concept that we need to think carefully about how justice claims have been and could be used in efforts to address climate change. Frankly speaking, the situation is too important to sideline debates about justice. If justice tensions are not addressed in the climate context now, they will re-emerge to be addressed later.

Moreover, failing to seriously engage with justice tensions now could erode our collective capacity to achieve the depth of action needed to meet the core objectives of the UNFCCC. The global regime committed in 1992 to avoid dangerous anthropogenic climate change. Keeping average global increases to below 2°C – much less 1.5°C – compared to preindustrial levels and ensuring adequate protections for those most likely to be affected requires greater collective action by all actors than ever seen before due to shifts in where emissions have been, are, and will be produced. Now would be an ideal time to chart a path that will result in the long-term legitimacy and effectiveness of the climate regime. We argue that, based on lessons from transitional justice experiences worldwide, achieving this long-term legitimacy demands a systematic vision of how justice concerns could be addressed.

The motivating insight behind this book was that although the dilemmas at the heart of climate change justice tensions are profound, they are not unique.

There is, unfortunately, no shortage of situations in which unavoidably interdependent people have had to manage the differential implications of historically rooted harms while collectively attempting to build a more just future. Transitional justice processes have been widely used to help people navigate the moral and political challenges of simultaneously addressing backward-oriented justice claims and forward-oriented efforts toward solidarity.

Broadly speaking transitional justice emerges from the recognition that historically rooted events, systems, and norms responsible for imposing harms on particular populations must be included in any viable pathway toward a future in which all people are able to lead full, flourishing lives. In this tradition, the voices and experiences of those who have been harmed are essential, even though, politically speaking, they may also be peripheral to the centers of power. Peripheral voices are necessary, not only due to the obligations of morality, but also because it is precisely the experiences of those who have been harmed and previously excluded that must guide efforts to build a more just, peaceful, and ultimately legitimate new regime. One of the challenges for those engaged in designing and implementing a transitional justice process is finding ways of systematically decentering privileged voices and actively building space for voices and concerns on the periphery. It is not about replacing one set of privileges or claims with another, but about building a foundation for greater solidarity across the divisions that have characterized the specific political, social, economic, and ecological contexts.

From this perspective transitional justice is not just a collection of tools, but a lens through which to view the challenge of building cooperation across deep fractures in a context of unavoidable interdependency. And when we look at the global climate regime through this lens, we see that far from being irrelevant to the climate context, transitional justice approaches are already, albeit informally, being used in the climate context. As is common across many transitional justice processes, the Paris Agreement emerged out of sustained conflict centered on how to balance responsibility for the past with the demands of the future at precisely the time when the sheer scope of the mitigation and climate impact challenges were starting to be understood.

Charged with the seemingly impossible feat of integrating 'common but different responsibilities and respective capabilities' in a regime that would be 'applicable to all,' the Paris Agreement sketched out a 'package deal' that aims to provide a foundation for long-term cooperation. Without calling it reparations, the agreement includes some provisions for adaptation and loss and damage. Without calling it amnesty, the agreement lays down some boundaries to states parties' liability for climate impacts. Without calling it institutional reform, the Agreement establishes a number of new institutions, and tweaks several others, designed to facilitate the ultimate goal of the UNFCCC: avoiding dangerous anthropogenic climate change. Without calling it transformation, the Agreement hopes to trigger 'momentum for change' across a far broader set of actors than are legally included in its provisions.[1]

The climate regime's informal application of measures common to transitional justice makes especially relevant the answer to the question: How could lessons from transitional justice be used in the climate context? Many transitional justice processes have not been successful. Some efforts have resulted in sustained, and sometimes intensified, conflict. Other efforts have looked like they would be successful but failed to follow up on wider, more transformational efforts that addressed underlying conflicts and challenges. The concern here is that the Paris Agreement alone is going to be insufficient for enabling the depth of change needed – in this case more ambitious climate action than ever before seen. One of the strengths of explicitly examining this challenge through a transitional justice lens is that it forces us to think more broadly about what is needed to create and sustain the kinds of solidarity and cooperative collective action that achieving these goals will require. No one is solving the emissions challenge alone. And no one is immune to the impacts of significant climate change.

Despite the many references to notions of solidarity in and around the negotiations (UNDP 2008; Rajamani 2010; Burkett 2015), the Agreement cannot be expected to build cooperation automatically. Without explicit thought about how solidarity – or at least recognition of mutual interdependence – is established and nurtured, we may miss opportunities to build trust and find common ground. As has been learned, and relearned, by so many social movements, solidarity does not come from ignoring differences in position or privilege. In fact, the opposite is true. Although it is rarely comfortable, solidarity emerges when we thoughtfully and courageously engage with our privileges and disadvantages, and are able to hear each other's concerns and claims. Writing about the persistent difficulties in building solidarity between black and white women in America, bell hooks argues that "creating a context where we can debate and discuss without fear of emotional collapse, where we can hear and know one another in the difference and complexities of our experience is essential. Collective feminist movement cannot go forward if this step is never taken" (hooks 1994).

In the climate space, debates on the role of historical responsibility in a context of (albeit unevenly) growing emissions in developing countries, persistent and profound inequalities within and across states, and uneven climate impacts provide plenty of scope for mistrust and missed opportunities for cooperation. Without dealing with these tensions from within a spirit of solidarity, it may not be possible to enable the future-oriented shifts required for achieving adequate mitigation and adaptation in ways that reduce pre-existing global inequalities. The attitude with which we attempt to build the future may be as important as the specific actions we take in doing this.

Creating new approaches along existing pathways

Within the frame of these broad reflections about what using a transitional justice lens could add to the climate context, we have explored common transitional justice mechanisms to see how they could contribute to building the depth of solidarity and collective action needed to achieve adequate climate action. We examined the lessons suggested by the mainstream mechanisms of transitional justice, which largely focus on 'top-down' incremental reform: amnesty, individual (and collective) legal accountability, truth commissions, reparations, and institutional reform. We also looked at the implications of more transformative approaches to transitional justice, which focus on historical injustices and structural inequality while often promoting 'bottom-up,' locally relevant, and participatory processes. Using these experiences as inspiration, we explored what a transitional justice approach to climate change might look like. This process yielded a number of insights.

The first major outcome of this work was the identification of a wide variety of possible climate-specific variations on common mechanisms. The full list of these mechanisms, detailed in the preceding chapters, can be viewed in Table 7.1. Some of our transitional justice-inspired proposals require substantial institutional

Table 7.1 Overview of transitional justice–inspired mechanisms proposed for the climate context

Proposed mechanism	*Status compared to existing UNFCCC institutions and processes*
Responsibility	
Process of acknowledgment	New process
Truth commission–like process	New institution, could build on existing civil society reviews
Legal accountability mechanisms (individual and collective)	Processes exist and could be augmented
Reparations	
Reparations Commission	New institution
Expand notions of repair and include greater range of resources	New process, could build on NAPA process
Root reparations in experiences of harm	Could adapt and expand NAPA process
Forward-oriented institutional reforms (in addition to above)	
Broaden range of contributors to financial mechanisms	Adapt and expand existing practices for Adaptation Fund and LDCF
Broaden range of types of contributions to climate action	New institution, could build on Adaptation Fund and LDCF
Increase transparency of support	Could adapt NDC and global stocktake processes
Due process mechanism	New institution
Loss and damage scoping studies (and national experts panel)	Could adapt and expand NAPA process
Education and capacity commitments by states	Could adapt NDC and stocktake processes
Education and capacity commitments by nonstate actors	New processes

change, whereas others tweak existing institutions or processes within the UNFCCC. Take, for example, conventional pathways for managing responsibility that have repeatedly resulted in stalemate in the climate negotiations. We offer several suggestions for including responsibility in the climate regime without amplifying the tensions it has elicited. One of these – a process like a truth commission – would require building an entirely new institution, although it could integrate a number of existing practices. A second proposal, developing a process of acknowledgment by which states would formally recognize historical emissions and request amnesty for some portion of these emissions, would build on existing practices of national communications and expert reviews, but would also require the creation of a new process to facilitate it. Meanwhile the legal accountability strategies we discussed are all extensions of existing efforts. A similar mix of brand-new institutions and alterations of existing ones is seen in our proposals regarding reparations and forward-oriented institutional reforms.

Although developing new institutions and building on existing ones is an essential aspect of a transitional justice approach, one of the limitations of these processes is precisely their focus on state actions and the creation of institutions. Critical scholars have suggested that more in-depth engagement is needed with individuals and communities most affected by harms, and with the broader systems that may prevent them from realizing or enjoying their human rights. As we discuss in Chapter 6, climate change faces at least two, usually oppositional, narratives of transformation. On the one hand, the sheer size of the mitigation challenge looming over us tends to privilege accounts of transformation based on mobilizing forces to address emission reductions as quickly as possible. The common resources relied on in this narrative are green growth and technological development (and deployment). On the other hand, grassroots climate justice organizers have insisted that climate change is only one of a larger set of ills. This bottom-up narrative stresses a wider and deeper approach to transformation that includes challenging capitalism and (re)engaging with indigenous knowledge.

Out of the creative tension generated by juxtaposing these two approaches to transformation we have proposed a set of three broader changes. These efforts are not bound by the creation of an institution within the UNFCCC or within a state, but encompass a wider set of actors and forms of action. For instance, inclusive low-carbon development that is both participatory and culturally engaged requires mobilization of a much broader set of actors than would usually be included in a more technocratic approach to low-carbon development. Similarly, stressing the development and use of justice-focused analytical tools and strategic capacity building (in the global South and North) also revolves around shifts to norms and practices far beyond states or the UNFCCC. It is possible that these broader changes might actually be more powerful in helping create a low-emission future in which all people can enjoy their human rights, but they may also be relatively slow. We suggest simultaneous attention to the institutionally focused adaptations identified earlier.

The second, and related, major outcome of this work is the recognition that multiple parts of a transitional justice approach to climate change could be used in concert. This is not a new insight: transitional justice scholars and practitioners have repeatedly stressed the importance of thinking about the integration of mechanisms. Because each context is unique, however, the exact interconnections in the climate context bear examination.

As seen in Figure 7.1, there are many possible lines of interaction across the suite of proposals we have made. For instance, developing a process for creating site-specific loss and damage scoping studies would provide documentation that a Reparations Commission could use to ensure that there is an appropriate match between the types of repair it supports and the actual needs of those experiencing harm. Scoping studies could be included along with the initial request for repair. Using these in conjunction with the wider notion of possible reparations, commissioners could assist governments in designing and financing appropriate reparative strategies based on addressing concrete needs. Moreover, these studies could either emerge out of or contribute to a truth commission–like process. For instance, a truth commission could request the creation of such studies to inform its truth-seeking efforts. Alternatively, a possible outcome of this type of process could be the recommendation that states do these scoping studies in order to establish the basis for reparations and nonrecurrence. Either way, maintaining a panel of national experts associated with the scoping studies, instead of disbanding them as happened in the NAPA process, could also feed into long-term strategic capacity building.

In some cases, the lines of interaction between our proposed alterations are fairly direct. For example, a truth commission–like process that facilitated

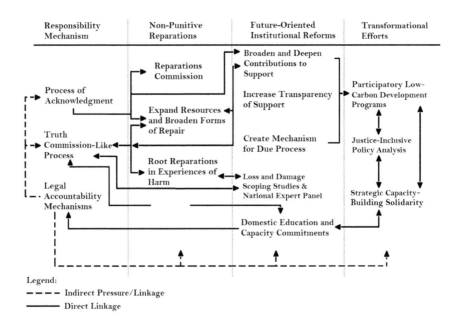

Figure 7.1 Integration of transitional justice–inspired mechanisms proposed for the climate context

contributions from both state and nonstate actors could be directly linked to an expanded set of resources for repair (both financial and nonfinancial). In a direct link such as this, state and nonstate actors could contribute to reparative efforts as recommended by the truth commission in order to generate a wider set of resources for repair. The administration of this expanded set of resources could be facilitated by altering existing institutions (such as the Adaptation Fund and the LDCF).

Other lines of interaction, however, would be indirect. Strengthening legal pressure for accountability aimed at either individuals or collectives (states or corporations) could be directly linked to another mechanism, such as a depository for reparations, although these could also be left indirectly linked. Indirect linkages with legal accountability measures are common. Because legal mechanisms cannot possibly accommodate all claims anyway, they are often used to generate pressure on otherwise insulated actors and to encourage them to participate in other mechanisms (such as a truth commission or a process of acknowledgment). From this angle continuing to develop legal resources for addressing climate change is important, if for no other reason than that it could help indirectly facilitate a range of other mechanisms.

There has been substantial debate in transitional justice about the ideal sequencing of multiple mechanisms. Over time, however, it has become clear that sequencing may be less important than the ability to draw on several mechanisms. Each context is unique and unfolds as the political space allows. Accordingly, although we have drawn attention to the points at which these proposals could reinforce or contribute to one another in the climate context, we have not attempted to argue for a particular sequence.

The final major outcome from this work has been a sense of the extent to which scholars embedded in the transitional justice and climate change contexts could learn from one another. Conversations about the scope and shape of justice in both the climate context and the transitional justice field generally are being developed against the broader context of rapid change, not only ecological but also moral. Interestingly, each field has typically highlighted different manifestations of these changes. For instance, within transitional justice a great deal of attention has been devoted to both understanding and actively engaging with shifts in norms about what harms are and what kinds of obligations individuals, states, and other actors have to address them. In some situations, such as the Canadian TRC process, this conversation has focused on the ramifications of colonialism and the necessity of addressing harms that are both still evolving and emerge out of much earlier decisions. In general transitional justice starts from, and contributes to, the premise that moral and legal norms change and that this change can be purposefully sought. In contrast this narrative of purposeful norm change in the scope and content of moral obligation has not been dominant in the climate context.

Simultaneously, the climate discourse is full of in-depth efforts to describe and understand large-scale demographic, economic, social, and technological shifts and their likely ramifications for claims of justice and global institutional arrangements. For example, debates about green growth (see Chapter 2) or scenario-based explorations of climate impacts over time (see Chapter 6) have relied on highly sophisticated efforts to integrate independent but interconnected multiscalar processes responsible for shaping people's capacities to flourish in the context of rapid global change. Comparably, systems-based analyses of current and possible future global arrangements, including in-depth consideration of ecological stress and planetary boundaries (Rockström et al. 2009), have featured less in transitional justice. Only recently have scholars started to work on acknowledging the linkages between these types of global socioecological shifts and the potential for harm through a transitional justice lens (Bradley 2017).

One of the strengths of attempting to integrate transitional justice and climate change discourses about global change, governance, and justice is that it helps us question the lenses each field has used to narrow its vision. We need to engage with the potential for norms to change, but we also have to face the extent of ecological devastation facing many communities. Moreover, if any of our decisions are to have relevance over time, we need to think hard about how we are connecting our understandings of what is with our projections of what could be. If we are attempting to build greater solidarity across communities with vastly different, and at times conflicting, needs and demands over time, we need to understand the deeply held concerns and experiences of all those involved from both a past-oriented and a future-oriented perspective.

Which harms from the past need to be seen in order to facilitate widespread participation in public life at local and global scales? Which opportunities moving forward need to be built into institutions to erode inequalities over time? What kinds of techniques might we use to test our intuitions about the development of peace, solidarity, or institutional change? How could we better incorporate ecological considerations into peace building and non–climate-related transitional justice processes? Integrating the complementary lenses used by climate change and transitional justice scholars and practitioners offers a pathway for advancing both fields.

Balancing idealism and pragmatism

Throughout the writing of this book we have been guided by both idealism and pragmatism. We recognize that implementing any of the proposals we have made would be difficult, and some may argue that they push the bounds of what is politically feasible. But many of the institutions we now benefit from on a regular basis were initially seen as idealistic. In less than a century the claim that every person ought to have their human rights recognized went from being a philosophical ideal to a widely accepted and legally enforced norm. Climate change itself changed from a relatively unknown area of obscure science to one of the most prominent debates in domestic and international politics within about thirty years. Humans all too often assume that what is will always be, but norms and institutions change. And these changes do not happen by accident but through the purposeful efforts of activists, scholars, negotiators, citizens, private-sector representatives, and policy makers to shape how we see what is and what could be. As we face substantial emission gaps and growing climate impacts, we must develop new pathways, and this effort is, at its heart, idealistic.

However, we have also sought to be pragmatic. Institutions can change, but this requires substantial effort, and in a situation of limited time and resources we must be thoughtful about which changes we see as essential. We also need to be clear-eyed about the extent of the challenge and the limited power of our proposals. This is why we have sought to build proposals as connected to current practice as possible, while also designing them in full recognition that what we need is transformation from our current pathway – the status quo, although pragmatic, is not an option.

Even as concepts and tools from transitional justice may be useful in the struggle for adequate climate action in the face of growing mitigation pressures and increasing climate impacts, these alone will be insufficient. We are offering these insights with the knowledge that transitional justice is not a panacea. Moreover, the power imbalances and mistrust among actors that are common in all transitional contexts, not only the climate one, make efforts to build solidarity and collective action even more tenuous.

Justice claims do not go away readily, and failing to build them into our efforts is unlikely to result in paths that take us where we want to go. At the same time, justice is contested, and messy, and visceral. Yet, if we are to achieve a climate regime that has long-term legitimacy, that is able to advance rapid climate action, and that will provide adequate protection and assistance to those facing the worst climate impacts without deepening inequalities in a context of radical global inequality, then this approach to imperfect justice may be our best bet. Achieving the ultimate goal of the Convention will require many leaps of faith, and each one of these would be easier in a context of trust and solidarity. It is time we gave our full attention to just how we are planning on nurturing these two crucial components of the world we would like to inhabit. Now, this all may seem impossible. And indeed it may be. But ultimately we would rather try and fail than not try at all.

Note

1 The Momentum for Change initiative is coordinated by the UNFCCC secretariat and aims to inspire and recognize 'lighthouse' activities that demonstrate leadership on any aspect of climate actions. These activities have been undertaken by individuals, civil society organizations, corporations, and government bodies (UNFCCC n.d.).

References

Bradley, Megan. 2017. "More than Misfortune: Recognizing Natural Disasters as a Concern for Transitional Justice." *International Journal of Transitional Justice* 11(3): 400–20.

Burkett, Maxine. 2015. "Rehabilitation: A Proposal for a Climate Compensation Mechanism for Small Island States Symposium: Environment and Human Rights." *Santa Clara Journal of International Law* 13: 81–124.

hooks, bell. 1994. *Teaching to Transgress: Education as the Practice of Freedom*. New York: Routledge.

Lerner, Melvin J. 1975. "The Justice Motive in Social Behavior: Introduction." *Journal of Social Issues* 31(3): 1–19.

Rajamani, Lavanya. 2010. "The Increasing Currency and Relevance of Rights-Based Perspectives in the International Negotiations on Climate Change." *Journal of Environmental Law* 22(3): 391–429.

Rockström, Johan, Will Steffen, Kevin Noone, Åsa Persson, F. Stuart III Chapin, Eric Lambin, and Timothy Lenton. 2009. "Planetary Boundaries: Exploring the Safe Operating Space for Humanity." *Ecology and Society* 14(2).

UNDP. 2008. "Fighting Climate Change: Human Solidarity in a Divided World." *Human Development Report 2007/2008*, 1–18.

UNFCCC. n.d. "Momentum for Change." http://unfccc.int/secretariat/momentum_for_change/items/6214.php.

About the authors

Sonja Klinsky is an Assistant Professor in the School of Sustainability at the Arizona State University. Broadly speaking her research seeks to understand how humans have tried, are trying, and could try to deal with the integrated challenges of climate change and inequality. Within this she has worked on both domestic and international aspects of this challenge, including on the social-psychological dimensions of climate justice dilemmas.

Jasmina Brankovic is a Senior Researcher with the Centre for the Study of Violence and Reconciliation, South Africa, and the Associate Editor of the *International Journal of Transitional Justice*. Jasmina conducts research on comparative transitional justice, civil society and victims' groups, and the intersection of transitional justice and social transformation. She is co-editor of *Advocating Transitional Justice in Africa: The Role of Civil Society* (2018).

Index

For Product Safety Concerns and Information please contact our EU
representative GPSR@taylorandfrancis.com
Taylor & Francis Verlag GmbH, Kaufingerstraße 24, 80331 München, Germany

9 780367 430221